MIND, CULTURE, AND GLOBAL UNREST

D1570513

MIND, CULTURE, AND GLOBAL UNREST
Psychoanalytic Reflections

Salman Akhtar

Routledge
Taylor & Francis Group

LONDON AND NEW YORK

Chapter One is a slightly enlarged version of 'Psychoanalysis and culture: Freud, Erikson, and beyond,' that appeared in *Psychoanalysis in Asia*, eds. A. Gerlach, M.T. Hooke, and S. Varvin, pp. 19–42. London: Karnack Books, 2013. Chapter Two is a slightly enlarged version of 'Religion and politics,' that appeared in *Immigration and Acculturation* by S. Akhtar, pp. 103–140. Lanham, MD: Jason Aronson, 2011. Chapter Three was first published in *British Journal of Psychotherapy* 30: 136–153, 2014. Portions of Chapter Four have previously appeared in 'From unmentalized xenophobia to messianic sadism,' in *The Future of Prejudice*, eds. H. Parens, A. Mahfouz, S. Twemlow, and D. Scharff, pp. 7–20. Lanham, MD: Rowman and Littlefield, 2007. Chapter Five has appeared under the title 'The tripod of terrorism' in the *International Forum of Psychoanalysis* 26: 137–150. 2017. Chapter Six has appeared under the title 'Dehumanization: origins, manifestations, and remedies,' in *Violence or Dialogue*, eds. S. Varvin and V.D. Volkan, pp. 131–145. London: Karnac Books, 2003. All this material is re-printed in this book with the pertinent authors', editors', and publishers' permission.

First published 2018
by Routledge
2 Park Square, Milton Park, Abingdon
Oxon OX14 4RN

and by Routledge
711 Third Avenue, New York, NY 10017

Routledge is an imprint of the Taylor & Francis Group, an informa business

Copyright © 2018 Salman Akhtar

British Library Cataloguing-in-Publication Data
A catalogue record for this book is available from the British Library

Library of Congress Cataloging-in-Publication Data
A catalog record has been requested for this book

ISBN-13: 978-1-78220-067-3 (pbk)

Typeset in Palatino
by V Publishing Solutions Pvt Ltd., Chennai, India

To
J. ANDERSON THOMSON, JR.
in friendship

CONTENTS

ACKNOWLEDGMENTS

Besides my patients and my friends in diverse regions of the world from whom I have learned much about the human condition, I am grateful to many professional colleagues who have helped me in subtle and not-so-subtle ways. Prominent among these are Drs. Aisha Abbasi, Masood Aslam, Jennifer Bonovitz, Ira Brenner, Mitchell Cohen, Fayez El-Gabalawi, Hossein Etezady, April Fallon, Anique Forrester, Gerard Fromm, Rao Gogineni, Jaswant Guzder, Joyce Kay, Rolands Lappuke, Afaf Mahfouz, Mali Mann, Henri Parens, Christie Platt, Nadia Ramzy, Shahrzad Siassi, J. Anderson Thomson, Jr, Stuart Twemlow, Madhusudana Rao Vallabhneni, and Vamik Volkan. Other friends, especially Drs. Nina Ahmed, Shantanu Maitra, Carl Schieren, Priti Shukla, Ashwini Tambe, and a few others who wish to remain anonymous also provided useful feedback. Belonging to diverse disciplines including information technology, women's studies, diplomacy, journalism, African studies, plastic surgery, and business, these individuals shed fresh light on aspects of prejudice, problems of minorities, migration, and terrorism. My assistant, Jan Wright, prepared the manuscript of this book with her usual diligence and good humor. Oliver Rathbone, Kate Pearce, and Cecily Blench, at Karnac Books, shepherded the project along the various phases of publication with grace and patience. Finally, I must mention Dr. Muge Alkan who "held" me in myriad ways as I labored through this project. To all these individuals, I offer my sincere thanks.

Salman Akhtar
Philadelphia, PA

ABOUT THE AUTHOR

Salman Akhtar, MD, is professor of psychiatry at Jefferson Medical College and a training and supervising analyst at the Psychoanalytic Center of Philadelphia. He has served on the editorial boards of the *International Journal of Psychoanalysis*, the *Journal of the American Psycho-analytic Association*, and the *Psychoanalytic Quarterly*. His more than 300 publications include eighty-nine books, of which the following eighteen are solo-authored: *Broken Structures* (1992), *Quest for Answers* (1995), *Inner Torment* (1999), *Immigration and Identity* (1999), *New Clinical Realms* (2003), *Objects of Our Desire* (2005), *Regarding Others* (2007), *Turning Points in Dynamic Psychotherapy* (2009), *The Damaged Core* (2009), *Comprehensive Dictionary of Psychoanalysis* (2009), *Immigration and Acculturation* (2011), *Matters of Life and Death* (2011), *The Book of Emotions* (2012), *Psychoana-lytic Listening* (2013), *Good Stuff* (2013), *Sources of Suffering* (2014), *No Holds Barred* (2016), and *A Web of Sorrow* (2017). Dr. Akhtar has delivered many prestigious invited lectures including a plenary address at the 2nd International Congress of the International Society for the Study of Personality Disorders in Oslo, Norway (1991), an invited plenary paper at the 2nd International Margaret S. Mahler Symposium in Cologne, Germany (1993), an invited plenary paper at the Rencontre Franco-Americaine de Psychanalyse meeting in Paris, France (1994), a keynote address at the 43rd IPA Congress in Rio de Janeiro, Brazil (2005), the plenary address at the 150th Freud Birthday Celebration sponsored by the Dutch Psychoanalytic Society and the Embassy of Austria in Leiden, Holland (2006), the inaugural address at the first IPA-Asia Congress in Beijing, China (2010), and the plenary address at the National Meetings of the American Psychoanalytic Association (2017). Dr. Akhtar is the recipient of numerous awards including the American Psychoanalytic Association's Edith Sabshin Award (2000), Columbia University's Robert Liebert Award for Distinguished Contributions to Applied Psychoanalysis (2004), the American Psychiatric Association's Kun Po Soo Award (2004) and Irma Bland Award for being the Outstanding Teacher of Psychiatric Residents in the country (2005). He received the highly prestigious Sigourney Award (2012) for distinguished contributions to psychoanalysis. In 2013 he gave the commencement address at graduation ceremonies of the Smith College School of Social Work in Northampton, MA. Dr. Akhtar's books have been translated in many languages, including German, Italian, Korean, Portuguese, Romanian, Serbian, Spanish, and Turkish. A true Renaissance man, Dr. Akhtar has served as the film review editor for the *International Journal of Psychoanalysis*, and is currently serving as the book review editor for the *International Journal of Applied Psychoanalytic Studies*. He has published eleven collections of poetry and serves as a scholar-in-residence at the Inter-Act Theatre Company in Philadelphia.

INTRODUCTION

This book emanates from two motives. The first pertains to my wish to say something—both as an ordinary citizen and as a psychoanalyst—about the current global turmoil. The second involves my desire to expand the purview of my discipline, psychoanalysis, by forging links between the internal world it has mapped out so well and the external reality it has only lately come to recognize as important.

Regarding the first matter, it is my sense that the unrest, strife, and bloodshed that we are seeing all over the globe are the end-products of the annihilation anxiety that both West and East are experiencing. European nations are feeling threatened by the influx of immigrants and refugees (especially those who are African and/or Muslim) and by the so-called "radical Islamic terrorism." Asian nations and more specifically the Middle Eastern countries are feeling threatened by the juggernaut of Western culture and by devastating military interventions (especially those by the United States). Both West and East are fearful of losing their regional identities. As a result, both are witnessing the rise of conservative movements, hyper-nationalism, and paranoia. Being a psychoanalyst, it is my striving to view this crisis from a "depressive position," that is, by avoiding simplistic, linear, one-sided etiologies and remedies for the enormously complex and multiply determined problems at hand. And, this forms the basis of the book's chapters on the political dimensions of migration, the mental pain of minorities, prejudice, terrorism, and dehumanization.

But this is not all. As I said above, a second motive for putting this book together is my desire to push for a shift from "psychoanalytic anthropology" to "anthropological psychoanalysis." The former regarded culture to be a product of the human mind, described personality development in Eurocentric terms, and minimized the role of external reality in considerations of psychopathology, therapy, and goals of treatment. The latter regards culture and human mind to be dialectically related, views personality development to be context-bound and culturally relativistic, and accords variables of external reality significant place in the assessment of psychopathology, treatment technique, and therapeutic goals. In writing the opening and closing chapters of this book, it has been my aim to advance anthropological psychoanalysis. Doing so has, however, required that I point out where our discipline has failed and committed errors. Some readers might find my criticism of psychoanalysis, especially in its educational and training functions, not to their taste. It is my hope, though, that their discomfort would not mobilize further denial and projection but honest self-scrutiny and attempts for betterment.

The spirit of my discourse (regardless of whether it pertains to the needed growth and maturation of psychoanalysis or to the nature of prejudice, problems of minorities, and origins of terrorism) is one of candor, self-examination, owning one's own contributions to the suffering being felt, and attempting to make reparation. It would therefore be no surprise to the reader that the individuals I uphold as my intellectual forebearers in writing this book even more than Sigmund Freud and Erik Erikson, are Melanie Klein and Noam Chomsky.

PROLOGUE

CHAPTER ONE

Psychoanalysis and culture: theory and technique

The interior dimension of human experience is the subject matter of psychoanalysis. It does pay attention to conscious thoughts and feelings, fantasies, daydreams, perceptions, values, and beliefs. Its heart and soul, however, are in the subterranean strata of psychic life. What lurks beyond awareness, beneath intellectual grasp, and beside platitudes and rationalizations is of greatest interest to psychoanalysis. Puzzling obsessions, utterly unrealistic phobias, bizarre convictions, embarrassing parapraxes, incomprehensible dreams, and, yes, miraculous feats of resilience and creativity draw the attention of psychoanalysis with irresistible magnetism. To find meaning in the seemingly meaningless and to add an undiscovered layer of hermeneutics to the flatness of logical existence is what psychoanalysis is about. To put it bluntly, if one were forced to select the most outstanding contribution of the discipline's founder, Sigmund Freud, the three word answer would be: unconscious mental life.

Such life, at least from the viewpoint of early psychoanalysis, grows out of the dialectics between the pressures of instinctual motivation and the experiential precipitates of formative years. The former are universal and ubiquitous. The latter are specific to circumstances, particular to each lived life, and idiosyncratic in their internal processing. The consequence is that all human beings are fundamentally alike and yet each individual is unique in its own right. Psychic needs are universally the same but wishes are experience-bound and thus highly variable with era, culture, and individual circumstances (Akhtar, 1999a). Human dilemmas are mostly the same all over the world, two cardinal ones being that some things are impossible and a few others are prohibited. The strategies people devise to deal with these quandaries are, however, variable.

This unique, specific, and whimsical dimension of human experience became the focus of investigation by psychoanalysis. What was ubiquitous and universal got relegated to the periphery. The fact that early psychoanalysis was largely a mono-ethnic (i.e., Jewish)[1] and mono-skin-color (i.e., white) enterprise made this latter step possible. It also helped jettison curiosity about what besides genes, upbringing, early trauma, and phase-specific fantasies might contribute to personality development. The role of cultural variables thus received short shrift. Everyone seemed more or less satisfied till things began to change and the psychoanalytic world crashed against the real world at large.

Cataclysmic events in mid-twentieth-century Europe made it clear that the sociopolitical history of a people could deeply affect the minds of its individual members. This impacted upon psychoanalytic theory and technique. Moreover, a gradual shift occurred in the demographic ranks of its practitioners and its patients. While Jews did not lose their predominant place in the field of psychoanalysis, Christians, Hindus, and Muslims[2] started to enter the field as well. Whites remained the majority but the so-called "people of color" (e.g., blacks, Indians, Pakistanis) and "Orientals" (e.g., Chinese, Japanese, Koreans) also joined the professional ranks. The languages in which psychoanalysis was practiced and inscribed multiplied too. A rainbow of cultural heterogeneity now appeared in the heuristic and technical sky of psychoanalysis. There was no turning back now. But wait. Let me not get ahead of myself. Let me recount the story from its beginning.

Psychoanalytic anthropology

The breadth of Freud's vision was astonishing. He plumbed the unconscious depths of "everyday life" and neuroses, mapped out to the epigenetic unfolding of development, argued against the irrationality of religious belief, speculated about the gnawing pull towards nonexistence in all living beings, delineated the toll extracted by the powers of civilization, wondered about the need for war, and grappled with the mysteries of dreams, perversion, and creativity. Absorbed in the theatre of clinical praxis, he maintained a robust interest in the fodder provided by the external world. Whether it was a piece of fiction (1907a) or a statue carved out of stone (1914b), a personal memoir (1911c) or a visit to a historical spot (1936a), group regression (1921c) or war (1933b), Freud brought his metapsychology to bear upon his understanding of them. Referring to himself as a "conquistador" (Freud, cited in Gay, 1988), Freud saw cultural artifacts largely as outward iconography of the repressed. In other words, culture was the product of the human mind and the origin of its constituents (e.g., art, poetry, festivals, and taboos) could be traced back to what could not be permitted into conscious mental awareness. Contributions of such a sort by Freud inaugurated the "era of psychoanalytic anthropology." Characteristic of such theorization was to set aside the "in-culture perspective," that is, principles and determining variables of the concept under study (e.g., music, poetry, art) and give premium to the psychoanalytic viewpoint *per se*.

Freud's pupils and early collaborators perpetuated this variety of "applied psychoanalysis." Among the salutary outcomes of the trend were (i) Abraham's (1912) investigation of the monotheistic cult of Aton, (ii) Jones's essays on chess (1931), figure skating (1936), and Hamlet (1948); (iii) Fenichel's (1946) analysis of anti-Semitism, and later, (iv) Kris's (1952) "regression in the service of the ego," a notion of great heuristic value in the study of creativity. Not all the contributions of this ilk turned out well, however. Heavy-handed speculation and "wild psychoanalysis" (Freud, 1905d) were also noticeable in such approaches to culture. Illustrations of this tendency include Rickman's (1924) designation of photography as "pseudo-perversion" and Sterba's (1947) simplistic equation of black-white tension in the United States to sibling rivalry. A more disastrous example of mindless psychoanalytic colonialism is constituted by the British analysts Berkeley-Hill's and Dangar-Daly's condescending diatribes against the Hindu character and India's struggle for independence, respectively. Both these analysts published articles portraying Indians as inferior and infantile. They even spoke of a need for the British to take the role of enlightened parents for the Indian people. Berkeley-Hill (1921) wrote a paper entitled, "The anal-erotic factor in the religion, philosophy, and characters of Hindus," in which he used the emerging psychoanalytic work on anal eroticism as a springboard for describing a model Hindu character as given to greed and hoarding, besides being "insanely short-tempered and vindictive" (p. 336). He stated:

> No one can deny that as a general rule the Hindus exhibit a disastrous propensity to quarrel, especially in the family circle, and to this trait is added, what is still worse, vindictiveness. Reference has already been made to the miserliness, meanness and pettiness of the Hindus, and as these traits are so well known there is no call to notice them further … . The tendency to dictate and to tyrannise is such a notorious trait of all Oriental character that it is not surprising to find it a prominent feature of Hindu character. (p. 336)

Dangar-Daly, who did not work with a single Indian patient, stated, "In the Hindu, we have a psychology that differs considerably from the European, its equivalent with us being found in pathological cases" (1930, p. 210). In the same applied psychoanalytic paper, entitled "The psychology of revolutionary tendencies," he expressed his opinion about the Indian freedom fighters such as Gandhi and Bose. He portrayed them as displaying childlike reactions to their overwhelming and pathological love of India, which he said symbolized the oedipal mother. Daly added:

> When we realize the nature of the Hindu's unconscious tendencies, we must see how easy it is for the young Hindu to form revolutionary groups … . They have engraved on their ego an ideal of the mother whose incestual love is denied them, and insatiable unconscious hate of any power that comes between them and their primitive desires. (p. 209)

Having thus "established" Hindu infantilism as the basis of the Indian freedom movement, Dangar-Daly found it logical to recommend that the British act as parents for them. He even felt that psychoanalysis could help the British adopt and maintain this role:

> It is only by a deep study of the psychology and needs of the Indian people, and the application of the knowledge obtained by

psychological research, that the British government can hope to continue to rule them to their best advantage in the present, and perhaps guide them to final liberation from their psychological fixations in the future. (p. 197)

What is striking in all this is the utter unawareness of distortions arising from a racist countertransference, confusion of group with individual psychology, and the disregard of actual sociopolitical variables in an oppressed people's rebellion. In all fairness, however, it should be acknowledged that in 1930, when Dangar-Daly's paper was written, psychoanalysis was too intoxicated by the discovery of the unconscious, and omissions of the sort mentioned above were hardly rare. Yet the prejudicial attitude is difficult to overlook. As a result of it, such writings come across as having more to do with British imperialism and its racist propaganda than with genuine psychoanalytic study. They also reflected the author's defensively contemptuous reaction to the Indian independence movement, which threatened the British colonizers' identity and existence within India.

In a far less malignant way, psychoanalytic developmental theory remained Eurocentric through the remaining twentieth century. Western models of childhood development were implicitly assumed to be universally applicable. Encountering Eastern variations in their duration, intensities, dramatis personae, and graphic details resulted in unfortunate phrases like "too much skin-to-skin contact between mother and child," "protracted symbiotic phase," "prolonged breast-feeding," "inadequate separation," "undue reverence towards authority," "enmeshed selves," and so on. Such phraseology betrayed the fact that the Western models of upbringing had been smugly taken to be modal or even normal and other pathways were regarded as exotic and needing explanations.

Let me hasten to add here that even in this intoxicated era of mono-theoretical supremacy, dissident voices, both within and outside psychoanalysis, could be heard. The most prominent among the "extra-mural" voices of this sort was that of the German philosopher and sociologist, Theodore Adorno. In a series of monographs and collected papers (Adorno & Horkheimer, 1944; Adorno & Frenkel-Brunswick, 1950; Adorno, 1951, 1956), he offered a penetrating critique of modern society, especially of its dark pockets of fascism. His best known and most psychoanalytically informed work, *The Authoritarian Personality*

(Adorno et al, 1950), established links between the character traits of ethnocentrism, politico-economic conservatism, anti-democracy stance, and anti-Semitism. On the "intra-mural" side (i.e., specifically psycho-analytic), the most prominent voices included those of Karen Horney, Erich Fromm, and Geza Roheim. The following three passages provide a brief glimpse of their views.

- Horney's (1937) *The Neurotic Personality of Our Times* and *New Ways in Psychoanalysis* (1939) are two shining examples of this more con-ciliatory trend between psychoanalysis and cultural anthropology. Through these texts, Horney sought to redefine psychoanalysis by replacing Freud's biological orientation with an emphasis on inter-personal relationships and culture.
- Erich Fromm's *Escape from Freedom* (1941) went a step further in syn-thesizing Freud's ideas with those of Max Weber and Karl Marx.[3] Fromm's later writings spoke of "existential humanism" and attempted to bring Zen Buddhism to bear upon psychoanalytic notions (Burston, 2002).
- Geza Roheim (1934, 1943, 1947), an anthropologist-turned-psychoanalyst, conducted real-life fieldwork in remote corners of the world and with mostly non-European societies, including central Australia, Melanesia, and the Horn of Africa.

Horney, Fromm, and Roheim were exceptions, however. The momen-tum was mostly in the reductionist direction of "applying" psycho-analytic psychology to understanding cultural phenomena. Those who dared to declare that the traffic flows in the opposite direction as well were banished as "culturalists." If they attempted to have their ideas affect clinical work, they got labeled as "interpersonalists" and, not infrequently, were regarded as traitors to psychoanalysis, the exalted science of the mind.

All in all, the "era of psychoanalytic anthropology" had the fol-lowing features: (i) culture was seen as a product of the human mind, (ii) personality development was worked out in Eurocentric terms, (iii) an individuated and self-observant psychic constellation—the "psychoanalytic self" (Roland, 1996)—was regarded to be universal, and (iv) cultural matters were not permitted to alter views of psycho-pathology, treatment technique, and therapeutic goals. Then something happened that jolted the field of psychoanalysis into recognizing that external reality, history, and culture-at-large have a far greater role in mental functioning. This was something big.

Anthropological psychoanalysis

This monumental event was the Nazi Holocaust. The devastating impact of the atrocities committed by Hitler and his lieutenants extended far beyond those killed in concentration camps. Effects of this "massive psychic trauma" (Krystal, 1968) lingered not only in the survivors of the Holocaust but were trans-generationally transmitted to their offspring and their offspring's offspring. When such individuals began to be psychoanalytically studied—either in individual treatments or in ethnographic interviews—some things became undeniably clear. History matters. Ethnicity matters. Politics matters. Prejudice matters. Leaving one's land matters. Being hated and facing the threat of extermination matters. This meant that psychoanalytic notions that were true under an "average expectable environment" (Hartmann, 1939) might not remain valid when the external reality became radically transformed and diabolical.

Encounter with the offspring (and their offspring) of Holocaust survivors taught psychoanalysis that sociopolitical matters did not just exist "out there"; they were inside the psyche, shaping and coloring its phantoms of dread and desire. Yes, mind could produce culture but now psychoanalysis discovered that culture could produce mind as well. Moreover, the history of a group was found to be present in the clinical chamber, affecting the dialogue and the process of treatment. Thus arose new theoretical notions, for example, "survivor's guilt" (Niederland, 1968), "empty circle" (Laub, 1998), "multisensory bridges" (Brenner, 1988), and "concretism" (Grubrich-Simitis, 1984). Technical innovations were also made for psychoanalytic treatment of Holocaust survivors and their subsequent generations. The most prominent illustration is the proposal of "joint acceptance of reality of the Holocaust" (Auerhahn & Laub, 1987); it declared that without an explicit acknowledgement of the great tragedy, "the analyst's silence may approximate too closely the silences of the survivors' Holocaust world, the absence of any response to his or her messages of need" (p. 57).

Given this, it is only proper to assume that such "joint acceptance" would be extended to all African-Americans undergoing psychoanalysis. After all, they have a deeply traumatic and centuries long legacy of psychosocial ostracism and slavery to contend with. And what about African, South Asian, and Middle Eastern patients in analytic treatment in England, France, Italy, Spain, Portugal, and Holland? Are we to pretend that the nefarious impact of European colonization does not color their object world, their immigration histories, and their transferences? Or, can we be courageous and accommodate Edward Said's (1978) and Frantz Fanon's (1952, 1959) penetrating deconstruction of the Western gaze at the colonized people of Africa and Asia[4] into the psychoanalytic corpus?

As we ponder such questions, we cannot but notice that a cultural transformation of psychoanalysis is indeed in the offing. But before attributing it all to the last two decades—indeed most productive in this regard—we must take a few steps back and pay homage to the "cultural pioneers" already mentioned (Fromm, 1941; Horney, 1937; Roheim, 1934, 1943, 1945) and the respectfully recognized doyen of this realm, namely Erik Erikson. The impact of Holocaust studies notwithstanding, Erikson single-handedly ushered in the "era of anthropological psychoanalysis."

In a series of contributions spanning over three decades, Erikson (1950, 1954, 1956, 1958, 1959, 1969, 1975, 1980, 1982) systematically delineated the role of society and culture upon the formation and functioning of the human mind. He replaced the Freudian epigenetic sequence based upon instincts and erogenous zones (e.g., oral, anal, phallic) with a multifactorial perspective which took account of ego capacities, anaclitic needs, drives for mastery and efficacy, social tasks, interpersonal feedback, and assimilation of handed-down group aspirations. At each step of the way, from childhood through adolescence and young adulthood to old age, Erikson spelled out psychosocial challenges that differed from the prevalent developmental models in three important ways: (i) the stages were conceived in terms of polarities of success and failure in achieving a particular psychosocial milestone, (ii) the unfolding processes of maturation were not seen as resulting from somatically anchored drives but from ego accomplishments, and (iii) the risks encountered and rewards reaped by the ego in the process of growth emanated not only from the microcosm of internal objects but also from the macrocosm of family, school, workplace, and society-at-large. This set up the groundwork for viewing human development as intricately context-bound and its derailment as embedded in the sociohistorical matrix of the individual. Erikson's concepts of "initiative," "identity," "industry," generativity," "intimacy," and "care" were all inherently interpersonal and socially anchored. His was the voice of "anthropological psychoanalysis" even though it remained rather unheeded by the profession's mainstream.

Two other developments were necessary before the full impact of Erikson's perspective could be registered. The influx of immigrant analysts into the United States, Canada, and England was one such development. Unlike the European analysts who were Jewish refugees of the Holocaust and who, due to the unfathomable severity of their "departure trauma," had not been able to write about linguistic and cultural differences between them and their patients, these voluntary immigrants began to record the impact of geo-cultural dislocation upon the human mind. A new genre of literature thus emerged and it supported the view that psychoanalytic developmental theory is culturally anchored, that estimates of what is psychopathological and what is not are context-bound, and that judicious alterations of the therapeutic frame might be essential in clinical work of bicultural dyads. The following list contains the most important contributions of this group of psychoanalysts.

- Garza-Guerrero (1974) introduced the concept of "culture shock" to denote the ego disturbance caused by a sudden and drastic change in one's environment.
- Grinberg and Grinberg (1989) described the fresh immigrant's destabilization upon entering a new land in terms of "disorienting anxieties," his psychic pain at parting from the motherland, and his need for a homoethnic community for psychic stabilization.
- Kakar, the most widely published psychoanalyst of India,[5] has an oeuvre list that is simply too vast to detail here. Suffice to say that he has published extensively and meaningfully on personality development, sexuality, youth, love relations, Hindu-Muslim conflict, and mysticism within the Indian context (1990a, 1990b, 1991a, 1991b, 1993, 1996). After Freud, Kakar is the only analyst throughout the world to receive the highly covered Goethe Prize; this was bestowed upon him by German Federal President Roman Herzog on March 22, 1998, in the Goethe town of Weimar, Germany.
- Akhtar (1995) introduced the term "third individuation" for the identity transformation consequent upon immigration. He also delineated guidelines to keep in mind during the psychoanalytic treatment

of immigrant patients (Akhtar, 1999b) and their offspring (Akhtar, 2011a).

- Freeman (1993, 1996, 1998, 2009) explored the intricacies of child-hood development, especially the phase of separation-individuation, in Japanese culture. He deftly integrated mythology, folklore, and child-rearing practices while evolving a cross-cultural perspective on the role of mutual affect regulation in character formation (see also Settlage, 1998).

- Bonovitz (1998) wondered "[I]f Mahler had emigrated to India rather than the United States, what theory of separation-individuation would she have woven from observations of Indian mothers and their babies?" (p. 178). Bonovitz concluded that in many non-Western patients, not just those from India, "infantile objects are relinquished very gradually, and this process does not take place to the degree necessary in cultures where the child is being prepared to live an adult life that is independent of the extended family" (p. 182).

- Roland (1996) questioned the universality of a "psychoanalytic self"—highly individuated and reflecting upon itself—and proposed a "we-self" for Asian Indians who live in the ongoing state of partial merger with their objects. Later he introduced the concept of the "spiritual self" (2011) that refers to "an underlying being and consciousness in all human beings ... [and] to a far deeper awareness of the underlying relationships in the universe" (p. 133).

These contributions reflect the first of the two developments I mentioned as having contributed to the more meaningful contemporary "culturalization" of psychoanalysis. The second development was the spread of psychoanalysis to the Far East. Japan had had some psychoanalytic presence since 1925 and even a formal, IPA-recognized psychoanalytic society since 1955; over the years, Japanese analysts made many significant contributions to psychoanalytic literature (Kitayama, 1998, 2004, 2009; Kosawa, 1931; Okinogi, 2009). South Korea and China were, however, new territories for Freud's thought.[6] What aspects of it might be found applicable and useful under cultures that are drastically different from the one where psychoanalysis was evolved? Equally significant—to those with truly open minds—was what can psychoanalysis learn from the philosophical systems of these regions?

Preliminary answers to such questions began to emerge as analysts from Europe, Australia, and North America conducted psychotherapy and even psychoanalysis in China, Japan, and Korea, and individuals from these countries travelled abroad for (of necessity, abbreviated) analytic training and supervision. The information exchange turned out to be very productive. But before giving some examples of such newly acquired knowledge, one must acknowledge the contributions of Irmgard Dettbarn, the German analyst who practiced psychoanalysis in China for a long time, and a group of German and Norwegian analysts (under the leadership of Alf Guerlach and Sverre Varvin, respectively) who have worked tirelessly to advance the knowledge of psychoanalysis in that country. Also noticeable are the efforts of Teresa Yuan, an Argentinian analyst with a Chinese background, Maria-Teresa Hooke from Australia, and Peter Loewenberg and Elyse Snider from the United States in conducting teaching workshops on psychoanalytic ideas in China. Similar efforts have been carried out in South Korea by Sander Abend, Allan Compton, Abigail Golomb, Richard Lightbody, Robert Tyson, and David Sachs.[7]

That being said, let me enumerate some important insights that have emerged in this realm:

• Heisaku Kosawa (1931) described the *Ajase complex*, named after a character from an old mythological fable of India. In this tale, Prince Ajase imprisons his father, King Bimbsara, on the political instigation of a senior member of their court. Then he learns that his mother, Queen Vaidehi, is secretly sending the king food and other supplies. He attacks his mother with a sword and nearly kills her. Later in his life, however, he begins to feel a strong sense of remorse which leads him to break out in pustular sores all over his body. Kosawa contrasted the tale of Oedipus with that of Ajase. Oedipus killed his father in order to possess his mother, but Ajase tried to kill his mother because he felt that he was losing possession of her. Kosawa stated that both parricidal and matricidal impulses result in guilt, but such guilt is stronger when the hostility is primarily directed at the mother.

• Takeo Doi (1962, 1989) introduced the term *amae* in the psychoanalytic literature. It denotes an intermittent, recurring, culturally patterned interaction in which the ordinary rules of propriety and formality are suspended, allowing people to receive and give affectionate ego support to each other (see also Taketomo, 1996). Daniel Freeman (1998), a North American psychoanalyst with extensive knowledge and experience of Japanese culture, regards *amae* to be an "interactive mutual regression in the service of ego, which gratifies and serves the progressive intrapsychic growth and development of both the participants" (p. 47). While echoes of early maternal refueling of a growing child's ego can be discerned in it, the interaction typical of *amae* extends beyond childhood to spread over the entire life span of the individual. In a more recent paper, Freeman (2009) has elucidated the nuances of *amae* in Western societies.

- Osamu Kitayama greatly enhanced the psychoanalytic understanding of guilt (1991) and shame (1997, 2009) in the context of Japanese culture. He also elucidated the phenomenon of transience (1998) and discussed the cross-cultural variations in expressing various affects (2004). More recently, Kitayama published a monograph on the "don't look" taboo in Japanese folklore and clinical situations.

- Yasuhiko Taketomo (1996) described *teacher transference*. This denotes the Japanese analysand's respectful desire to be mentored by his or her analyst. The basis of such feelings is in the important connection a Japanese child makes with the kindergarten teacher (often, a male) since he is the first major extra-familial and truly paternal object in the child's experience. An implication here is that Japanese fathers are often more maternal and hence the child's first father-like experience occurs in the relationship with the kindergarten teacher.

- Stuart Twemlow (2009) noted that psychoanalysis has much to learn from Zen Buddhism and even from the martial arts of the Far East. He emphasized that "non-attachment" is different from detachment. The former relieves greed for possessing objects and hence permits letting alone of the phenomenon so that it can manifest as it is.[8]

- Ming Dong Gu (2006) proposed that oedipal themes in China are configured by Confucian morality and take the disguised form of parental demands for filial piety and children's commitment to the resulting duties. The manifestations of such *filial piety complex* include (i) the mother's possessiveness towards her son coupled with a strong antipathy towards his wife, (ii) the son's profound longing for a woman who is a surrogate mother or an aunt with complete obliteration of the parricidal dimension of the usual Oedipus complex, (iii) the daughter's fears and blind loyalty to her father, often accompanied by an "incomprehensible inhibition against love and marriage" (p. 189). In essence, the Chinese Oedipus complex is muted, fragmented, and couched in terms of family roles and moral duties.

Libidinal dimension is accentuated and aggression minimized, though it certainly lurks under the surface.

• Adeline van Waning (2007), a Dutch psychoanalyst, described her experience with *Naikan*, a Japanese introspective practice for self-transformation. This involves a silent retreat and immersion in reviewing one's life along three basic questions: (i) what have I received from such-and-such person?, (ii) what have I given to him or her?, and (iii) what difficulties and hurts have I caused him or her? One generally begins with applying these questions to one's parents but one can proceed later on to include siblings, a spouse, children, and others. Of note here is the elimination of externalization ("what hurts have they caused me?") and the ready-made conduit to the "depressive position" (Klein, 1940). Van Waning compared and contrasted *Naikan* and psychoanalysis in a most thought-provoking essay.

• Lois Choi-Kain (2009) provided a psychodynamic deconstruction of *haan*, the widespread phenomenon of suppressed anger and covert grievances in the Korean culture. She noted that while *haan* tends to serve masochistic aims, it can also lead to productive stoicism and heroic deeds.

• Mark Moore (2009) elucidated the relational dynamics of *wa* or harmony in Japanese culture. He noted that the Japanese *kanji* (or lexical character) for the term is made up of two constituents: a rice stalk and a mouth. This implies an orally gratified and tranquil state. Moore also discussed the intricate relationship between *ama* and *wa*.

• Gohar Homayounpour (2013), an émigré analyst who returned to her native country, Iran, found that contrary to the popular portrayal of Iranians as unable to voice their opinions, her patients were quite talkative and candid with their concerns. She also observed that, unlike Western countries where conflicts over narcissism and aggression predominate, in Iran, anxieties over sexuality are foremost on patients' minds.

Pooled together, the Holocaust studies, the work of Erik Erikson, the immigration literature, and the emergent psychoanalytic insights from and about the Far East constitute what I call the "anthropological psychoanalysis." Add to this list the psychoanalytic work with the urban poor in the United States (Altman, 2004; Sklarew, Twemlow, & Wilkinson, 2004), the collection of essays upon psychoanalysis and

India (Akhtar, 2005a), psychoanalysis and the Islamic world (Akhtar, 2008b), psychoanalysis and the problems of ethnic divide in Australia (Hooke & Akhtar, 2007), psychoanalysis and the Far East (Akhtar, 2009a), and upon psychoanalysis and African Americans (Akhtar, 2012), and you have got the up-to-date picture of the field. This new "anthropological psychoanalysis" differs from early "psychoanalytic anthropology" on the grounds that it (i) regards personality development as being context-bound and culture-based to a considerable level, (ii) views degrees of separation and individuation to be relative, without a priori declaring one pole to be normative and the other deviant, and (iii) accords cultural matters a place in the assessment of psychopathology, treatment technique, and therapeutic goals.

Concluding remarks

In this contribution, I have traced the history of the tedious relationship between psychoanalysis and anthropology. I have divided the 112 year history of the discipline into two eras, namely (i) the era of psychoanalytic anthropology, and (ii) the era of anthropological psychoanalysis. The former was characterized by viewing culture as a product of mind, giving primacy to psychoanalytic metapsychology, and excluding cultural matters from clinical work. The latter is characterized by viewing mind as a product of culture, giving primacy to the bilateral flow of information between psychoanalysis and the humanities (e.g., history, political science, economics, sociology),[9] and permitting cultural variables in the chamber of clinical praxis. However, enthusiasm for didactic clarity must not make us overlook that "psychoanalytic anthropology" and "anthropological psychoanalysis" are actually conjoint twins that are better left unseparated. The enriching complementarity between these two vantage points is nowhere more evident than in the genre of "psychobiography"—which has become increasing sophisticated and, paradoxically, less imperious in its conjectures.[10]

And, we can hardly overlook that it was Freud (1930a) himself who saw culture as an outgrowth of repression and repression as an outgrowth of culture. Pursuing the second part of this equation, he went to the extreme of declaring that human suffering emanates from the very existence of civilization. In that way, he seemed to be ahead of us all. But Erikson put Freud's message on its head. He declared that our pride and joy come from our abiding with—and, strengthening—civic

9

institutions and our suffering comes from failures in negotiating with
the world. Analysts inspired by Freud, Erikson, and many other pioneers have elucidated their ideas and given them even more color and
texture.

The resulting transformation of psychoanalysis has been salutary.
This is evident in our greater respect for pathways of personality
development across the globe, the deeper understanding of what is
and what is not pathological and the social context in which such
decisions are made, and a more flexible application of psychoanalytic treatment method to diverse cultural populations. In the realm
of development, we are now respectful of varying degrees of the
self's autonomy, different types of parent–child relationships, and
variable mixtures of masculinity and femininity in the modal personality configuration. In the realm of psychopathology, we have
responded to changing cultural norms and normalized what was
earlier regarded as morbid (e.g., homosexuality).[11] In the realm of
technique, we have permitted judicious alterations of frame and
process in treatments where the dyad is bicultural and/or bilingual
(Abbasi, 2008; Akhtar, 1999b, 2011a; Amati-Mehler, Argentieri, &
Cansestri, 1993; Antokolitz, 1993; Movahedi, 1996). We have also
evolved the concepts of "racial" (Holmes, 1992, 2012; Leary, 1995,
1997) and "colonial" (Akhtar, 2007b, 2009b) transferences and
countertransferences.

A little more detail regarding the technical refinements of psychoanalysis and psychoanalytically informed therapies might not be out
of place here. Three different, though somewhat overlapping, contexts
have especially elicited a bold new turn from the early, rigidly uniform,
applications of our treatment method.

- *Working with immigrant patients.* Here, I (Akhtar, 1995, 1999a, 1999b,
  2006, 2011a) have provided important guidelines which include:
  (i) allowing the patient a greater physical latitude while settling in
  the office; (ii) validating his or her feelings of geo-cultural dislocation; (iii) affirmatively as well as interpretively dealing with the
  patient's forays into nostalgia; (iv) paying attention to the various
  functions served by the patient's bilingualism in the clinical situation; (v) conducting "developmental work" (Pine, 1997) in regard to
  the patient's changed external reality, and (vi) staying receptive to the
  possibility of nonhuman transferences and countertransferences.[12]

- *Working with non-immigrant but racially or culturally different patients.* Here, the contributions of Holmes (1992, 2006, 2012, 2016), Leary (1995, 1997), Davids (2006, 2011), Altman (2004), Abbasi (2008), and Tummala-Narra (2016) are of great importance. Together, these clinician-investigators have underscored the importance of the analyst's scanning the patient's associative material for disguised references to racial, religious, or class differences within the clinical dyad. Such references, they note, can serve as important points of access to a patient's deeper transference to the analyst. These clinicians also leave the space open for judicious accommodations of the therapeutic frame to the patient's reality and for empathic validation of social marginalization and prejudice experienced by many such patients.

- *Working with refugees.* Here, psychoanalytically informed outreach by Dahl (1989), Papadopoulos (2002), Varvin (2003), Kirmayer et al. (2011), Guzder (2011), and Leuzinger-Bohleber, Rickmeyer, Tahiri, Hettich, & Fischmann (2016) are of paramount importance and so are the educational programs at Harvard Medical School and Tavistock Clinic that train mental health individuals in working with refugees. Culled from this burgeoning data are the following guidelines: (i) assuring physical and psychological safety, (ii) providing space for the individual to narrate not only what has happened (e.g., persecution, leaving home, dangerous travel) but also what is happening (e.g., the conditions in the refugee camp); (iii) preventing social withdrawal and apathy; (iv) creating safe public spaces for children and helping them express their inner states through drawing and painting; (v) group work with adolescents, with the preventive eye towards gang formation and substance abuse, and, perhaps most important, individual and group interventions with pregnant women and women who have recently become mothers since mothering in a chaotic atmosphere and that, too, in a foreign land is no easy task (see also Harrison, 2016; Tummala-Narra & Claudius, 2016).

Equally impressive are the attempts by psychoanalysts to address the societal problems of prejudice (Parens, Mahfouz, Twemlow, & Scharff, 2007), school bullies (Twemlow & Sacco, 2008, 2012), ethnic conflict (Volkan, 1988, 2004, 2006), terrorism (Akhtar, 1997; Hollander, 2010; Varvin & Volkan, 2005; Volkan, 1997), and genocide (Kaplan, 2008; Varvin, 1995). Such community-directed applications are now interdisciplinary in orientation, giving due recognition to other than intrapsychic variables (e.g., economic, historical). Psychoanalysis no longer butts heads with sociology, anthropology, and other related disciplines. It has become both their teacher and their student. And, that is indeed an occasion to celebrate with, of course, a tip of the hat to Sigmund Freud and Erik Erikson!

Notes

1. Nearly all of Freud's early associates and pupils were Jewish. The Wednesday Psychological Society that he founded in 1902 had an exclusively Jewish membership that consisted of Alfred Adler, Hugo Heller, Max Graf, Paul Federn, and Wilhelm Stekel. And, by 1908, when this select group expanded to become the Vienna Psychoanalytic Society, most members or frequent visitors (e.g., Karl Abraham, Max Eitingon, Sandor Ferenczi, and Otto Rank) were Jewish.
2. For a history of Muslims in the psychoanalytic world, see Akhtar (2008a).
3. Fromm was not alone in his devotion to Marxist ideology. Many early analysts subscribed to it; these included Wilhelm Reich, Otto Fenichel, Ernst Simmel, and Siegfried Bernfield. Herbert Marcuse (1955) attempted to synthesize Freud and Marx in his widely read book, *Eros and Civilization*.
4. See Khanna (2004) also in this context.
5. The history of psychoanalysis in India goes back to 1921, when Girindrashekhar Bose (1887–1953), a Kolkata-based psychiatrist, started a correspondence with Freud. The correspondence lasted until 1937 and has been published in its entirety (Ramana, 1964). The Indian Psychoanalytic Society was formed in 1922 with the assistance of Ernest Jones and continues to be active to this day. For more details on psychoanalysis in India, see Akhtar and Tummala-Narra (2005).
6. Detailed histories of the development of psychoanalysis in Japan (Kitayama, 2011; Mori, 2011; Okinogi, 2009), South Korea (Jeong, 2011; Jeong & Sachs, 2009), and China (Kirsner & Snyder, 2009; Varvin & Gerlach, 2011), and Taiwan (Liu, 2011) have recently been published.
7. Do-Un Jeong (Jeong & Sachs, 2009) provides a more complete list of psychoanalysts who have been teaching in South Korea.
8. Such perceptual realism of the philosophical systems of the Far East is also to be found in aspects of Bion's (1962b) work implicitly, and in some of Coltart's (2000) writings explicitly.
9. The forays by contemporary psychoanalysis into the realms of music (Feder, 1981; Nagel, 2007, 2010; Nagel & Nagel, 2005), sports (Brearley,

2018; Marcus, 2015), and architecture (Weiner, Anderson, & Danze, 2006) clearly show such advanced thinking.

10. See the books on Gandhi (Erikson, 1969), Joseph Conrad (Meyer, 1970), Houdini (Meyer, 1976), Lawrence of Arabia (Mack, 1976), Kemal Ataturk (Volkan & Itzkowitz, 1984), Nixon (Volkan, Itzkowitz, & Dodd, 2001), George Bush (Frank, 2004), and Osama Bin Laden (Olsson, 2007).

11. We have also found "new" and culture-bound etiologies of certain psychopathological syndromes. Holmes's (2006) perspective on the so-called "success neurosis" is especially enlightening in this regard.

12. For further explication of these guidelines and for illustrative clinical vignettes, see Akhtar (2011a, pp. 17–26).

CURRENT GLOBAL UNREST

CHAPTER TWO

Religion, politics, and migration across national borders

In the focus upon economic and emotional aspects of immigration (Akhtar, 1999a; Grinberg & Grinberg, 1989), the role of religion and politics in the causes and consequences of people moving across national borders often gets overlooked. The aim of this chapter is to fill this gap. The ensuing discourse will be divided into sections dealing with: (i) the intricate relationship between religion and immigration, including reactive changes in the intensity of religious commitment, (ii) the politics of immigration, including the impact of immigration upon national economy, social fabric, and family values, (iii) the tension between the "new" immigrants and African Americans, (iv) the immigrants' politics, including the post-migration hypernationalism and immigrant-generated secession movements, (v) the societal debate over the status of illegal aliens as well as the marginalization and suffering of individuals in this group, (vi) the troubling state of refugees and asylum seekers across the globe, and (vii) some concluding remarks that will bring the foregoing material together and underscore the inoptimally addressed matters in this realm. Separated for the purpose of didactic ease, these sections will inevitably have some overlap, especially while tackling the thorny issue of multiculturalism and its implicit "challenges to American national identity" (Huntington, 1996).

23

Religion and immigration

Although inoptimally noted in the psychological and psychoanalytic literature on immigration (e.g., Akhtar, 1999a, 1999b; Elovitz & Kahn, 1997; Grinberg & Grinberg, 1989), the relationship between religion and immigration is multifaceted and capable of having a significant impact on the psychosocial lives of immigrants (Cadge & Ecklund, 2007). The intersection between religion and immigration is especially noticeable around the religion-based motives for migration, religion's role in post-immigration identity change, and the multiple functions of religious organizations founded by immigrants.

The place of religion among the motives for leaving one's country

Faced with prejudice, hostility, and violence directed at them for no other reason than their belonging to a particular religion, its members might decide to emigrate. The scale of this might range from the unnoticed exit of a small group to a monumental exodus of masses. Human history is replete with examples of such persecution-based immigrations. The twelfth century BC exodus of the Jews from Egypt, the flight of Mohammad from Mecca to Medina in 622 AD, and the eastward relocation of the Zoroastrians during the mid-seventh century are some of the well-known early illustrations. Closer to home, restrictions on religious practice also played a part in the earliest Anglo-Saxon arrivals in North America from England and Scotland. The bloody Hindu-Muslim "population exchange" during the tragic partition of India in 1947 was similarly triggered by real and imagined threats of religious persecution. Better known to the Western world is the post-Holocaust Diaspora which sent European Jews scurrying for safety and cover in nations as far apart and diverse as England, United States, Brazil, Chile, Mexico, Spain, and Australia; the same mass immigration resulted in the creation of the state of Israel. More recently, a working paper released during Pope Benedict XVI's visit to Cyprus notes that many Catholics have fled the Middle Eastern countries from Iran to Egypt fearing discrimination by Muslims and many Catholics have arrived in the same countries from the Philippines, India, and Pakistan, fearing discrimination by Hindus (Simpson & Hadjicostis, 2010). To be sure, even more examples of the sort given above can be added but the point is made: Religious persecution can lead to mass immigration.

That said, it should be added that immigration can also be a result of human religious striving and search for meaningful experiences in the realm of spirituality. Some devout American Jews move to Israel for this reason and many individuals from the Western countries find themselves living in *ashrams* across India, Nepal, Tibet, and Japan in their search for an encounter with the Divine.

Religion's role in post-immigration identity change

Becoming unmoored from familiar cultural anchors and encountering unfamiliar social customs and values leads to a slow and painful identity transformation among immigrants (Akhtar, 1995, 1999b). Issues of temporal continuity, optimal distance, language, food, music, history, political memory, and nostalgia play an important role in the psychic reconfiguration of the self after immigration. Religion can also matter in this regard. Choi-Kain (2009), for instance, notes the role of Protestant Christianity in both the migration and subsequent assimilation of Koreans in the United States:

> The strong ties between Koreans in America and Protestantism may be the single greatest factor for Koreans assimilating in mainstream culture since Korean values founded in Protestant beliefs neatly converge with the religious basis of American culture and economy. First generation Koreans who came to this country for opportunity became well-known for their work ethic and business success. Because of their Protestant roots, Koreans in America not only worked hard to earn money, they eschewed spending such money on luxurious items or status symbols, but rather invested that money primarily into the education of their children. (p. 222)

The religious aspect of identity can become more salient for the immigrant in his new country than in his country of origin because of religion's frequent contribution to ethnic identity. For instance, in a study of two Hindu subpopulations in the United States, Kurien (1998) has demonstrated that Hinduism helps a group of Indian immigrants ease the transition between being Indian and being American. By asserting pride in their Hindu heritage, they can claim a position for themselves at the American multicultural table. A similar observation has been made by Mohammad-Arif (2002) regarding South Asian Muslims living in New York City.

Such adaptive outcomes, however, do not exhaust the strands of interface between religion and immigration. Many other pathways exist. Some immigrants, for instance, become less devout and somewhat lax in their religious practices after immigration. Muslims who hid their transgression of the Islamic prohibition of drinking while living in their country of origin often become more "relaxed" (or "brazen," depending upon the values of the observer) in this regard. Likewise, some Hindus break the taboo against eating beef once they arrive in the West. More often, though, one sees an intensification of religiosity as Third World immigrants encounter the more liberal social customs of the West. Many Muslims feel threatened by the pervasive presence of alcohol and by the sexual liberation of women. Many Indian Hindus feel narcissistically injured by their "demotion" to a minority status and by discovering that Muslims (who were a minority back home in India), with their multiple nationalities, outnumber them in the United States. The less educated among such Muslims and Hindus are especially ill-equipped for the rigors of acculturation. Separated from their native cultures and unable to internalize Western ways, they feel a void within and often resort to hyper-religiosity to fill this gap. Their emotional life becomes focused upon the scriptures and practices of their respective religions.

An opposite outcome is also seen sometimes. This involves the immigrant's converting to the preponderant religion of the country of adoption in order to consolidate his new identity. Paradoxically, this can make it easier for him to express his ethnic characteristics. Ng (2002), for instance, argues that converting to the mainstream Christian religion in the United States often helps Chinese immigrants developing their own appropriations of cultural icons and rituals.

Immigrant religious organizations

The religious organizations founded and/or attended by immigrants often play an important role in determining whether, how, and to what extent would an immigrant participate in the civic matters of his adopted land. Immigrant churches, temples, and mosques constitute the psychosocial hub of immigrant activities (see also Chapter Four for homoethnic enclaves). These religious centers at times help their congregants navigate the process of becoming a citizen by offering help with learning the English language and/or with studying for the US citizenship test (Ebaugh & Chafetz, 2000). They also provide the members with a moral narrative and enhance their desire for community service. In this way immigrant religious organizations influence the development of a civic identity. Such positive contributions are, at times, eclipsed by problematic scenarios. When dealing with a religion that is too closely tied to the national identity of the country of origin, these organizations risk creating the civic identity as an "Other" in the mainstream culture (Rajagopal, 2000). Worse, the organization may turn into a cover for ethnocentric paranoia and even terrorist activities. Fortunately this happens on an infrequent basis. More often, the immigrant religious organizations make positive contributions though the forms these take can, at times, vary. One determining factor here is whether a particular religious group held a majority or minority status in the home country and whether this status is altered in the host country. The differing sociopolitical strategies of the Hindu and Muslim immigrant groups from India in the United States is a case in point (Kurien, 2001). Yang and Ebaugh's (2001) comparison of a Chinese Buddhist temple and a Chinese Christian church in Houston, Texas, sheds even sharper light on this matter:

> Chinese Buddhist immigrants commonly retain a secure Chinese identity because Buddhism has deep roots in Chinese tradition. However, Buddhism is a minority religion in the United States. Therefore, the Hsi Nan Temple strives hard to achieve an American identity, and one way of doing that is to recruit non-Chinese Americans. Meanwhile, the "authentic otherness" of Buddhism is an attraction to some Americans who seek an alternative to dominant, majority religions. Consequently, the Hsi Nan Temple is slowly but successfully gaining non-Chinese members. In contrast, Christianity is a minority religion in Chinese society, and Chinese converts to Christianity are sometimes chastised for becoming non-Chinese. Thus, the Chinese Gospel Church faces the task of asserting a Chinese identity for Christians in its efforts to convert fellow Chinese. However, the emphasis on Chinese culture sabotages the church's attempts to go beyond ethnic boundaries. Christianity is a majority religion in the United States and many evangelical churches exist in the community to serve Americans.

Consequently, in the course of Sinicizing the church, the Chinese church has a more difficult time attracting non-Chinese Americans. (p. 376)

Regardless of such nuances, the fact remains that the positive contributions of religious organizations are considerable and range from giving help in identity consolidation, assuring continuity with ancestral conditions, and encouraging community service. To top it all, there is evidence (Lien, 2004) that immigrants who are involved with their respective religious organizations are more likely to vote in elections. Moreover, since religious identity sometimes overlaps with racial and ethnic identity, these religious centers have the potential for forging and sustaining new types of political coalitions. The fact that they are able to accomplish all this is in no small measure due to their colorful celebration of traditional festivals, offer of ethnic food, and sponsorship of visiting dignitaries from "back home."

The mention of such overlap between immigration, religion, and politics brings up the tension that has arisen vis-à-vis the large Muslim migrations (from North Africa, Bosnia, Turkey, and Iraq) to the West. While Sweden and France have the largest immigrant populations from Muslim countries, the "problem" also affects the UK, Germany, Holland, and, to a lesser extent, the United States. Needless to add that both parties—the immigrant Muslims and the native hosts—contribute to this tension. The former often find the magnitude of difference between their native cultures and those of the Western countries too much to bridge; they chafe at the West's ignorance of their culture and insensitivity towards their religion (e.g., the publishing of cartoons involving Mohammad by Denmark's newspaper, *Jyllands-Posten*). The latter deride the homophobia, marital rape, veiling of women, and polygamy they consider rampant among Muslim immigrants. The specific assertions of these opposing factions might be debatable (Bawer, 2007; Huntington, 1996; Said & Jensen, 2006) but far more important are the challenges this tension poses to the fundamental notions of free expression and, ultimately, to the institution of democracy itself. In Romano's (2006) words:

To whom does any country's physical territory belong? Those who have been there longest? A simple majority? The best educated? Must the cultural rules of longtime societies last forever? Or might

> it make perfect democratic sense for officially secular France to
> change should its Muslim population reach 50 percent, just as the
> English-speaking United States might need to accept Spanish as an
> equal language if Spanish speakers reach that mark? (p. H-12)

The jury is still out on this matter but the clock is certainly ticking.

The politics of immigration

To say that the issue of immigration is replete with political implications is a gross understatement. The fact is that laws and social policies regarding immigration feature prominently in political debates all
over the industrialized and "developed" nations of the West. European
countries (e.g., the UK, France, Holland, Portugal) that colonized parts
of Africa and Southeast Asia during the nineteenth and early twentieth
centuries now face the influx of "natives" of those regions. Germany,
which did not have many colonies, receives immigrants (mainly from
Turkey, but also from the former Yugoslavia and Italy) for filling the
labor force, especially at the lower rungs of the monetary ladder. And,
the United States—the golden land of promise—draws not only the
ambitious and industrious fortune-seekers from all over the world but
also its neo-colonial subjects (e.g., from the Philippines, Puerto Rico)
and refugees from nations where it has militarily intervened.

The traffic across national boundaries of the West is thus heavy.[1]
More heavy are the sociopolitical concerns of such influx and the group
emotions that are associated with it. To be sure, the impact of immigration and the host population's response to it varies from era to era
and from region to region. Also important as determining variables are
the magnitude of the new population being added to a country and
the skill level (i.e., highly educated professionals versus menial labor)
of the new entrants. Taking all this into account, the following discussion is mostly focused upon the situation in the United States, though
occasionally referring to other nations as well. The proposal here is that
the "politics of immigration" mostly revolves around four variables:
(i) old versus new immigration, (ii) the impact of immigrants upon the
national economy, (iii) the impact of immigrants upon the social fabric,
especially North American family values, and (iv) the movement from
the "melting pot" dream to the ideology of multiculturalism. A brief
elucidation of each of these realms follows.

Old versus new immigration

Putting aside the "pre-historic" fact that some 32,000 years ago, wandering tribes from Mongolia and neighboring Himalayan regions walked across the Bering Strait into what is now Alaska and then southwards into the current United States and were later called "American Indians," the history of immigration to this country can be divided into three phases: (i) *first immigration* (1619–1803 AD) which brought white, mainly English-speaking Protestant individuals from Western Europe; (ii) *second immigration* (1820–1924) which brought "darker" Europeans, such as Italians, Greeks, and Russians, more non-English speaking people, and those belonging to Catholic and Jewish faiths, and (iii) *third immigration* (1965-present) which brought people from the Third World, that is, poor countries of Latin America and Asia, predominantly non-English speaking, and of quite diverse religions (e.g., Catholics, Hindus, Muslims).[2] Each of these waves was mobilized by "push" (from the countries of origin) and "pull" (from the United States) factors of their own kind. The *first wave* of immigration was largely the result of a search for religious freedom—away from being forced to comply with uncompromising tenets of the Anglican Church by a succession of English queens and kings. Elizabeth I (1558–1603), James I (1603–1625), and Charles I (1625–1649) would not allow members of other religious groups to worship God in the ways they believed to be correct. Even if the groups fled to other European countries where their religious faith was tolerated, they could not flourish economically. Thus, the rush towards America was initiated. The *second wave* was caused by the breakdown of the traditional agricultural system in Europe and facilitated by a transportation revolution that made America more accessible. An additional "pull" factor, that especially involved immigrants from the Philippines, China, and Mexico, was constituted by need for labor in the United States. The promise of higher wages was alluring but not sufficient; deliberate recruitment seemed necessary. Between 1902 and 1905, nearly 7,000 Koreans were brought as plantation laborers to Hawaii, 1,000 of whom subsequently moved to the mainland (Houchins & Houchins, 1974). Mexican immigration too was initiated by large farming operations and railroad companies in the United States. By 1916, five or six trains full of Mexican workers hired by the American agents were being run every week from Laredo to Los Angeles (Portes & Rumbaut, 1996). The *third wave*—religion-wise and ethnically more diverse than the previous two—has resulted from the postcolonial hunger in poor countries of Asia for the West and the worldwide increase in the awareness of economic disparity between the United States and Third World countries. Dreams of monetary success largely propelled this wave. At the same time, those arriving on the shores of America in this period also included exiles and refugees produced by the Second World War as well as those dislocated due to the United States' own armed interventions in distant locations (e.g., Vietnam, Cambodia, Iraq).

The three waves have had somewhat different fates with the passage of time. The *first wave* of immigrants has gradually acquired the status of "original inhabitants," eclipsing the vanquished natives of the land. This development in the United States parallels similar occurrences in many other countries (e.g., Australia, Canada, Israel, New Zealand, and South Africa), though the relationship between the actual natives and the early settlers is hardly the same everywhere. The *second wave* has largely been assimilated within the culture established by the first and in the process has altered it to a certain extent. Despite this, a sense of their being on a lower rung of social status persists in the minds of the so-called original inhabitants. The *third wave* is constituted by the darker-skinned Asian and Latin American immigrants and is still struggling to find its place in the mainstream culture; this is especially true for the individuals of lower socioeconomic status of these groups.

The three waves also differ in their magnitude. Census figures, to the extent these are available, tell this story. In 1850, foreign-born persons constituted about 7 percent of the total population of the United States. In 1910, the number had risen to 14.7 percent. Anti-immigration sentiment rose around this time; this was partly due to sheer numbers and partly because a lot more non-English speaking Europeans, Catholics, and Jews had begun migrating to the country. A consequence of this negativism was the passage of the National Origins Act in 1924 which severely restricted immigration from Southern and Eastern Europe, while continuing the exclusion of Asians. The economic depression of the 1930s also discouraged immigration. By the mid-1960s, the population of foreign-born persons living in the United States dropped dramatically to a mere 4.4 percent. However, a coalition of Jews, Catholics, and political liberals, who had fought for years against the discriminatory slant of the 1924 law, succeeded in getting the Immigration and Nationality Act passed in 1965. The amendment put limits upon European immigration for the first time. More important, it abolished restrictions on immigration from Asian countries and discarded all efforts to distinguish between immigrants on account of their race or their historical link to America. Consequently, the proportion of immigrants in the general population began to rise: 4.4 percent in 1965, 6.2 percent in 1980, 7.9 percent in 1990, 11.1 percent in 2000, and 12.8 percent in 2004 (Guskin & Wilson, 2007).

Seemingly high, this number is actually *lower* than that in 1910 when the immigrant population stood at 14.7 percent. So why is there now all this social uproar about immigration? Why is the "new" immigration construed as bad for the country while the "old" immigration is upheld as having been good? Could it betray the quintessentially short American memory which overlooks the previous high numbers and focuses on the present only? Or, could feelings of alarm at the magnitude of the "new" immigration be a cover for racial and ethnic biases against darker-skinned immigrants from Asia, Africa, and the Caribbean? The fact that a considerable proportion of these "new" immigrants do not belong to the Christian faith might also be a contributing factor. The current anti-immigrant sentiment might thus be a modern-day reincarnation of the xenophobia directed at Catholics and Jews and immigrants from Italy, Greece, Poland, and Russia around the turn of the twentieth century.

Impact upon the national economy

In the early period after their arrival in the United States, some immigrants might indeed cost the nation money. They might put less money into the system than they draw from it in the form of benefits. This is because they tend to be younger than the general population as a whole.

> The National Academy of Sciences calculated in 1997 that households headed by immigrants were costing households headed by native-born citizens some $166 to $266 a year, mostly in public education and health expenses for children. The number was even higher for states with large immigrant populations: in California, the cost was $1,178 for households headed by native-born citizens. Taken out of context, this number seems like ammunition for immigration opponents. But native-born young people with families are

also a "burden" on the system in exactly the same way—they too
make less money and pay less in taxes when they are raising children. (ibid., p. 63)

However, both groups—immigrants and young native-born citizens—
end up putting more into the national monetary stream than they take
out as they grow older and their children finish public schooling. The
deficit of their earlier years is mitigated by the positive balance of their
later years. The notion that immigrants make the national economy
bleed thus turns out to be false.

Three other widely held beliefs also contain more myth than reality.
These include the following:

- *Immigrants take American jobs*: This notion is hardly applicable in current times. "In fact, today's economy is so globally integrated that
the idea of jobs having a national identity is practically useless"
(Chomsky, 2007, p. 3). American businesses, seeking to reduce costs,
have increasingly moved production lines to poor countries. Even
the service-based industries (e.g., credit card providers, health care
records) rely upon such outsourcing. It is not the immigrants who are
taking "American" jobs, it is the American employers who are sending them away.
- *Immigrants reduce the number of jobs available to native-born citizens*:
This notion is based upon the assumption that the number of jobs in
a given society is finite. This is not true. The number of jobs available
is elastic and dependent upon a large number of variables. Moreover,
population growth (in this case, by the addition of new entrants to the
country) creates jobs at the same time as it provides more people to
fill them. Growing communities offer more, not fewer, jobs. In 1994,
the conservative Alexis de Tocqueville Institution found evidence
that immigrants create at least as many jobs as they take and that
"their presence should not be feared by the U.S. citizens" (Moore,
Gallaway, & Vedder, 1994, p. 103). And, "[T]welve years later, the liberal Pew Hispanic Center came to a similar conclusion based upon a
study of employment trends in the 1990s and early 2000s" (Guskin &
Wilson, 2007, p. 68).
- *Immigrants drain the economy by sending their earnings back to their countries of origin*: It is true that immigrants in the United States tend to
send money to their less affluent relatives back home. For certain

countries (for instance, Mexico, Haiti), these remittances constitute a significant part of the national economy. And yet, the monies sent out benefit the United States. This happens in two ways. First, the money goes to countries which have close business ties to the US and purchase a lot of US goods and services. Second, considerable fees are generated in connection with monetary remittances to foreign countries. "In 2002, immigrants paid about $4 billion in fees for sending remittances to Latin American and Caribbean countries; most of this went to US banks or to US corporations like Western Union" (ibid., p. 67). Moreover, remittance money, when spent locally in the immigrants' countries of origin, can help improve the regional economy and therefore reduce migration (Chomsky, 2007).

All in all, it seems that the negative impact of immigration upon the national economy is a myth concocted and perpetuated by immigrant opponents and their spinmeisters. What actually propels this need to fuel xenophobia is hard to say. It is, however, not far-fetched to imagine that the economically rationalized nativism might be hiding some anti-immigrant racism.[3] And, the ubiquitous need for societies to have an enemy (Volkan, 1988) might also play a role here especially because the United States, if not the entire West, is undergoing a socioeconomic turmoil and requires "external" causes to explain it.

Impact upon the social fabric

A sentiment prevails across the nation that immigrants, especially those recently arrived, have a negative impact upon American culture. Speaking in 1992, conservative pundit Patrick Buchanan declared that a block-by-block war was coming to "take back our culture" (cited in Fukuyama, 1994, p. 151). Such rhetoric intentionally or unintentionally fueled the societal dread that somehow the American way of life is endangered, if not about to become extinct. Immigrants, in this line of thinking, are seen as eroding our culture, our love of family, while benefiting from our system of "the three m's—money, mobility, and meritocracy" (Noonan, 1994, p. 177).

Such anti-immigrant propaganda is spun out of the yarn of distortion. *First*, a highly idealized picture of the "American culture" is presented. Note the following statement by Peggy Noonan, a conservative spokesperson and the official speech writer for Ronald Reagan and

George Bush from 1984 to 1989: "Deep in its heart the world thinks that America is the bravest, sweetest, toughest, funniest place on earth" (ibid., p. 178). Add to this the self-exalting drumbeat of how "our" system encourages life, liberty, and the pursuit of happiness for all; it is founded upon regarding all persons to be equal.[4] America, in such a portrayal, is fair, just, and a haven that forever welcomes (and has welcomed) disenfranchised people from all over the world. What this rosy picture does not include are the horrific facts pertaining to the genocide of American Indians; the centuries of slavery and related abuse of African Americans; the dropping of an atomic bomb on Japan that killed nearly 173,000 innocent civilians; the pillage of Cambodia, Laos, Vietnam, and Iraq; and the rampant breakdown of the family structure across the nation. The anti-immigrant sentiment depicts the foreign-born as arriving in a heaven with mud-strewn shoes and soiling the idyllic scenery. Nothing can be further from the truth. It is true that the United States is more affluent than the countries they leave behind but it is hardly the blissful terrain the political right would have us believe.

Second, the current anti-immigrant sentiment seems directed at those who have come from the so-called Third World countries of Africa, Latin America, and Asia. Many of these immigrants belong to religions unfamiliar to Americans (e.g., Hinduism, Islam), and many are dark-skinned. What passes for an anti-immigrant stance might thus contain elements of religious and racial prejudice as well. This is not accorded proper consideration in debates centering on the issue of immigration.

Finally, the anti-immigrant sentiment overlooks that immigrants might bring more solid family and communal orientation than exists in the United States. On the parameters of divorce rates, single parent family households, and respect for elders, the immigrants seem to do better than the American-born citizens. They have stronger family values than middle class suburban Americans, to be sure. For instance, 78 percent of Asian and Pacific Islander households are two-parent households compared to 70 percent for white Americans *and* while Asians are as likely to be married as whites, they are half as likely to be divorced (Fukuyama, 1994; Smith & Edmonston, 1997). Of note is also the fact that households without fathers comprise about 13.5 percent for whites, 46.6 percent for African Americans, and 24.4 percent for Hispanics (Fukuyama, 1994). However, when corrected for social class, the Hispanic population comes very close to the white population. Finally, immigrants, especially from the Far Eastern countries of

China, Korea, and Japan, as well as those from Bangladesh, India, Iran, and Pakistan, show much greater respect for the elderly and often take care of parents at home through aging and infirmity.

Such unmasking of the hollowness of the assertion that immigrants have a negative impact upon family values in America does not mean that family structure is not in trouble here. It is. However, the roots of the cultural breakdown are to be found in the disruptive nature of capitalism which creates false consumer needs, fuels human greed, pulls mothers prematurely away from their infants in order to earn money, lulls people to live their entire lives in debt, and puts a premium on material acquisitions at the cost of family cohesion. The sexual revolution, the institution of no-fault divorce, the growing anomie of urban life, and the widely prevalent cynicism towards government have also contributed to the current cultural meltdown. And, these detrimental vectors have originated in the heart of white Anglo-Saxon America; they are not brought to the shores of this nation by Third World immigrants.

From "melting pot" to multiculturalism

Massive immigration over the last three decades has resulted in dramatic changes in the cultural climate of the nation. This wave of immigration has a large proportion of people from Third World countries. Their cultural difference from the mainstream American is far greater than the Russian, Italian, and Greek immigrants who preceded them. As a result, the "melting pot" of American society (into which the newcomers could submerge their unique identities) has given way to the potpourri of multiculturalism. The process of "melting" into the "pot" has become slower and subject to greater resistance. Moreover, the various minorities have established their own ethnic enclaves, started celebrating their festivals with gusto, and created museums of their history. In tandem, academia has begun to include the important figures of ethnic minorities in textbooks as well. The business world too has responded by managing cultural diversity in ways that enhance organizational performance (Cox, 2001; Nemeth, 1985).

Reactions to such changes have been swift and, from the right wing of the political stage, expectedly negative. Patrick Buchanan (1992, quoted in Fukuyama, 1994) and Peggy Noonan (1994) are hardly alone in lamenting the loss of "our culture." Lawrence Auster, the author of

The Path to National Suicide: An Essay on Immigration and Multiculturalism (1990) emits a similarly injured groan.

> Across the country, America's mainstream identity is being disman-
> tled in the name of "inclusion." Half of New York City's Shakespeare
> Festival in 1991 was given over to Spanish and Portuguese trans-
> lations of Shakespeare. Christmas has been replaced in many
> schools by a non-denominational Winterfest or by the new African-
> American holiday Kwanza, while schools in areas with large His-
> panic populations celebrate Cinco de Mayo. The exemplary fig-
> ures of American history have been excised from school textbooks,
> replaced by obscure minorities and women. (p. 169)

The implication is clear: what is happening to the American culture at large is bad and undesirable. Instead of upholding the moral validity of all cultures and subcultures and the individual's freedom to express, celebrate, and live according to his or her ancestral traditions, these self-appointed guardians of (white) conservatism assert that the cultural change happening as a consequence of Third World immigration is a death knell for Western civilization. They therefore oppose both immigration and multiculturalism. "Neoconservatives," however, de-link the two; they are willing to tolerate immigration as a labor necessity but vehemently oppose multiculturalism. They even propose that multiculturalism has little to do with the new immigrants and, in a strange twist of logic, put the entire responsibility for this social movement on the threshold of the African American population. A prominent representative of such thinking is Irving Kristol (1995) who states that multiculturalism:

> ... is propagated on our college campuses by a coalition of
> nationalist-racist blacks, radical feminists, gays and lesbians, and
> a handful of aspiring demagogues who claim to represent various
> ethnic minorities. In this coalition, it is the blacks who provide the
> hardcore of energy, because it is they who can intimidate the fac-
> ulty and the administration, fearful of being branded "racist." This
> coalition's multiculturalism is an ideology whose education pro-
> gram is subordinated to a political program that is, above all, anti-
> American and anti-Western ... . What these radicals blandly call

multiculturalism is as much a "war against the West" as Nazism
and Stalinism ever were. (p. 52)

Besides invalidating the aspirations (and right) of the new immigrants
to preserve and celebrate their uniqueness, Kristol's diatribe does dis-
service to the African Americans striving for a belated recognition of
both the injustices done to them and of their profound contributions
to the American culture. Publications of this kind also have the potential to create rifts between African Americans and the Third World
immigrants.

The tension between the new immigrants and African Americans

An important aspect of the recent influx of Third World immigrants
is its socioeconomic impact upon the African American population of
the country. The myriad ways in which this occurs and the complex
relationship between the two groups (putting aside all the subtleties
and nuances of subgroups within each, for the time being) constitutes
a vast topic that can hardly be addressed meaningfully in this section.[5]
Three aspects deserve special attention, though. These include the following: (i) racism of the immigrants from colonized countries, (ii) competition between "new" immigrants and African Americans for jobs,
and (iii) the special situation of immigrants of African origin.

- *Racism of the immigrants from colonized countries*: Immigrants from
  countries that were colonized by white majority nations (e.g., Great
  Britain, France, Spain, Holland) are inflicted with the dual irony of
  overly idealizing the West and succumbing to their erstwhile mas-
  ter's devaluation of the "natives." Often dark-skinned, these immigrants secretly regard themselves as inherently inferior to white
  people. Upon entering a country with a predominantly white population (e.g., the United States), they align themselves with the majority, often projecting their own shame-laden self-representations on
  to the African American people. Consequently, they develop strong
  anti-black sentiments; this is a reversal of what they had suffered
  directly at the hands of their white colonizers or what had been trans-
  generationally transmitted to them by their colonized ancestors.
  Displaying an "identification with the aggressor" (A. Freud, 1946),
  the victims of yesterday become the perpetrators of today. Shifting

social alliances—some plausible, others curious—facilitate such developments. Immigrants from India, for instance, are often information technology or medical professionals and readily move up the economic ladder. This affords them greater contact with the white majority with whom they establish an imaginary kinship. Distancing themselves from African Americans buttresses their sense of "belonging." Since most of them are Hindus and are experiencing a minority status for the first time, such narcissistic repair—even though unfortunate and tinged with hostility helps restore their self-esteem. More curious in this context is an expression used by some Muslim immigrants from Pakistan and Bangladesh. They declare that the least reliable people in the world are *Malus* and *Kalus*[6] (Hindus and blacks). That such unlikely pairing could only result from regressed, unthinking, and hateful (and self-loathing) minds goes without saying. It should also be added that the anti-black sentiment is hardly restricted to South Asian immigrants; the intonation in which many Jewish immigrants from Poland, Russia, and Hungary refer to the *schwartzas* leaves little doubt about their racist attitudes. In all fairness, though, it should be added that African Americans might also harbor ambivalent feelings towards Asian immigrants. While lack of familiarity with the latter's way of life and forms of communication might fuel the African American xenophobia (Bailey, 2000), a greater role is played by their sense that the newcomers seem to have equal, if not greater, access to the economic protection programs that have become available to them only after centuries of abuse and decades of civic struggle. The situation is akin to an older child having misgivings about a younger sibling who is born after the family's financial status has significantly improved. While the African American vs. new immigrants tension has the ring of such sibling rivalry, such resemblance is largely metaphorical. There are broader economic, historical, and social factors at work here.

• *Competition for jobs:* Immigrants from "developing nations" impact upon the lives of African Americans in another way. They compete with them for jobs, especially when it comes to the lower scales of employment. In a sophisticated essay dealing with this issue, Jackson (1988) states:

> Anecdotal data, labor market statistics and simple observation show a pronounced trend during the past two decades of immigrant

and refugee workers replacing many native black unskilled, semi-skilled and supervisory workers in such businesses as hotels, restaurants, fast food outlets, light manufacturing firms, construction firms and taxicab companies in metropolitan areas with heavy concentrations of recent immigrants and refugees. Indications of these trends have been confirmed by sectoral and regional studies during the past decade that suggest that undocumented workers displace low-skilled native workers and depress wages. (p. 247)

Jackson acknowledges that there have been studies that assert the contrary (McCarthy & Burciaga Valdez, 1985; Muller & Espenshade, 1985; see also Guskin & Wilson, 2007 for a more recent iteration of this position) but point-by-point shows their methodological errors. She concludes that even if the "new immigrants" do not displace African Americans in significant numbers on a nationwide basis, they do create a stiff competition; this can have discouraging effects on the poorest African Americans who have little hope for economic ascendance anyway. Jackson also notes the "linguistic discrimination" that has cropped up in certain regions, like Florida, where employers prefer to hire Spanish-speaking and bilingual workers.[7] Finally, there is also some evidence (Mines, 1985) that poor Hispanic immigrants drive the hourly labor wages down since they are willing to work for lesser amounts. This, in turn, leads unscrupulous employers to prefer them over African American workers.

• *Immigrants of African Origin*: Whether coming from the various countries of the African continent itself (e.g., Ethiopia, Ghana, Nigeria, Sudan) or "secondarily" from other places (e.g., the Caribbean region), immigrants of African origin constitute a special group when it comes to the encounter with African Americans, that is, people of African origin who have been in the United States for centuries. Though often distinct in language, accent, and at times, attire, rituals, and bodily gestures, immigrants of African origin are often mistaken for African Americans. They become "invisible immigrants" (Stephen Shanfield, personal communication, April 11, 1994) and, in this limited way, seem akin to Canadian or Australian whites living in the United States. Such ready-made blending-in has its pros and cons. On the positive side, it offers them a quick sense of fraternity and protects them from feeling the unease of being viewed as "foreigners." On the negative side, it glosses over the profound differences in history, politics, religion, and social customs between them and the "local" African Americans. Age at the time of immigration plays an important role in this context. The "negative" impact seems to be greater in older immigrants. Their identities are soaked in their original culture (including religion, art, music, family values, and social customs) and they find it disconcerting to be lumped with African Americans whose idiom of life is often quite distinct form theirs. In contrast, those who come to the United States as children internalize American ways of being to a greater extent and thus feel close to being African American. Anique Forrester, a young physician in the Philadelphia area who migrated from Jamaica to the United States as an eight-year-old child testifies to such a development.

> It is not obvious when you look at me or talk to me, as it may be with others, that I am an immigrant. I am more often thought of as African-American and I don't often correct others or make a distinction in being Jamaican. I feel like I have two identities, I am both. I feel American when I interact with people from Jamaica who are shocked that I lost my accent and maybe don't believe that I'm one of them. I feel Jamaican the rest of the time but it's hard to say what that actually feels like. I think there is an ease and familiarity that comes over me when I'm with family or in Jamaica that I don't think I could get from anyone or anything else. However, it is also true that I have so much in common with some of my American colleagues that my identity as a foreigner sometimes gets lost. That sometimes puts me in a difficult situation with myself. Am I supposed to integrate myself in the workplace to the point that the core of who I am is lost? Or do I make it a point to highlight my differences and let others know that I am not native to this country? I think sometimes I do a combination of both in different circumstances. I think that those who know me know most of who I am and where I come from but I do know that in unfamiliar situations and sometimes as a way of getting along I do take the easier path of blending in as just one of the others. (personal communication, April 23, 2010)

Besides the age at which immigration took place, the socioeconomic status of the African immigrants also affects the degree of their assimilation into the American culture. In a study of black West Indian immigrants, Waters (1999) found that:

> Immigrants and their children do better economically by maintaining a strong ethnic identity and culture and by resisting American cultural and identity influences … those who resist becoming American do well and those who lose their immigrant ethnic distinctiveness become downwardly mobile … When West Indians lose their distinctiveness as immigrants or ethnics they become not just Americans, but black Americans. (p. 5)

In other words, assimilation for African immigrants can often imply a downward economic mobility. This is especially true of those who are less skilled and it shows that the association between cultural assimilation and economic gain is an idea derived mainly from the experience of white immigrants.

The immigrant's politics

Refugees and exiles are often preoccupied with the political issues that led to the departure from their home countries. On formal or informal bases, they gather in groups and discuss the situations "back home," often planning strategies for returning there and improving the sociopolitical scene. In contrast, immigrants—unless they come from politically unstable nations—are far less politically conscious. This is especially true in the early period of their arrival in a new country. Interest in political events "back home" at this stage in time is largely in the service of nostalgia and maintaining connection with what, in reality, has been left behind. Interest in political events of the country of adoption is similarly a screen which masks the drive to assimilate and be like the "local" people. In other words, the political awareness of the early immigrant is hardly civic-minded at its heart. It is intended more towards the amelioration of internal anxieties than towards the betterment of external realities.

Genuine political consciousness and praxis in the immigrant evolve over a long course of time which might span more than a generation or two. Assurance of financial security, a deeper encounter with the local culture in the course of raising children, and intrapsychic transformations of middle age often contribute to the dawn of political consciousness in the immigrant. This is not true of all immigrants though, and many lead lives of political indifference and absorption in essentially personal concerns. When political awakening does take place, it tends to take two pathways. The first is centered upon matters pertaining to the country left behind. It is often characterized by a powerful resurgence of nostalgic idealization of the "motherland" left behind and an alarming sort of ethnic grandiloquence. Elsewhere, I (Akhtar, 2005b) have illustrated this type of development in the context of some Hindu Indian immigrants to the United States. While forming a minority among the entire Hindu Indian immigrant population here, this particular faction manifested a "hyper-nationalism" that had many problematic aspects, including:

> (1) the mistaken equation of Indian culture with Hinduism; (2) a conviction that mankind's wisdom sprang only from Hindu religious thought; (3) an insistence that while Hindu culture provided concepts and imaginative potential to both the West and Far East, nothing significant from those regions contributed to the Hindu culture; (4) an exaggerated and paranoid sense of cultural victimization by the West; and, (5) a doomsday scenario suggesting that Christian evangelists proselytizing in India would gradually convert so many people to their faith that the demographic dominance of Hindus would be threatened. (pp. 118–119)

Not surprisingly, a close liaison developed between this group of Hindu fundamentalists and the right-wing "nationalist" political parties in India; significant money was raised in the United States to finance the activities—often anti-Muslim and anti-Christian—of these parties. In accomplishing such sociopolitical praxis across oceans, the "hyper-nationalistic" Hindus were following a path that had been earlier taken by certain Muslim immigrants from India to England who had brewed the idea of carving out Pakistan (Akhtar, 2005b) and a group of Sikhs in Canada and the US who fueled the failed effort to create Khalistan (an independent nation of their co-religionists) in the Northwestern part of India. To be sure, such immigrant fervor to affect politics back home, often to the extent of initiating or supporting secession movements, is not restricted to the people of the Indian continent. Many other immigrant groups (e.g., Irish, Cubans, Palestinians) may provide financial and emotional support to political movements back home.

In contrast to such excursions into the political landscape of the nation left behind, one notices the emergence of political awareness that is relevant "locally," that is, pertains to social and civic issues in the land of adoption. Usually such development occurs only after an immigrant has lived in his or her new country for quite some time and has either become fully acculturated or has personally transformed the difficulties of acculturation into a voice of social activism. Some immigrants, however, bring a sense of social ethics and a keen eye for communal malaise from the very start. Joyce Kay, a geriatric psychiatrist who migrated to the United States from Ireland, forms an illustration *par excellence* of such civic mindedness. She states:

> My husband and I entered the United States on June 11, 1964, not long after the assassination of President John F. Kennedy. My eldest daughter was born in August of that year. Although in our eyes, there were many problems in the country, it was the beginning of Lyndon B. Johnson's "Great Society," and we felt the government was trying to remedy them. My second child was born in February of 1968, about eight months following the murder of a potentially great leader, Robert F. Kennedy. Two months later on April 8, I listened to the news of the death of Reverend Martin Luther King, Jr. At that time we were living in an integrated neighborhood with a busy shopping hub, served by "shoppers' special" buses. Enclosed shopping malls were yet in their infancy. I was greatly upset by the news, but as was my usual habit, I did go out for a walk with the baby that day. I was stunned to find myself in a deserted street— no pedestrians, no cars, no buses. A beautiful but uncannily silent spring day. Suddenly, I wondered whether we had made an error in coming to the United States. Did I wish to bring up my children in a country that murdered its great men? (personal communication, April 4, 2010)

While poignant tales like this touch our hearts, it takes something more to channel such emotional grace into nuts-and-bolts political participation. Early childhood experiences, especially those involving a sense of being unfairly treated due to one's minority status, often play an important role in such development. Identification with socially conscious and active parents (and/or other important family members) too is a facilitating factor. Finally, the era in which one is growing and to the degree it is suffused with political happenings also influences the extent of one's civic mindedness. The fact that adult life political activism in an immigrant is derived from such complex sources is confirmed by the experience of Nina Ahmad, a Philadelphia-based research scientist from Bangladesh. Eloquently, Ahmad traces her current political participation in ethnic minority affairs to the multiple layers of experience, exposure, and identification during her formative years.

> Lunch time recess was noisy and chaotic. A mosaic of images: bright blue sky, big black crows swooping down to snatch lunch out of our tiffin boxes, noisy rambunctious kids running around on a concrete playground. This was Karachi Grammar School, the elite institution in Pakistan, founded in 1847 by the British. Sharply etched in my memory: on that playground, a kid I knew was from East Pakistan, proclaiming he was from the West when being teased by fellow West Pakistani students. I was confused and had glimpsed a fleeting expression of shame on that little boy's face. East Pakistanis were definitely second class citizens in their own country: this was much discussed by the Bangali expatriate community in Karachi, to which my family belonged. My first overtly political act at around age six to seven was my decision not to speak Urdu. I even refused to answer the phone at home. I had no inkling of the Language Movement of 1952 etc., no idea how this feeling of injustice fueled the birth of Bangladesh. I was just protesting in my own little way of what I perceived as unfairness that would make a little boy be ashamed of his roots.
>
> We are an amalgam of many forces that shape our lives. Our genes, our environment, the impact of political and historic events shape personal lives and affect the trajectories of the future. I was raised in a two-parent, two-child home (older boy and younger girl) in which my mother was the overt "liberal," the social worker who trained as a Montessori teacher, the one who took cooking classes and made us exotic dishes from Africa and Indonesia, from Ireland and Poland! She was the one who came from a lineage of "liberal" politics with her uncle Humayun Kabir, an Education Secretary and then the Minister of Culture and Scientific Research in India during its early post-independence years. Currently, my mother's cousin is a Judge on the Supreme Court of India. From her I heard stories of struggles of Indian Independence, the

divided loyalties during the World War II, *Ramayana,* and she was my constant cheerleader in all I did! My father was my source of stability, the one who had a practical take on matters, but also always my cheerleader! He was the eldest son of a conservative landowning family (from the then eastern Bengal), whose father was also a politician, but within the frame of being a Muslim in India. It was fascinating for me to watch my mother influence my father's views as I grew up, expanding his frame of reference and making him a much more tolerant man. It was significant that religion was a social/cultural construct in our home, even though my mother practiced her own questioning brand of Islam especially in her later years.

The single most defining historic event that has imprinted my brain in a myriad of ways was the Independence War of Bangladesh. Watching people from all walks of life band together, ready to sacrifice their lives for the freedom to be who you are (culturally) was very powerful to an adolescent. My life affirming moment was sitting in a sea of people (amazed that my parents allowed me to go with my young adult neighbors) in one of the biggest rallies in the newly minted Bangladesh, welcoming the Father of our nation, Sheikh Mujibur Rahman, who had been just released from prison by Pakistan. It was then I truly felt the power of political oratory. I don't remember the words but I remember how I felt—energized, part of something bigger than myself and truly feeling one can make a difference!

I brought this feeling that "I mattered" to the United States when I came for college. After completing my Ph.D., starting a job, having my first child, I was clearly looking for meaningful ways of contributing and belonging. Always having followed global politics as an observer, I felt moved to be more involved. My sustenance of spirit needed a community that held my beliefs and I found politics to be a sure way to root out "who was who" with respect to fundamental principles. Having always been an immigrant, I segued easily into "democratic" politics which seemed to honor the minority opinion. I felt immediate kinship with the Civil Rights Struggles that still persist, but I seemed to have developed a more nuanced approach to accepting "principled" compromise, understanding that is necessary for things to move forward at certain junctures.

Identity politics as an Asian American has certainly been a natural fit for me, albeit uncomfortable at times, since intellectually I feel we need to be beyond this frame. The sense of self I have developed along the way, nurtured by my parents and now by my own nuclear family, has afforded me some ease in negotiating the halls of power. I have developed a deep love for my city, Philadelphia, while still maintaining my affection for Dhaka. I don't experience this as divided loyalties, but rather a sense of loss from time to time. Frequent trips to Bangladesh and maintaining relationships with those I care about there has certainly helped with this dichotomous feeling. Ultimately, I am involved in politics in order to feel that I "matter" in this vast global village! (personal communication, May 10, 2010)

All in all, it therefore seems that the immigrant's politics displays five features (a) early pseudo-political interest which is largely in the service of post-migration stabilization of the self, (b) a relatively long period of political difference during which the immigrants establish them-selves socioeconomically in their new land, (c) continued political apathy in some immigrants, (d) a rise of nostalgic hyper-nationalism towards the land left behind and associated manic and paranoid operations, and (e) genuine political praxis that tackles the palpably real problems of minority politics.

Illegal aliens

The topic of illegal aliens is emotionally laden. Immigration opponents continually strive to restrict the rights of such people and many go to the extent of advocating mass deportations. Immigrant-rights activists assert that "[A] globalized political and economic system creates illegality by displacing people and then denying them rights and equality as they do what they have to do to survive—move to find work" (Bacon, 2008, p. vi). The realm of illegal aliens is thus not only affectively charged but complex and multifaceted. The following passages will address the topic under five subsections: (i) the label itself, (ii) the use of fake identification for getting jobs, (iii) impact upon economy, (iv) becoming legal, and (v) adverse psychosocial effects upon such immigrants themselves.

The label

The first matter of note when it comes to the consideration of illegal aliens is the label itself. Both components of the label ("illegal" and "aliens") evoke negative emotions. The term "alien," by definition, declares a group of people to be strange, incompatible with the host population, and even a bit uncanny. The prefix "illegal," when applied to a group of people rather than to a set of actions, acquires a quality that is simultaneously absurd and sinister. To designate people as "legal" or "illegal" is silly since these categories refer to varieties of an individual's behavior and not to his mere existence. Indeed "[O]ne of the most heartfelt slogans shouted in the huge immigrant marches and printed on millions of signs and buttons is: 'No human being is illegal'" (ibid., p. v). There is a sinister element as well to declaring some people as "illegal" since it encourages others to view all their actions with suspicion. No wonder then that the label "illegal alien" comes across as pejorative and discriminatory. Immigrant-rights activists fiercely oppose its use and prefer the terms such as "unauthorized migrants" (Passel, 2006), "out of status immigrants" (Guskin & Wilson, 2007), or "undocumented immigrants" (Bacon, 2008) in its place. And, the United Nations High Commission on Human Rights has declared that the expression "illegal migrant" should be discarded in favor of "undocumented migrant." And yet, the term "illegal aliens" keeps appearing in public discourse. Perhaps its irresistible appeal is due to the pressure all of us feel to externalize the illegal and alien aspects of our own selves. Thus by using the term "illegal aliens" thoughtlessly, we can locate outside what we actually dislike within our own selves.

The use of false documents

A second issue pertains to the use of false documents by such "out of status immigrants" in order to secure employment. To be sure, this is criminal. However, this crime is not committed by such immigrants in isolation; their employers frequently know who they are hiring and, for their own financial benefit, turn a blind eye to the forged documents. This is not emphasized in the immigration debates where the anti-immigrant bias puts the entire blame on only one party in the interaction. Note the following as well:

Working for a living doesn't harm society, and most people consider it to be a good thing. But for some reason, immigrants face more public condemnation—and harsher legal consequences—for using fake IDs to get honest jobs than US born teenagers do when they use fake IDs to buy liquor. Why are immigrants held to a higher standard than US citizens? Most US born citizens have broken some laws during their lifetimes, yet no one calls them "illegals." (Guskin & Wilson, 2007, p. 40)

At the same time, it can not be denied that the use of forged documents has all sorts of adverse psychosocial consequences. On the psychological front, it can lead to living with perpetual fear, guilt, and low self-esteem. On the social front, one can become beholden to criminal elements in the society and be exploited and abused by them.

Impact on economy

A related third issue (which contributes to the negative attitudes about undocumented immigrants) is that they adversely affect the nation's economy. There is some truth in it insofar as the children who are "out of status," or who are the offspring of "out of status" immigrants are entitled to free public education up to high school in the United States. This costs the nation money. Financial burden on the state is also caused by those undocumented workers who work "off the books" and are paid "under the table." Their employers do not report their income and income taxes are not deducted from their salaries. This too is a loss to the national economy. Highlighting such facts and embellishing them with fierce rhetoric is the trademark of anti-immigration forces. The following statement exemplifies such a stance.

Immigration—especially that of illegal immigrants, recent amnesty recipients, and refugees—is a major contribution to the growth of adult illiteracy in the United States. To this degree, immigration, by adding to the surplus of illiterate adult job seekers, is serving to diminish the limited opportunities for poorly prepared citizens to find jobs or to improve their employability by on-the-job training. It is not surprising, therefore, that the underground economy is thriving in many urban centers. Moreover the nature of the overall immigration and refugee flow is also contributing to the need for

> localities to expand funding for remedial education and training and language programs in many urban communities. Too often these funding choices cause scarce public funds to be diverted from being used to upgrade the human resource capabilities of the citizen labor force. (Vernon Briggs, cited in Miles, 1994, p. 129)

While containing a kernel of truth, statements of this sort overlook that the monetary scenario involving illegal aliens has other facets as well.

> Out-of-status workers and their employers also pay an estimated $6 billion to $7 billion in Social Security taxes each year and about $1.5 billion in Medicaid taxes. This account amounts for about 10 percent of Social Security's annual surplus. Very few of these workers are able to get back what they paid in. Most never expect to apply, but if they did, they would be barred by the Social Security Protection Act of 2004. This law in effect confiscates these workers' benefits because they worked here without authorization. (Guskin & Wilson, 2007, p. 65)

Such compensations for the deficit-producing leakage in money are, however, infrequently brought to public attention. This implies that political "spin" often affects how facts in this realm are presented. To complicate matters further, the methodology by which such facts are deduced might also be imprecise. For instance, in a highly publicized report, Huddle (1993) concluded that immigrants present in the United States in 1992 cost the government that year more than $45 billion above and beyond the taxes they paid. However, a close examination of his data by Passel (1994) revealed that, far from costing that staggering amount of money, immigrants actually contributed a net surplus of $28.7 billion. Such gross discrepancies confirm that the study of fiscal implications of immigration is far from precise.

Becoming legal

Whether an illegal immigrant can become legal and get permanent resident status ("Green Card") depends upon whether the individual entered the United States with a valid visa (e.g., tourist, student) which has expired or whether the entry itself was illegal, that is, without a visa. For the former, three ways are open: getting an employer to sponsor one, getting a parent or adult child[8] to sponsor one, or getting married to a US citizen. None of these are easy. Employers are reluctant to put up with the paperwork necessary to demonstrate that they tried unsuccessfully to fill the position by hiring a US citizen or a permanent resident. Parents and/or adult children might be more forthcoming but the process can take a long time and involve significant bureaucratic hurdles. Marrying a US citizen puts the burden on the applicant to prove that the union is not fraudulent and entered into only for the purposes of obtaining a Green Card. One is required to have filed joint taxes, cosigned leases, opened a joint checking account, and received utility bills in the names of both marital partners. Even with all this in place, the process can take two to three years before the nonresident spouse gets a permanent resident status.

Becoming legal for those who entered the country illegally is an entirely different matter. Individual effort has no meaning in this context. Group activism and legislative change is what matters. For instance, the passage of the Immigration Reform and Control Act (IRCA) in 1986 allowed anyone who could prove his or her continuous presence in the United States for at least the preceding four years to apply for permanent residency. Over 1.5 million illegal people became legal under this provision.[9] However, such amnesty[10] programs are short-lived. Within the next two decades more immigrants arrived and a fresh underclass of undocumented and illegal immigrants cropped up. According to recent estimates (Griswold, 2010; Tucker, 2010), 11 million people are living in the United States illegally and have no options at all to legalize their status. Another wave of amnesty seems in order even though this too may provide only a short-term solution. On the other hand, granting amnesty to illegal aliens will release them from the bondage to an underground, cash economy. Employers will have less opportunity to cheat on taxes. Trading in forged documents will also lessen. And, the travel industry might get a boost since, equipped with Green Cards, these immigrants will become able to visit their lands of origin. Even more useful than amnesty might be the introduction of a strong and viable temporary worker program. Allowing more legal workers could turn out to be good for the American economy since it would permit the expansion of important production lines and create more middle-class employment opportunities for Americans (Griswold, 2010). Moreover, legalization of such work-related entry would free up the border patrol to focus upon intercepting real criminals.[11]

Adverse effects upon the immigrants

Undocumented immigrants tend to live with fear and shame. They often avoid hospitals—even though they have more job-related accidents (Franklin & Little, 2006)—and cannot obtain valid driving licenses. They are compelled to take menial jobs and accept less than minimum hourly wages. Unprotected by labor laws, underpaid, and overworked, they remain vulnerable to exploitation and blackmail. They can be readily fired and lack the courage to ask for a raise. They are often mistreated by their landlords. Lacking proper papers, they cannot travel back to their countries of origin to visit family and friends. Such unavailability of "emotional refueling" (Mahler, Pine, & Bergman, 1975) saps their emotional strength and weakens their psychic resolve. The situation is further complicated by the fact that the road to higher education is blocked for most of them.

> There are many thousands of immigrants who came here as young children, have been educated in U.S. public schools, speak perfect English, feel as "American" as anyone else, and yet still lack legal status. Now they find themselves without a future. Denied in-state tuition, unable to quality for financial aid under federal rules, and unable to work legally, they get stuck in low-paying jobs and shut out of more promising opportunities. (Guskin & Wilson, 2007, p. 54)

Working in unison, these economic and social factors lead to considerable emotional distress in these immigrants. Fractured self-esteem, irritability, fear, shame, bad temper, and regressive daydreaming are thus common in this subpopulation. The clandestine and, at times, dangerous, ways of their entering the country also leaves post-traumatic residue. Such psychic sediment is even more marked in the case of refugees and asylum seekers.

Refugees and asylum seekers

Employing the term "exile" interchangeably with "refugee," I have elsewhere (Akhtar, 1999b) delineated the variables on which such an individual differs from the "usual" immigrant.

> *First*, the immigrant has left his country voluntarily while the exile has been forced out of his land. *Second*, the immigrant has usually

had more time available for preparing to leave, while the exile has had little or no notice for his departure. *Third*, less traumatic events are generally associated with the immigrant's leaving his home; the exile has often fled a catastrophic sociopolitical situation in his country. *Fourth*, the immigrant retains the possibility of revisiting his home country while the exile, having broken the tether of belonging, lacks this important source of emotional refueling. *Finally*, the manner in which the two groups are received by the host population might also vary. The immigrant arrives with less sociopolitical baggage and is therefore likely to encounter greater hospitality than the exile, who is viewed with suspicion and accepted reluctantly by the host population. (p. 124, italics in the original)

Putting aside this earlier use of the word "exile," it is better to consult the lexicon of UNHCR (United Nations' High Commission for Refugees) and align our current discourse with its terminology. The following designations seem pertinent.

- *Refugee*: someone who has been forced to flee his or her country because of persecution, war, or violence.
- *Internally displaced person*: someone who has been forced to flee his or her home for the same reason as a refugee, but remains in his or her own country and has not crossed an international border.
- *Stateless person*: someone who is not a citizen of any country. A person can become stateless due to a variety of reasons, including sovereign, legal, technical, or administrative decisions or oversights.
- *Asylum seeker*: someone who seeks sanctuary in another country and applies to be recognized as a refugee and to receive legal protection and material assistance.

As one considers these categories and their implications, it is useful to keep the following global agreements in mind.

- *The Universal Declaration of Human Rights* (1948) underlines that every individual has the right to a nationality.
- *The Geneva Convention* (1951) is the main instrument of law that stipulates what sort of assistance and protection a refugee must get from signatory nations and what obligations the refugees have to their host countries. The Convention was limited to the post-World War II

refugees, but a later document, the 1967 Protocol, expanded the scope of the Geneva Convention to all countries across the globe.

• *The Dublin Convention* (1990) states that a refugee is the sole responsibility of the country in which he or she first arrives after leaving his home country. This convention is, at times, overruled due to humanitarian concerns and for the sake of equitable distribution of refugees.

The UNHCR estimates that there are 65.3 million forcibly displaced people world-wide, of which 10 million are "stateless people" and 21.3 million qualify to be called "refugees." An astounding 53 percent of refugees come from three countries: Somalia, Afghanistan, and Syria. And, refugees are relocated in various parts of the world, including the USA, Europe, and many other countries of Asia, Africa, as well as Australia.

The situation in the United States

The number of refugees arriving in the United States and their countries of origin have varied over time. The Pew Research Center's most recent study (Krogstad & Radford, 2017) provides the following data. During the mid-1970s, nearly 150,000 refugees arrived in the US. During the 1990s, about 112,000 refugees arrived each year. This number dropped by over 75 percent following the 9/11 terrorist attacks in 2001. This number went up a few years later and peaked in 2016. It has dropped dramatically since January 2017 when US President Donald Trump severely curtailed the admission of refugees into the country. The refugees during the mid- to late 1970s were largely from Vietnam and Cambodia, during the 1900s from Kosovo and from various countries of the former Soviet Union, during the early 2000s from Laos, Cuba, and Somalia, and more recently from the Congo, Rwanda, Myanmar (formerly Burma), Bhutan, and from Afghanistan, Syria, and Iraq. Nearly 39,000 Muslim refugees entered the United States in 2016, the highest number for a single year on record. Apart from the foregoing Pew Research Center data, there also exists the up-to-date tabulation from the US Department of State's Bureau of Population, Refugees, and Migration, which reveals that between October 1, 2016, and March 31, 2017, a total of 39,093 refugees have been legally accepted into the United States. Less than 10 percent of them are from Europe and more than 50 percent are from "Near East/South Asia."

While the American general population has always had disapproving attitudes about the arrival of refugees, this has slightly shifted towards acceptance. A public opinion survey of 1,580 US citizens conducted by Brookings Institution (Telhami, 2016) revealed that 59 percent of them support taking in Middle Eastern refugees (after proper security screening) and a little over 50 percent believe that the United States has a moral obligation to help refugees from Iraq and Syria.

The impact of refugees arriving in the US, especially those who have come after the 9/11 attacks, has been politically polarizing. Among those who support accepting Middle Eastern refugees, 77 percent are Democrats and among those who oppose, 63 percent are Republicans. And, when it comes specifically to refugees from Syria, 73 percent of those willing to take them in are Democrats and 61 percent of those unwilling, are Republicans. Economic and humanitarian concerns undergird such attitudes to the plight of these dislocated people. There also exists the fear that these refugees would commit terrorist acts once permitted into the country. This fear is a cornerstone of the ultra-right wing's propaganda and has influenced recent governmental policies regarding the acceptance of refugees. However, the actual number of refugees arrested for terrorist acts since 9/11 is a mere three (ibid.)!

What also tends to get lost in the paranoid drumbeat of the right is that the Middle East is not the only origin of refugees currently relocated into the United States. Countries from Latin America, Africa, and Far Eastern Asia also are represented in the refugee population. Yet another important point to note is that the strict vetting measures and relatively well-run rehabilitation policies preclude the abysmal conditions associated with "refugee camps" scattered over other countries.

The situation in Europe

In a dramatic reversal of nineteenth- and early twentieth-century patterns of immigration whereby Europeans were fleeing to other parts of the world to avoid famine (e.g., from Ireland) and politico-religious persecution (e.g., from Nazi Germany and the Soviet Union), the period from the mid-twentieth century onwards till the present has witnessed a massive influx of immigrants and refugees from Asia and Africa into the EU (European Union) nations. First, there was a wave of post-colonial subjects (e.g., from India, Pakistan, Algeria, Suriname) ending up on the idealized lands (e.g. England, France, Holland) of their erstwhile masters. The assimilation of such wide-eyed economic migrants into the culture of their adopted European lands was relatively slower than it was in the United States, since regional identities in Europe were relatively monolithic. The presence of Asian, African, and Caribbean immigrants aroused ambivalent feelings in the national majority populations and this, in turn, created difficulties for the newly arrived people (see Chapter Three for more details). The situation has become more complex with the recent and massive influx of citizens of the war-torn Middle East, as well as of Kosovo, Albania, Ukraine, and various African countries, especially Eritrea and Nigeria. Here are some up-to-date facts.[12]

• Syria, Afghanistan, and Iraq are the three top countries from which people are applying for asylum in EU nations.
• Germany and Hungary are the two top countries for asylum applications. The former received more than 476,000, and the latter, 177,130 new applications for asylum in the calendar year 2015. That year and over the time that has followed, Germany has been far more open to taking in refugees as against Hungary. The latter country has fortified its border with Serbia to keep refugees out; more recently, it has established detention camps surrounded by razor wire that are reminiscent of Nazi concentration camps (Lyman, 2017). In contrast, Sweden has taken in a large number of refugees.
• The International Organization for Migration (IOM) estimates that in 2015 more than 1,000,000 migrants arrived by sea and almost 35,000 by land.
• According to the IOM, in 2015, nearly 4,000 migrants died in the course of their sojourn. Most died while crossing from the northern shores of Africa to Italy, and many died in crossing the Aegean Sea from Turkey to Greece.

The origins of such massive emigration lie in regional civil wars, the mayhem unleashed by ISIS and American "counter-terrorism" (see Chapter Five for more on this), widespread societal unrest, and pervasive hunger. The consequences of such immigration are myriad and exist on both international and intra-national levels. On the international front, tensions have arisen between nations that, owing to their geographical status as gateways to Europe, have received high numbers of refugees (e.g., Greece and Italy) and nations that have firmly warded off such influx (e.g., Macedonia and Poland). In Scandinavia too, marked differences have emerged. Sweden opened its doors wide while Denmark made its unwelcoming attitude quite clear. Consequently, some pressure to "redistribute" the migrant population across Europe has evolved. *A European Agenda on Migration* issued in May 2015 proposed a "mandatory and automatically triggered re-location system" (Traub, 2016, p. 3) to share the burden of caring for refugees in the face of an emergency. Little attention was paid to this proposal, however. Most EU nations remained content, it seems, with the 1990 Dublin Convention which declares that refugees "belong" to the country they first arrive in and are solely that country's responsibility.

A careful look at the situation reveals that the refugee crisis in Europe has actually undergone three phases (ibid.): (i) *a humanitarian phase*—this showed much outpouring of sympathy for the suffering masses of dislocated people. In Malmo and Munich, volunteers welcomed refugees and the German chancellor, Angela Merkel, declined to stand by the Dublin Convention, declaring that her nation will accept refugees no matter where in Europe they had first arrived; (ii) *a mandatory shared relocation phase*—this phase saw the transfer of a few thousand refugees from Greece and other European "border" countries to more "inland" EU nations, and (iii) *a sovereign reassertion phase*—in this phase, EU nations made a deal in which Turkey received billions of euros in aid in exchange for staving off the flow of refugees (mainly from Syria and Afghanistan) into Europe and to repel or absorb those showing up at its own borders.

In addition to such international intrigues and alliances, the European refugee crisis has had significant intra-national consequences, as a recent Pew Research Center report (September, 2016) demonstrates. Here are some of its salient findings.

- Between 76 percent (in Hungary) and 60 percent (in Italy) of the general population fears that the arrival of refugees will increase the incidence of terrorism.
- In eight out of ten EU nations surveyed, those on the political right perceive refugees as a major threat more often than those on the political left. This distinction is most marked in France.
- Negative views of refugees are closely tied to negative views of Muslims.

- Few Europeans say that diversity makes their countries better. This is in sharp contrast to the fact that 58 percent of Americans say that growing cultural and demographic diversity makes the US a better place to live.

These developments are dialectically related to the rise of politico-economic conservatism in Europe. Each fresh wave of unfamiliar migrants (read Muslim, African) fuels the rhetoric of right wing parties and such hatred, in turn, renders those arriving in Europe more likely to retreat into ethnocentrism and fundamentalism.

The situation elsewhere in the world

According to 2016 UNHCR data, the top four countries "hosting" evacuees are Turkey, Pakistan, Lebanon, and Iran, with estimated refugee numbers of 2.75 million, 1.6 million, 1.1 million, and 979,400 respectively. Turkey has the most refugees in the world. This is a source of national pride but also poses significant absorptive, financial, and political challenges. At first, the situation was manageable and appeared temporary. However, with Europe threatening to close its doors (with the exception of Germany), Turkey has to accept that most of the Syrian refugees are going nowhere. The fact that most of them are Sunni Arabs adds a sectarian dimension to the problem. Liberal and secular groups, as well as other ethnic communities (e.g., Alawis, Kurdish nationalists) fear that political leaders are exploiting refugees to transform the Turkish national identity and re-frame the country's role in the Middle East as more Arab, Sunni, and hegemonic.

Pakistan, Lebanon, and Iran have their own refugee crises to deal with. Pakistan is now home to nearly 2 million refugees. Most of them (about 85 percent) are Afghanis, while the remaining are Uzbeks, Tajiks, and other ethnic groups. Lebanon has over a million refugees; most recent arrivals are from Syria, and the earlier ones from Palestinian territories. And, Iran is the host country for nearly a million Afghani citizens who have fled their war-torn nation. In addition to these properly registered refugees, there is an equal number of those who have entered Iran illegally.

Other countries of the world also have seen influx of refugees. India has a long history of accepting persecuted people from other lands: Zoroastrians from Iran in the late eighteenth century, Hindus and

Sikhs from what became Pakistan in 1947, Tibetans since the 1960s, Bangladeshi Hindus and Afghani Muslims since the 1970s, Tamils from Sri Lanka since the 1980s, and more recently, the Rohingya Muslims (declared by UNHCR to be the most persecuted ethnic group in the world) from Burma. In all, over a million refugees have arrived in India during the last four decades. In contrast, Australia has accepted only 13,750 refugees as of 2014 and has turned away a multitude of asylum seekers (from Iran, Syria, Somalia, Sudan, and Afghanistan), hundreds of whom are still languishing in Australian-run detention camps in the Pacific island nation, Nauru.

Regardless of where they come from and where they end up, most refugees suffer great hardships. Many have undertaken risk-laden travel and in its course, experienced much psychological trauma. Upon arrival in a new country, they face rejection and, even when accepted, they encounter difficulties with respect to economic opportunities, access to health care, obtaining education, and finding much needed legal protection. Since political turbulence, ethnic strife, and war turns ordinary citizens into refugees, the link between religion, politics, and migration across national borders becomes amply evident. In situations of the sort described above, the individual and intrapsychic "trauma of geographical dislocation" (Akhtar, 2011a) gets combined with the socio-cultural injuries that comes with the newly acquired status of being a minority in a strange land.

Concluding remarks

In this chapter, I have elucidated the relationship between religion, politics, and immigration. I have noted that religious prejudice often makes people leave their countries of birth. However, upon arrival in a new country immigrants themselves tend to develop prejudices; often this leads to their forging alliances with groups that have similar prej-udices but little else in common with them. Increase and decrease in the degree and intensity of religiosity is also seen in association with immigration.

On the political front, matters seem equally multifaceted. Immigration is an emotionally laden issue and gets readily caught up in political agendas of all sorts. Within the United States, the contrasting atti-tudes regarding "old" and "new" immigration emanate from com-plex socioeconomic and historical variables including, regrettably, racism. The "new immigrants" (mostly from the so-called Third World countries) are frequently portrayed as adversely affecting the national economy, the moral climate of the country, the institution of family, and the finer literary and artistic dimensions of the American culture at large. Such anti-immigrant propaganda is driven by the conservative, right-wing politicians. This prejudicial perspective, especially directed toward the Third World and undocumented immigrants, is clearly delineated in this chapter. Empirical evidence to demonstrate the hollowness of such assertions is also provided. Also considered are the political attitudes of immigrants themselves, especially their vulnerability to the contrasting attitudes of socio-political apathy and nostalgic hyper-nationalism. Separate sections have been devoted to the plight of undocumented immigrants and to the occasionally tense relationship between the new immigrants and African Americans.

Perusal of such discourse might lead mental health profession-als of varying stripes (e.g., psychologists, psychiatrists, psychoana-lysts, and social workers) to question if it is of any relevance to their work. The answer to this question is an emphatic "yes." Allow me to elaborate this point a bit further by underscoring that the dramatically changed demography of the country has made contact—even close contact—with immigrants inevitable. All of us deal with Nigerian and Bangladeshi cab drivers, Chinese dry cleaners, Korean manicurists, Filipino nurses, Indian physicians, and so on.[13] Immigrants of diverse origins live in our neighborhoods and our children go to school with their children. Such intermingling has psychic consequences that range from prejudicial repudiation through the thawing of "unmentalized xenophobia" (see Chapter Four in this book) to assimilative internaliza-tion. Mental health professionals are no exception in this regard. They are psychosocially affected by immigrants around them; indeed many are immigrants themselves.

The clinical population is also changing rapidly and more and more immigrants are appearing on the threshold of mental health profes-sionals. While clinics specializing in dealing with immigrant and refu-gee patients and their families (e.g., Nafsiyat in London; PHAROS in Amsterdam; Intercultural Child Traumatic Stress Center in Portland, OR; Coalition for Asian American Mental Health in New York; Richmond Area Multi-Services in San Francisco; and Across Boundaries in Toronto) have emerged, the usual mental health facilities also cater to clientele that is increasingly diverse in terms of religion, skin color, ethnicity, and national origin. Even the relatively "elite" psychoanalysts are now treating more patients from Asian, Latin American, and African countries. All mental health professionals are thus vulnerable to new countertransference reactions and require a culturally sensitive "tune-up" of their technique.

While not optimally brought under the purview of theory, the fact is that economic, racial, ethnic, and religious differences within the clinical dyad have the potential to significantly affect the clinical process (Akhtar, 1999a, 2008a; Altman, 2004; Bonovitz, 1998; Kareem & Littlewood, 1992; Perez-Foster, Moskowitz, & Javier, 1996; Roland, 1996; Sklarew, Twemlow, & Wilkinson, 2004). Even less recognized are the subtle influences of the therapist's political orientation on his or her listening capacity and ability to empathize with certain kinds of patients; the meager literature that does exist in this realm (Garcia & Rodriguez, 1989; Gorkin, 1996; Layton, Hollander, & Gutwill, 2006) tends to suggest that politics does enter, albeit silently, the chamber of clinical dialogue. The therapist's attitudes toward immigration, admixture of cultures, national economy, and people of race and religion other than his own can alter how he relates to them. Matters involving abortion, homosexuality, impending death, and life after death especially tend to evoke countertransference reactions that are, at least in part, governed by the analyst's beliefs. The specific religion to which the analyst belongs can also come to play an important, even if subtle role in the clinical exchange involving these issues. Consider the following examples as well.

- A Hindu surgeon reports that he bows his head to the elephant-headed deity, *Ganesha*, that sits on his office desk before walking toward the operating room.
- A Jewish lawyer declares that Muslims are basically primitive and praises Israel for the assassination of the Hamas leaders.
- A Catholic college student struggles with difficulty in finding boyfriends and potential marital partners owing to her religiously based refusal to have premarital sex.
- A Muslim analysand expresses his outrage at the recent newspaper cartoons ridiculing the Prophet Mohammed; he says that the murder of Theo van Gogh, the Dutch documentary maker, was a legitimate retribution for his mockery of Muslim customs.

Now, ask yourself whether religious and nonreligious Christian, Hindu, Jewish, and Muslim analysts would listen to these associations in exactly the same manner? As much as we would like to believe that they would, the doubt that this might not be the case nags at our theoretical conscience. We would like to believe that the religious backgrounds of these analysts would not preclude their receiving this material with equanimity and that they will all attend similarly to the surface as well as the in-depth and symbolic aspects of these communications, especially as they pertain to transference-countertransference developments. However, this view may be idealistic. It overlooks the fact that countertransference experience in such situations becomes quite vulnerable to the tricks of "shared ethnic scotoma" (Shapiro & Pinsker, 1973), "acculturation gaps" (Prathikanti, 1997), "excessive culturalization of the analytic ego" (Akhtar, 1999a), and "nostalgic collusions" (Akhtar, 2006). To be sure, this does not have to happen, but the fact is that it can happen. And, that is the point, namely, that the religious background of the analyst (and the sociopolitical stances consequent upon it) can come into play under certain circumstances and alter the pathways of empathy and interpretation. The analyst's political views—especially those pertaining to immigration—also have the potential to affect his emotional attitude and listening capacity vis-à-vis patients from cultures other than his own.

Matters of religion and politics, in the setting of immigration, therefore merit serious attention. Alongside the variables of work and money, sex and marriage, and friendships and socialization, these issues impact upon the psychosocial adaptation of the immigrant population and should be of concern to mental health professionals.

Notes

1. This does not imply that people do not move from the West to Eastern countries such as China, Japan, Korea, or India. However, the West to East traffic is lesser in magnitude than that which flows East to West. On the other hand, migration from rural to urban areas is more marked within Eastern countries (with the exception of Brazil where such migration is of huge proportions). China's rural to urban migration is perhaps the largest in human history, involving nearly 130 million people. With the enforced residency rules of the Mao regime now gone,

almost every worker in urban factories, restaurants, and construction sites is a rural migrant (Chang, 2009).

2. The fact that the "import" of slaves from West Africa during the mid-eighteenth century is not included in such categories of immigration to the United States is simultaneously curious and understandable. The omission is curious because the arrival of African slaves in the country was after all an example of immigration. Given this, it came with all the problems attendant upon geo-cultural relocation. The omission is understandable because this "wave" did not involve people leaving their lands voluntarily; they were seduced, bought, and obtained in barter with warring factions who had been bribed to "sell" their opponents away. Such migration differs from any other in the history and therefore would be diminished by being lumped with more voluntary and "affluent" forms of migrations.

3. Suspicion that such racism underlies the newly enacted (April, 2010) Immigration Law, S.B. 1070, in the state of Arizona (which allows the local police to demand identification of anyone they regard as a possible undocumented migrant) is the reason for the intense debate surrounding it. Fascinatingly, African Americans—who are often viewed by Hispanics as rivals—have joined the forceful opposition to this bill.

4. What is skipped here is that, in declaring all persons to be equal, the nation's founding fathers were referring only to white men. Blacks and women of all races were certainly not included in this lofty proclamation.

5. This topic includes cultural, linguistic, economic, historical, and political dimensions. One particular aspect of the occasionally noticeable friction between immigrants and African Americans comes from the proximity in which these groups often live. Resentment can be fueled by the fact that Third World immigrants have mostly settled in cities like Chicago, Los Angeles, Miami, and New York City, that is, the cities with significant African American populations. Since these early arrivals gravitate towards lower income housing, they can appear to push African Americans out of their neighborhoods.

6. *Kalu* (a denigrating word for people of African race) is derived from *kala*, the Urdu word for "black." The etymological root of *Malu* is, however, more curious. It seems to be an abbreviated and Urdu vernacular form of *malaa-oon*, the Arabic word for "the cursed." Using the denunciation for Hindus, perhaps, helps the prejudiced South Asian Muslims feels aligned with their so-called Arabic brethren.

7. An endemic issue of mild to moderate proportions now, the impact of Spanish-speaking workers on the labor market in Miami was severe in the wake of the Mariel Boatlift of 1980. This event involved a mass exodus of nearly 125,000 Cuban citizens to Florida, 50 percent of

whom decided to settle permanently in Miami. While its impact on the regional economy has received varying assessments (Card, 1990; Portes & Jensen, 1989), one solid piece of statistics speaks louder than all other discourse: the unemployment rate in Miami rose from 5 percent in April 1980 to 7.1 percent in July 1980!

8. Opponents of immigration call such children "anchor babies" implying that prospective immigrants often use their US-born children as a way of getting a permanent visa to remain here. However, giving birth to a child in the United States confers citizenship only upon the child and it is not until that child becomes twenty-one years old that he or she can sponsor a parent for permanent residency or citizenship.

9. A similar amnesty program was enacted during 2005 in Spain. Three conditions, however, had to be met in order to qualify: having been in the country for at least 6 months, having been employed, and having a clean legal record. Some 550,000 people were thus legalized.

10. Immigrant rights activists oppose the use of the term "amnesty" on the grounds that it gives credence to the idea that undocumented immigrants are criminals. They advocate the use of "legalization" or "regularization" in its place.

11. Such issues lie at the heart of the current immigration reform imbroglio between the conservatives and liberals. While they agree on the need for greater border control, their perspectives on other matters differ considerably. The conservatives advocate a mandatory employment-verification system and deportation of those who have entered the country illegally. The liberals find mass deportations financially prohibitive and objectionable on humanitarian grounds. They push for legalization (after a penalty and a waiting-period) and temporary work-related visas.

12. The data presented here is derived from the *BBC.com/news/world-Europe*, accessed March 23, 2017.

13. The use of stereotypes, transparent in this passage, is a deliberate literary device to kindle affects of familiarity and recognition.

CHAPTER THREE

Mental pain of minorities

The word "minority" is a loaded one. A quick look at its dictionary definition reveals references to "the period before attainment of majority," "the smaller in number of two groups constituting a whole," "a group having less than the number of votes necessary for control," and "a part of a population differing from others in some characteristics and often subjected to differential treatment" (Mish, 1998, p. 757). Implications of being small, childlike, weak, and different in some important way—often negative—abound here. The notion of "minority" thus appears to exceed its numerical connotations. Actually being lesser in number does not always coincide with being a minority. The British colonizers of pre-independence India, though miniscule in population when compared to their Indian subjects, hardly conceived of themselves as a "minority." The same was true of the white rulers of apartheid South Africa. And, Arabs who constitute only 20 percent of the world's Muslim population are not referred to as a minority among the followers of Islam. Such numerical de-linkage also works in the opposite direction. For instance, women might exceed men in number in a given community but may still be regarded as a minority group.

Other caveats have to be entered as well. *First*, there is often a blurring between "minorities" and "immigrants" in contemporary sociopolitical discourse. This is especially so if the latter are dark-skinned and originate from the so-called Third World nations; New Yorkers who have migrated to London, or French citizens who have chosen to live in Montreal are generally not included among "minorities." People from Suriname living in Amsterdam, the Netherlands, from Turkey living in Tubingen, Germany, and from Morocco living in Calais, France, are the ones designated as "minorities." *Second*, each nation has larger and smaller minorities and the majority's attitudes towards the two are often different. The larger minority is subject to greater paranoia and discrimination; the smaller minority is blithely ignored or exoticized. *Third*, the demographic make-up of the community-at-large also has salience in this context. Nations that are largely homoethnic (e.g., Iceland) and nations that are predominantly multi-ethnic (e.g., the United States) respond differently to an influx of new "minorities." *Finally*, the chronology of arrival in the host country also matters (Akhtar, 2011a). Referring specifically to the United States, it is clear that the first wave of immigrants (1700–1803; predominantly white English-speaking Protestants from Western Europe) has gradually acquired the status of "original inhabitants," eclipsing the vanquished natives of the land.[1] The second wave (1804–1924; "darker" Europeans—Italians, Greeks, and Russians—and more non-English-speaking people, and more Catholics and Jews) has largely assimilated within the culture established by the first wave and in the process has altered it to a certain extent. The third wave (1925-present; darker-skinned Asian, Caribbean, and Hispanic immigrants) is still struggling to find its place in the mainstream culture; this is especially true for the individuals of lower socioeconomic strata of these groups. Admittedly, such accounting of immigration to the United States overlooks the "import" of slaves from Africa (1519–1808) whose subsequent generations constitute the largest and the most discriminated against minority of the country.

What all this demonstrates is that numerical facts and historical layering of population matter less in labeling a population as "minority" than its social power, its having a communal presence and voice, its access to resources, and its participation in shaping the canonical narratives of a society or nation. A minority, regardless of whether it is that of race, religion, gender, ethnicity, nationality, language, or sexual orientation, is defined by the relative weakness of its social praxis, the lack of its governmental representation, the unfairness of the judiciary towards it, and the distorted gaze of the so-called majority on it. This sentiment was captured by the eminent North American sociologist Louis Wirth (1897–1952), when he stated that a minority is:

> A group of people who, because of physical or cultural character-istics, are singled out from others in the society in which they live, for differential and unequal treatment, and who therefore regard themselves as objects of collective discrimination. (1945, p. 347)

Belonging to a minority, therefore, acts like a "cumulative trauma" (Khan, 1963), whereby breaches in the protective and holding functions of the society-at-large accrue over time and put a silent but palpable strain on the ego, both at an individual and collective level. Elucidation of such "strain" in its myriad aspects and the search for its ameliora-tion forms the core of this chapter. In it, I will address four dimen-sions of the experience of belonging to a minority, namely, (i) presence, (ii) perception, (iii) participation, and (iv) progress. I will attempt to highlight the subjective, the objective, and the dialectically constructed scenarios in each of these realms, underscoring the sources of distress and discontent that lead to dysfunctional solutions. I will then sum-marize this material, enter a few caveats, and outline psychoanalyti-cally informed social strategies for the betterment of majority-minority interaction.

Presence

Minorities exist. They exist everywhere. All groups are visibly or invis-ibly divided into majority and minority factions. Each country has its own minority groups, big or small as these might be. In the United States, for instance, African Americans constitute 13 percent of the pop-ulation and represent the nation's largest minority; Hispanic Americans, Asian Americans, and Native Americans are other minorities of sizea-ble proportions. Fascinatingly, Jews, who make up only 3 percent of the country's population, are hardly ever described as a "minority" group; their success in academic and social realms accords them prominence, power, and exemption from being called a "minority." It is obvious that numbers do and do not mean much when it comes to recognizing the presence of a minority. And, here we note a clash between the subjective and objective perspectives; Jews might regard themselves as a minor-ity but others, especially those from relatively disenfranchised minority groups, might not see them in this manner. In other words, one might be both present and absent as a minority.

The schism becomes more pronounced when the camera is tilted towards iconic portrayals in the society-at-large. Members of a minority group find their representation to be minimal or absent. The portraits on currency bills or coins are those of majority individuals. Movies and television shows, unless specifically addressing minority issues, do not have proportionate representation of minorities on the screen. Few streets are named after figures from the minority groups. Few statues of their heroes decorate parks and boulevards. Few museums of their history exist. It is as if the majority refuses to "mentalize" (Fonagy & Target, 1997) their presence. I will return to the resulting syndrome of "unmentalized xenophobia" (Akhtar, 2007b) in my discussion of prejudice (Chapter Four). Here I wish to highlight a contradiction that exists in regard to the majority's reaction to the minority's presence.

On the one hand, the majority responds to the minority by ignoring its existence; not seeing becomes tantamount to eliminating or erasing those who seem different and "not like us." On the other hand, the majority craves for a minority group. The latter serves as a "suitable target for externalization" (Volkan, 1997) of the majority group's paranoid and depressive anxieties. This "need" for a minority group is ubiquitous. However, for the purposes of stark illustration, we can turn to two nations that were *created* by "minorities" so that they could be a homogenous majority in their own lands. I am referring here to Pakistan and Israel, founded respectively in 1947 and 1948 by separatist Muslims of the British imperial India, and Zionist Jews of the virulently anti-Semitic mid-twentieth-century Europe. The aspiration of a homoethnic enclave that would be joyous and conflict-free, however, did not materialize in either case. In 1971, Pakistan split up into two, owing to the Punjabi-Bengali linguistic and cultural divide, giving birth to the nation of Bangladesh. It is now rife with violence between Shiites and Sunnis. And, Pakistan's treatment of its Christian minority has come under question. Israel, though less violent within its boundaries, is torn apart between the liberal and the orthodox Jewish groups. It does not treat all groups of its largely immigrant Jewish population with equal regard. In commenting upon this, Abbasi (2008) states that:

> There can hardly be a more striking example of the negative power
> of blackness than the current plight of the Black Ethiopian Jews in
> Israel … . These are Jews who were brought back to Israel in 1991

and were extended full citizenship. However, their condition in Israel is already complicated by the development of ghettos, welfare dependence, and poor education. Even as a Jew, being black has become a problem for these people in a country that ostensibly welcomed them home. (p. 138)

The majority-minority tensions in Pakistan and Israel, highlighted here for didactic ease, are universal. Almost everywhere one looks, one finds that at the conscious level, the society feels unease at the existence of minority groups within it and strives to deny their presence. At the unconscious level, it longs for a minority group since that can be used as a "container" (Bion, 1967) for its own unmetabolized concerns. Oscillation between what the former US Senator Daniel Patrick Moynihan (D-NY, 1976–2000) called "benign neglect" and what the well-known psychoanalyst, Henri Parens, called "malignant prejudice" (2007), often characterize the majority's stance towards the minority. Furthermore, this contradiction between the majority's not wanting and yet needing the minority contributes to the latter's difficulty in locating itself properly in their relational matrix. If one is needed then one should, indeed must, exist, but how to accomplish that if the paraphernalia of existence (e.g., statues, museums, characters in movies, television shows) are denied to one? If one is not wanted but does exist, then what is one to do with one's existence?

Perception

The second source of the minority's distress lies in the realm of perception. The majority and the minority both contribute to difficulties that ensue. The majority, to extend the discussion in the preceding section, might simply refuse to "see" the minority and acknowledge its presence. Such "negative hallucination" (Green, 1999) or non-perception of an object expresses the majority's distress and hostility. In turn, it can lead to an uncanny sense of invisibility on the part of the minority. No more eloquent example of the latter experience exists in English literature than Ralph Ellison's (1947) novel *The Invisible Man*. Here is the book's opening paragraph.

I am an invisible man. No, I am not a spook like those who haunted Edgar Allan Poe; nor am I one of your Hollywood movie ectoplasms. I am a man of substance, of flesh and bone, fiber and liquids—and I might even be said to possess a mind. I am invisible, understand, simply because people refuse to see me. Like the bodiless heads you see sometimes in circus shadows, it is as though I have been surrounded by mirrors of hard, distorting glass. When they approach me they see only my surroundings, themselves, or figments of their imagination—indeed, everything and anything except me. (p. 1)

Ellison, giving voice to black subjectivity in the pre-civil rights America, astutely concludes that his invisibility to white folks is "a matter of construction of their *inner* eyes" (p. 1, italics in the original). Far from being restricted to his particular era and his particular part of the world, such majority myopia is ubiquitous. Who notices the Muslims in China, Jews in India, Catholics in Turkey, or Sikhs in Pakistan? How many of us even know who Abkhaz, Sami, Tupi, and Uighurs are and to which countries they belong?[2] Such people exist on a "subaltern" (Spivak, 1988) level and operate below the visual threshold; unmirrored by others, they become invisible over time. Their history goes unrecorded. Their slogans fade and their poetry is scattered as literary debris. They not only get excluded from the formative drumbeat of time, they also become unmoored from their own narrative and legacy. In Sartre's (1946) terms, this is "torture by separation" (p. 8).

In fact, matters are more complex. The eyes of the majority can change their pasty indifference into piercing accusation. Mesmerized by the fierce rhetoric of a narcissistic and paranoid leader, the majority's search for a scapegoat invariably ends up with the minority as the culprit. The unseen becomes the disliked. Imagine a burqa-clad Muslim woman on a subway train in Paris, a turbaned Sikh on a college campus in Oklahoma, or a black man driving his BMW through a pampered suburb of Boston and you will grasp what I am trying to convey. People either pretend that such protagonists are simply not there or stare at them with agonized disbelief. The "No coloreds allowed" signs might have disappeared from restaurants and buses, "No Jews permitted" from country club applications, but the stone-hearted attitudes behind those signs have not melted. Minorities all over the world continue to face prejudice. Each nation and each large group chooses its "favorite" target of ethnic, religious, or racial hatred. And, popular media play a big role in perpetuating such prejudices.[3]

I will discuss the topic of prejudice in greater detail later (Chapter Four). Here, suffice it to say that a narrow-minded vision of others assaults their complexity and reduces them to cardboard figures. Even the positive stereotypes that emerge vis-à-vis certain minority groups have deleterious consequences (McCauley, Stitt, & Segal, 1980). For instance, Asian Americans in the United States are called the "model minority" in view of their industriousness, excellence in science and mathematics, and rapid economic climb. This sounds good but it can result in school teachers' ignoring a Chinese American student who is not proficient in algebra and making such a student feel profoundly backward. And, what if an Asian Indian in New Jersey does not make a lot of money? Has he brought shame to the "model minority"? More-over, by not representing the "model minority" properly, so to speak, he has become invisible to the biased eyes of the majority and becomes hyper-visible to the members of his group; they look down upon him with unease and disdain. What happens to a Pakistani Muslim in London who is not at all religious and loves to drink and party? How is he perceived by the white majority or, for that matter, by his fellow Pakistanis in London?[4]

There is little indication for becoming maudlin about such out-comes, though. The "model minority" of South Asian Americans seeks to distance itself from other minorities, especially African Americans, and align itself with the white majority; it might even try "out-whiting whites" (Lee & Gandy, cited in Deo, Lee, Chin, Milman, & Yuen, 2008). Mitra (2008) states that the dislike of dark skin among South Asian Americans is:

> ... a likely product of three factors—a historical presence of color consciousness in the region, a history of colonialism whereby "white people" and thus, "whiteness," were constructed as supe-rior along with a denigration of "dark people" and "darkness," and the global hegemony of Western racism. The mélange of these negative feelings towards blackness carried from a pre-migration social context with the denigration of "dark" skin and celebration of "whiteness," associated with the American social context, are likely to have reinforced each other. (p. 308)

Nonetheless, in terms of being perceived by the majority, the minority feels both the anguish of invisibility and the torment of hyper-visibility.

This conundrum is reflected in the subjective experience of the minority individuals. At times, they feel invisible to the majority, and, at other times, they feel hyper-visible. Moreover, they feel invisible about certain aspects of their existence and hyper-visible about others. Their skin color or attire, for instance, might be noted by all, but the nuances of their humor might be shaved off to fit the dominant idiom of the majority. In an ironic twist to Freud's (1924d, p. 178) "anatomy is destiny" remark, the melanin content of skin and thickness of epicanthic folds are often accorded greater recognition than the poetry in a person's heart. The resulting pain is greater if the minority individual's mother tongue differs from that of the majority around him or her. François Cheng (1985), a Chinese émigré to France who did not know a word of French until age twenty, eloquently describes such a linguistic cleavage of his self. The same pain is reflected by Julia Kristeva (1988):

> Not to speak your own mother tongue. To live with sounds, logics, that are separated from the nocturnal memory of the body, from the sweet-sour sleep of childhood. To carry within yourself like a secret crypt or like a handicapped child—loved and useless—that language of once-upon-a-time that fades and won't make up its mind to leave you forever. You learn to use another instrument, like expressing yourself in algebra or on the violin. You can become a virtuoso in this new artifice that provides you with a new body, just as false, sublimated—some would say sublime. You have the impression that the new language is your resurrection: a new skin, a new sex. But the illusion is torn apart when you listen to yourself—on a recorded tape, for example—and the melody of your own voice comes back to you in a bizarre way, from nowhere, closer to the grumble of the past than to the [linguistic] code of today. (translation cited in Amati-Mehler, Argentieri, & Cansestri, 1993, pp. 264–265)

The disjunction is not restricted to the sphere of sounds. The minority individual feels a peculiar figure-ground disharmony that precludes, however subtly, his "going-on-being" (Winnicott, 1956), that is, his spontaneity, authenticity, agency, and temporal continuity. The fit between his corporeal self and his ecological surround is not seamless. The landscape, vegetation, architecture, and the big and small animals that populate his life are not congenial to the "waking screen" (Pacella,

1980) of his perception. His psychosocial idiom also does not fill his cultural envelope comfortably. The best way I can explain what I have in mind here is by recounting a personal experience. I was born and raised in India. I lived there till age twenty-six and then migrated to the United States. Now, the statement that from birth till twenty-six, I was "living in India" is not emotionally true for me, since I was simply "living," not "living in India." And, since my immigration, I have been "living in the United States," unlike my American-born friends and colleagues who are not "living in the United States" but are simply "living." In other words, for the native and/or the majority, the figure-ground relationship is smooth and unquestioned. However, for the immigrant and/or minority, the figure-ground relationship is jagged and a matter of awareness. This takes a toll—however gradual or subtle that might be—on the preconscious coherence and continuity of self-perception. Trying to fit in, one loses oneself. Holding on to oneself, one gets ruptured from the surround. One is either more aware or less aware of oneself than one needs to be. One also lacks the mutual enrichment that comes from the thoughtless ebb and flow between inner life and external reality. Isolated unduly, the former can become burdensome. Standing on its own, the latter can turn uncanny.

Participation

Participating in group activities and in the creation and sustenance of civic institutions generally has a positive impact upon the self-esteem of an individual. This is more true if the individual belongs to a dominant majority, however. For those belonging to racial, religious, or cultural minorities, participation in the societal rituals raises all sorts of questions. First and foremost, there is the issue of choice. Individuals belonging to a majority often have the option to associate or not associate with those from a minority. Individuals belonging to a minority lack such freedom. They are "forced" to interact with those from the majority. Having no recourse, should they retreat to ethno-racial conclaves? Should they split-off parts of their affective and cognitive apparatus and submerge themselves in the affairs of the majority? At their base, such questions (e.g., whose festival am I celebrating?, does this religious holiday have anything to do with me?) pertain to identity and acculturation issues. According to Berry and Kim (1988) four possibilities offer themselves to the minority, especially if they are entering a host society for the first time. They can choose to maintain their original cultural identity and develop new relationships with the host society (*integration*); they can choose to give up their original cultural identity and develop a new one based on their inclusion in the host society (*assimilation*); they can choose to maintain their original cultural identity alone, without developing ties with the host group (*separation*); or, they can give up their original cultural identity without developing a new identity based on their membership in the host society (*marginalization*).

Although couched in the context of the minority status of recent immigrants, these observations have applications for "preexisting" minorities as well. Also to be noted is that the emphasis on "choice" in the foregoing passage might be somewhat overdone. The sociopolitical praxis of the majority acts as a conduit either towards *assimilation* or towards *integration*. In contemporary social discourse, the two vantage points are termed "melting pot" theory and "multiculturalism" theory, respectively. The "melting pot" theory implies that the prevalent culture is superior to the one that might emerge as a consequence of the newcomers' or the minority's input. The proponents of this theory envision and engineer societal policies that keep the core aspects of minority cultures in abeyance.[5] The fact, however, is that all over the Western world, the process of "melting" into the pot has become slower and subject to greater resistance. Various minorities have established their own ethnic enclaves, started celebrating their own festivals with gusto, and are insisting upon the recording of their history. Reactions to such changes have been swift and, from the right wing of the political stage, expectedly negative. In the United States, Patrick Buchanan (1992, quoted in Fukuyama, 1994) and Peggy Noonan (1994) loudly lament the loss of "our culture." Lawrence Auster, the author of *The Path to National Suicide: An Essay on Immigration and Multiculturalism* (1990), emits a similarly injured groan (see Chapter Two).

Hateful voices can be heard all over Europe as well. The late Austrian politician, Jörg Haider (1950–2008), spewed fierce anti-Muslim rhetoric in public. Geert Wilders (1963–), the Dutch parliamentarian, openly voices contemptuous anti-immigrant and anti-Muslim sentiment. And, the recent rise of the Golden Dawn party in Greece attests to the increasing prejudice against ethnic minorities in Europe.

The implication of such xenophobia is clear: what is happening to the Western culture-at-large due to the impact of minorities is bad and undesirable. This assumption rests upon an idealized view of the Western culture which ignores the West's colonial exploitations, barbarianism of slavery, bloodshed of wars, and dreadful sin of the Holocaust. Moreover, the prevailing anti-immigrant sentiment overlooks the fact that the immigrants might actually bring more solid family structures and communal orientation than exists, for instance, in the United States (Akhtar, 2011a; Fukuyama, 1994; Smith & Edmonston, 1997). The roots of the West's cultural meltdown are not traceable to its minorities; they are to be found in the disruptive nature of capitalism which creates false consumer needs, fuels greed, pulls mothers prematurely away from their babies to earn money; and puts a greater premium on material acquisition than family cohesion. These detrimental variables have originated in the heart of the Western world and not brought to its shores by third world minorities.

And yet, instead of upholding the moral validity of all cultures and the individual's freedom to express, celebrate, and live according to his or her ancestral traditions, the self-appointed guardians of conservatism continue to declare that the cultural change, happening as a consequence of minorities asserting their rights and more and more immigrants from Third World nations pouring in the country, is a death-knell for Western civilization. The cultural conservatives therefore oppose both immigration and multiculturalism. Neoconservatives, however, de-link the two; they are willing to tolerate immigration as a labor necessity but oppose multiculturalism. Either way, these majority representatives strive to keep genuine minority participation at its minimum.

Conversely, minority members often feel that their participation in the festivities and celebrations originated by the majority has a destabilizing impact upon the deeper, historically grounded structures of *their* identity. Can a Native American be joyous on Thanksgiving Day, a reminder of innocence trumped by cunning? Does an African American celebrating the Fourth of July (America's Independence Day) "forget" that only the white people got freedom that day? Can one really expect that African and Asian immigrants from England's erstwhile colonies feel joy at the pomp and splendor of the nation's royalty? But what is the alternative? To go along with the majority enhances the chances of one's acceptance by it and can be salutary for self-esteem. However, one might have to sacrifice authenticity. To not participate can isolate one and expose oneself to the blame of communal sedition.

The dilemmas of minority participation in the whole group's operation acquire more serious hues when it comes to the electoral process, voting, and legislative representation. Freedom of movement, fairness in taxation, and the right to own property are other important challenges for minorities. The world's history is replete with inequalities and injustices in all these realms. Take a look at the following examples.

- While the United States gained independence from the British in 1776, women and blacks were not allowed to vote until 1920 and 1870, respectively, although blacks were still denied voting under many state laws until the civil rights era of the 1960s.
- Talking of civil-rights imbalance in Israel, former US President Jimmy Carter writes that "Each Israeli settler uses five times as much water as a Palestinian neighbor, who must pay four times as much per gallon" (1987, p. 121).
- Pakistan allows ten parliamentary seats for its non-Muslim population. However, these seats are nominated by the ruling party made up of Muslims and not elected by the masses.
- Both Israel and Pakistan, in declaring themselves as Jewish and Muslim states, respectively, automatically diminish the sense of belonging, pride, and safety for their bonafide citizens of other religions.
- Till recently, the German policy of *Jus Sanguinis* (right of blood) deprived children born to Turkish immigrant parents the right of German citizenship. Thus, an individual born and raised in the country did not have civil rights equal to others simply because of his or her ethnic origin.

To wit, these are all democratic nations. And, even though laws exist on paper in each of the places that reflect equality for all their citizens, the day-to-day life in the community at large is different. Even India, with its more than adequate record as a functioning democracy, has seen anti-Sikh carnage in New Delhi and anti-Muslim violence in Gujarat as recently as 1984 and 2002, respectively. And, as these inter-religious tensions have subsided, abuse of women, including rape, has become increasingly prevalent.

Minorities existing under totalitarian regimes have a worse fate; they have little recourse except to comply with the oligarchy of sadism. Women are not allowed to drive or travel without companions in Saudi Arabia. Homosexuals must hide their erotic preference in Iran.

The absence of provisions for divorce in Chile leaves a battered woman the option of pleading for a religious annulment of marriage or the indignity of staying married even when living a separate life altogether. The history of Europe's colonial rule in Africa and Asia, apartheid in South Africa, and various other disenfranchising strictures in nations across the globe provide many more illustrations of such "silence of the oppressed" (Akhtar, 2013).

In Fivush's (2010) terminology, these are not "instances of being silent"; these are illustrations of "being silenced." The former is elective, the latter enforced. The dominant narrative of the majority stifles societal experiences that do not fit its frame. This can take the form of depriving people of the right to assembly or by labeling their vision of reality as heretic, blasphemous, or mad. Such imposed silence can hamper the sharing of the present with the younger generations and preclude socially mediated interpretations of the past (Fivush, 2001; Fivush & Nelson, 2004). The history of the minority goes unrecorded and over time becomes too dissipated to assemble with coherence. Those whose participation was deliberately blocked are then registered as not having participated in generative acts of the group as a whole.

Progress

Minority individuals often feel that there is a limit to the number of rungs they can climb on the professional ladder. This is perhaps less marked in artistic and athletic fields and more marked in the realms of administration, politics, elected offices, and even the much hallowed sphere of academia. Minority individuals whose skin color or language or sexual preference is different from that of the majority, or those who are immigrants from erstwhile colonized nations are especially vulnerable to this feeling. Thus, in the United States, a Canadian guitar player or French sculptor is less vulnerable to feeling blocked by invisible barriers to professional advancement than a chartered accountant from Ghana or a social anthropologist from Pakistan.

The sources of this culturally modulated "glass ceiling" are both external and internal. Prejudicial attitudes of the majority can readily come into play and stop a minority individual from advancing beyond a certain point. Intrapsychic factors are operative as well. Minority individuals often feel unconscious guilt at having exceeded the productivity and social success of their relatives and friends. This can weaken their competitive strivings and, by projection, lead to a feeling that their success is being blocked by forces in the external reality.

Matters might go even deeper. Intrapsychic resistances to success are often traceable to decades, if not centuries, of the white devaluation of women and dark-skinned people. Margarita Sanchez-Mazas and Annalise Casini (2005, 2009), contemporary European sociologists, have conducted research studies which show that:

> Beyond the currently identified and well-documented impediments to women's careers stemming from the unequal distribution of housework and family tasks, the operation of norms and the implication of gender identity contribute to the reluctance that some women show in endorsing high positions in various fields. (2009, p. 50)

The pithy observations made by the Washington, DC-based psychoanalyst, Dorothy Holmes (2006), in connection with "success neurosis" among African Americans and among people of North America's lower socioeconomic classes, are equally pertinent here. She notes that "All transactions in our culture regarding race and social class are premised on the view that the non-dominant races and the poor are inferior and the Euro-Americans and the rich are superior" (p. 216). Holmes goes on to state that such attitudes get internalized by the racial minorities and by poor people, leading them to feel unentitled to success.

> In those persons of color and lower class who are so affected (i.e. who internalize the message that they are not to succeed, that they are not worthy of success), the pursuit of success is de facto taboo and, as such, must be punished. I argue that these views are set down in the mind extremely early and that they damage one's readiness to pursue that which one's society systematically opposes. Those societal opposing forces may also be internalized in one's superego, leading one to punish oneself for any pursuit of success, as well as to anticipate punishment from real opposing forces. So either success is denied by a real and later internalized perpetrator, or if pursued, it occurs at great personal cost, since one is haunted by one's essential "crime"—not by a fantasized oedipal or preoedipal one, but by a crime that our society indicts and condemns even more. (p. 219)

Consequently, the minority individual—often deprived in reality of helpful resources and thus ill-prepared for success—undoes his or her own progress in the social sphere. The variables of ontogenetically derived guilt (i.e., from pre-oedipal and oedipal sources), societally induced lack of entitlement, and prejudicial blockades in the pathways to success are compounded by the fact that achieving prominence can render the minority individual hyper-visible to self and others; preconscious anticipation of such discomfort can function as a brake in the psychomotor striving for success. Moreover, being used by the majority as a "token" of its liberal ways[6] and as a "mascot" of its achievements by the minority can deride the individual's authenticity and uniqueness. In a mirror image of the masochist for whom social failure becomes a psychological success (Bergler, 1949; Cooper, 1988), the minority individual can end up in a situation where social success becomes a psychological failure.

Ameliorative measures

The psychoanalytically informed social strategies that I am suggesting here are aimed to diminish the pain of minorities and to improve the majority-minority relations. The list of such strategies is neither exhaustive nor fully fleshed out. Additions can be made to it and the model is open to fine-tuning. The approach suggested here is informed by the vectors of economics, politics, history, and sheer pragmatism but it is fundamentally psychoanalytic in orientation. It emanates from psychoanalytic convictions which emphasize:

- That one must sustain a "belief-in-species" (Erikson, 1975), meaning that all human beings belong to the same species and any attempt to divide them into categories is misguided.
- That a sense of safety is the most basic requirement for normal psychic functioning (Sandler, 1960).
- That Freud's (1916–1917) declaring incest and murder[7] to be the "two great human crimes" (p. 333) applies to all human beings.
- That while solutions to these vary across cultures, human psychic problems, at their base, can be distilled to only two (i.e., some things are impossible and a few others are prohibited) all over the world (Bach, 1977).

- That human wishes are experience bound and hence culturally variable, but human needs[8] (e.g., for biological dignity, identity, affirmation and mirroring, intrapsychic and interpersonal boundaries, causality, temporal continuity, love, and generativity) are globally the same (Akhtar, 1999a).

With this uniform view of the essential humanity of all the world's people (the undeniable uniqueness of every single one of them not withstanding), social activism, judicial decree, legislative process, and administrative finesse can be mobilized. This, in turn, can result in significant emotional and moral uplift of minorities.

Providing access to, or restoring, full civil rights

Assuring that the minorities have civil rights equal and comparable to those of the majority is perhaps the most important social measure to diminish the minority's pain. To be sure, this is easier said than done and can apply only to states where a democratic system of government is in place. But as the foregoing discourse has demonstrated, equality of rights is not always the case even in democratic nations. With persistence of social activism, spread of empathy derived from knowledge and interaction, and with the appearance of a visionary leader, changes can be accomplished. Just note the improved situations of blacks, women, and homosexuals in the United States. Persistence pays. Keeping the dream alive matters. However, democracies which are simultaneously theocracies (e.g. Israel, Pakistan) would, of necessity, face difficulties in this path and might remain vulnerable to inner strife. The situation with autocratic governments and nations ruled by monarchs is far worse in this regard.

Acknowledging the majority's role in minority problems

This might be restricted to a simple statement of facts or might extend to the offer of an apology and of making reparations. For instance, the social policy debates over immigration to Europe and the United States would benefit from a clear and explicit reminder that their own import of labor and their colonization of Asian and African nations has served as a major impetus to such human traffic. If Moroccans and Algerians are in France today, is it partly because France was in Morocco and

Algeria yesterday. If Mexicans are crossing over the border into the United States, it is a "payment" for the trainloads of Mexican laborers that the United States imported during the early twentieth century, and so on. Such acknowledgement might extend to how the majority has treated the minority in the past. The salutary effects of Holocaust-related reparations upon German-Jewish relations, and the healing impact of the Truth and Reconciliation Commission's work upon post-apartheid South Africa are shining examples of what acknowledging the majority's role in putting down minorities can accomplish. And, in this context, just like in the bully–victim equation (Twemlow & Sacco, 2008), the role of "bystanders" acquires great importance. The bar is set by the degree to which they—in this case, other nations of the world—can remain silent (and therefore, complicit) in the face of a nation crushing its minorities.

Accepting a minority's culture

Since no race, religion, ethnicity, or language is inherently superior than another,[9] it would become the responsibility of the majority—who wields the power, anyway—to assure that all citizens receive this message. However, to convey it, the governing powers have to truly feel it. And, herein lies the difficulty. The temptation to preserve the majority society's "purified pleasure ego" (Freud, 1915c) and to extrude its inchoate and virulent aspects by projection is great indeed. As a result, one can come to believe that a Sikh's *pagdi*, a Jew's *yarmulke*, and a Palestinian's *kaffiyeh* are somehow unequal, with one or the other being better or worse. Were such biases limited to headdress or the attire in general (is a kilt strange?, a kimono weird?), matters might be simple. Unfortunately, this is not the case. The conservative streak in the human psyche pulls for retaining the status quo and responds to differences with derision. Thus one religious festival, one cuisine, one manner of discourse, and one music gets regarded as superior to its differing counterpart. Such essentialization has adverse consequences for the minority self-esteem for theirs is invariably the devalued culture. Communal efforts to rectify this bias can go a long way in diminishing the minority's anguish. Such efforts might include education in schools, civic support for ethnic neighborhoods, and government-sponsored displays and celebrations of minority cultures.

Including minorities in social iconography

The absence of minority faces from those depicted on currency bills, coins, and portrait galleries of the famous and the accomplished needs rectification. So does the lack of representation of minorities in the naming of streets, buildings, and bridges. Efforts should also be made, with the collaboration, if not sponsoring, of the minorities, to create museums of their history and their accomplishments. Significant cultural boost to an ethnic community can come from the (often belated) recognition of its heroes. The creation of a national holiday in honor of Martin Luther King, Jr. (1929–1968) in the United States and, even more profoundly, the 2008 election of Barack Obama to the country's presidency have, for instance, been of great social value to the African American community. These are big steps. Less monumental gestures can also have a remarkably uplifting impact; the fact, for instance, that seven US cities (New York, San Francisco, Chicago, Houston, Atlanta, Washington, DC, and Davie, FL) have erected statues of Gandhi is considerably morale-boosting for the Asian Indians in the country. Even smaller stimuli work. Movies that portray a minority's culture favorably can raise its self-esteem and its respect in the eyes of the majority. The Greek American and Indian American communities have thus greatly benefitted from the release of *Zorba the Greek* (Twentieth Century Fox, 1964) and *My Big Fat Greek Wedding* (Gold Circle Films, 2002), and *Gandhi* (International Film Investors, 1982), *Monsoon Wedding* (IFC Production, 2001), *Slumdog Millionaire* (Celador Films, 2008), and *The Life of Pi* (Fox 2000 Pictures, 2012), respectively. Museums of Jewish history in Baltimore, New York, and Philadelphia, and the Holocaust Museum in Washington, DC, have done similar service for North American Jews. And, the National Museum of African American History, recently inaugrated on Constitution Avenue in Washington, DC, promises a similarly uplifting impact upon the people it will celebrate.

Self-actualizing on the part of minorities

Lest the foregoing passages give the impression that what I am recommending is merely a passive nurturance of the minority, I hasten to add that my view could not be farther from this. I believe that minorities have to rise up and take control of their destiny (to the extent possible) themselves. They have to actively reject the centrifugal pull of masochism and a victim mentality. They have to gather themselves coherent spokespersons of pride, equality, and justice. Such protests can be vociferous. At times, however, the "rebellion" has to simmer below the surface of seeming collaboration with the majority. Nandi (1983) speaks of "cunning of the weak and victimized" (p. 111) which permits all-encompassing compromises that, at a deeper level, serve as refusals to be psychologically co-opted. This preserved core of authenticity can then plot uprisings and, in due course of time, overtly quest for justice and equality.

The path of minorities towards such goals might be full of hardships and even brutality by the majority (witness the scenes from the Selma, AL, march during the civil rights movements of the early 1960s led by the Reverend Martin Luther King, Jr.), but well-intentioned activism always pays in the end. And, things do not have to turn violent. Minority pride can be enhanced by imaginative slogans (e.g., "Black is beautiful"), assertive talent (e.g., Muslim film stars in Bollywood), and organized campaigns for fair treatment (e.g., the highly productive gay pride movement in the United States). Working in unison, such forces can lead to legislative reform and judicial edicts for the betterment of minorities' lives.

Concluding remarks

In this chapter, I have outlined the psychosocial distress of minorities by shedding light on the facets of their social presence, their perception by the majority and by themselves, their participation in the activities of the large group, and their impediments to socioeconomic progress. In each of these realms, I have delineated variables from both the external reality as well as the intrapsychic experience. With a modicum of anthropomorphization, my discourse has suggested that the discord between the subjectivity of the minority and its ecological and cultural "holding environment" (Winnicott, 1960b) causes minority individuals chronic mental pain or, in Freud's (1926d) terms, *Seelenschmerz*. Anesthetizing influence over such distress can be provided by retreat from social participation, nostalgic idealization of times and places where one was not a minority, soothing, even if grandiose dreams of times or places which would accord one the majority status again, exaltation of fundamentalism, and the discharge of impotent rage via acts of "terrorism" (see Chapter Five for more details). Far better than such turns of events are developments that follow minorities' asserting their rights and the majority's realizing the benefits of collaboration.

In conclusion, I would reiterate that the chronic unease felt by minorities arises from their being used as dehumanized targets of the majority's projections, as well as from the figure-ground discord in their subjectivity. Societal measures that assure their presence in textbooks of history and their representation in embodied communal narratives (e.g., statues, memorials) go a long way in diminishing their distress. Protection and/or restoration of their rights to vote, run for office, have freedom of movement and expression, and own property are also important. Finally, judicial provision of designating prejudicial acts of violence as hate crimes too increases the sense of minorities' safety. All this is not only good for them, it is beneficial for the society-at-large and, therefore, by implication, for the majority as well. It raises all sections of society to a higher humanitarian ground and this is what Gandhi, most likely, had in mind when he said, "A society is known by how it treats its minorities."

Notes

1. This development in the United States parallels those in many other countries, such as Australia, Canada, Israel, New Zealand, and South Africa, though the relationship between the actual natives and the early settlers is hardly the same everywhere.
2. Abkhaz are a Russian ethnic minority, mostly residing in the Black Sea region. Sami and Tupi are indigenous Scandinavian and Brazilian people, respectively. Uighurs are Turkish-speaking Chinese people.
3. Deo, Lee, Chin, Milman, & Yuen (2008) note that media frame racist ideologies by: (i) representing only certain images of a group to the exclusion of its other aspects, and (ii) choosing portrayals that directly resonate with existing stereotypes. However, popular media also have the potential of countering dominant ideologies, framing racism as contexted rather than essentialized, and offering positive images of a disenfranchised group.
4. The Pakistani novelist, Mohsin Hamid, addresses the anguish of such people in his book, *The Reluctant Fundamentalist* (2007).
5. The Chinese Exclusion Act, passed by the United States Congress in 1882, was the first of a number of federal and state laws established to ensure that certain immigrant groups would have minimal impact upon the emerging North American culture.

6. See Niemann (2003) for a comprehensive survey of the literature on the psychology of "tokenism."
7. I have taken the liberty here of changing Freud's (1916–1917) "incest with the mother" and "parricide" (both on p. 333) to "incest" and "murder," considering the former expressions to be unnecessarily phallocentric and restrictive.
8. For a thorough elucidation of the distinction between needs and wishes, see Akhtar (1999a).
9. Each culture has evolved in response to certain specific ecological, religious, economic, and political givens. Each has its strengths and weaknesses. Each has its realms of permissiveness and taboo. Each has its ways of giving voice to human desires, including those of affiliation, love, sexuality, competitiveness, and aggression.

CHAPTER FOUR

Racial, religious, and ethnic prejudice

While it relies upon simplification, certainty, and shallowness, prejudice itself is a deep and complex matter. Its roots can be traced back to evolutionary ontogenetic, historical, socio-political, and economic sources. Its myriad manifestations range from thoughtless discomfort with strangers through overt ethno-racial devaluation to communal violence and genocide. Its understanding requires an interdisciplinary approach with input from evolutionary sciences, history, political science, comparative religion, economics, media studies, and applied psychoanalysis. And its amelioration depends upon a harmonious blend of legislative, judicial, economic, educational, and psychodynamic interventions.

Formidable as all this might sound, it must not preclude our approaching the topic's threshold, namely, its definition. Indeed, such operational clarity is nowhere more important to have than in the realm of prejudice since the very nature of this concept rests upon distortion of perspectives. I will therefore begin my discourse with comments upon the nature and form of prejudice, that is, *what* constitutes prejudice and *how* prejudice becomes evident. I will divide my observations into sections dealing with the definition, varieties, and manifestations of prejudice. Labeling these sections ignorance, hostility, and externalization;

breaking the monolith; and six levels of intensity, respectively, I will provide a portrayal of the currently agreed-upon perspective as well as a brief elucidation of what seems unsettled and unsettling in each of these areas. I will conclude with some synthesizing remarks and by underscoring areas needing further investigation.

Challenging the conventional definition

The word *prejudice* is derived from the Latin *praejudicum*, which means a judgment formed in advance of a trial. The *Random House Dictionary of the English Language* (1966, p. 630) reflects this etymology in stating that prejudice is "an unfavorable opinion or feeling formed beforehand or without knowledge, thought, or reason." *Webster's Ninth New Collegiate Dictionary* (1987, p. 928) similarly declares prejudice to be a "preconceived judgment" including "an adverse opinion or leaning formed without just grounds or before sufficient knowledge," and "an irrational attitude of hostility directed against an individual, a group, a race, or their supposed characteristics." The thrust of these definitions is threefold: (1) prejudice implies arriving at a conclusion before considering pertinent facts, (2) prejudice is evident through derogatory and hostile attitudes, and (3) prejudice is directed at others. These three components can be termed the *ignorance factor*, the *hostility factor*, and the *externalization factor*. This tripartite construction is implicit in everyday usage of the word *prejudice*, and most scientific writings use the expression in the same way.

Finding this conventional tripod a bit wobbly, I propose an expanded definition of prejudice, hoping that it might provide us access to unlit psychosocial corners of the conceptual space that is always implicit in a definition. By deconstructing the prevalent lexicon, I hope to highlight aspects of prejudice that are not often considered. This might enrich interdisciplinary dialogue around such matters and enhance ways to ameliorate prejudice.

Ignorance and ignoring

The centerpiece of prejudice's definition refers to making a judgment before knowing the pertinent facts. This makes sense. However, in these days of postmodern relativism, what constitutes a fact is itself unclear. The so-called facts turn out to be slippery, if not to reside entirely in the mind of the beholder. Stalin and Mao had their "facts." Hitler had his "facts." Osama bin Laden, to be sure, had his. Even within our own country, not all facts seem based upon reality. From the Tuskegee experiments through the Watergate scandal to the recent Enron fiasco, we have been inundated with falsehoods masquerading as facts. Saddam Hussein's possessing weapons of mass destruction, invoked to justify the US invasion of Iraq, constitutes a current example. Whose facts were these? Were these facts or convenient fictions? To be sure, a vast majority of the world's nations, not to mention Iraq itself, regarded the American facts to be untrue; indeed there is now indisputable evidence (Clarke, 2004; Woodward, 2004) that the latter were closer to the mark.

Besides the issue of reliability, what does and does not constitute a fact is also unclear. Should we restrict ourselves to external reality, or do the facts in the internal, psychic reality matter as well? Even if we limit ourselves to the former, we can hardly deny that sociopolitical interests readily put a spin on available information to create suitable facts. Both current and historical realities are subject to such revisionist strategies. Take one look at Slobodan Milosevic's resurrection of the 600-year-old defeat of Serbian Prince Lazar by Ottoman Turks to justify his ultra-nationalistic agenda, and you will instantly grasp the power of these tactics. The fact is that facts can be invented.

Then there is the issue of knowledge of facts. The definition of prejudice states that a decision is made before (i.e., without) knowing the facts. However, it does not tell why the facts were not known. Were they actually not available? Or, did knowing them seem contrary to one's agenda? Is the ignorance because of not having information or denying and distorting it? Clearly, there is much to think about here. In fact, prejudice frequently exists despite our knowing facts. Lack of knowledge often plays a lesser role than the active jettisoning of available information that does not support one's emotionally needed convictions and plans. It is more often a matter of ignoring than of ignorance.

Hostility and undue idealization

The second component of the definition of prejudice refers to its disparaging, demeaning, and devaluing dimension. This certainly is true of most prejudices (e.g., anti-Semitism, Islamophobia, racism, homophobia). However, positive judgments in the absence of knowledge also qualify as prejudicial. Notable compromises of logic and mindless loyalty emanating from homoethnic idealizations are one example of this tendency. For instance, a Muslim individual's automatic assumption that anything that an Islamic nation does is correct, regardless of the outrageousness of the act and of world opinion against it, is an illustration of *positive prejudice*. The same applies to a Hindu individual's overlooking the pernicious impact of Hindu fundamentalism on the democratic fabric of India, and a Jewish individual's defense of all Israeli policies vis-à-vis the Palestinians. In other words, naïve idealization is as much a manifestation of prejudice as is ignorant devaluation. Freud's (1918a, p. 199) celebrated phrase, "narcissism of minor similarities" has a counterpart in Andreas Kraebber's "narcissism of minor similarities" (personal communication, January 21, 2004). The fact that customary usage of the word *prejudice* is limited to its hostile form does not make its positive version correct.

Externalization of "badness" and co-opting of "goodness"

The third and the final aspect of prejudice is that it is directed at other individuals. Ethnic and racial groups and nations other than one's own can also become "suitable targets of externalization" (Volkan, 1997) of one's hatred. Individuals with paranoid personality disorder especially show such a tendency. On a large group level too, similar projective mechanisms are witnessed. For instance, an actual or manufactured dread in the United States regarding Third World nuclear capabilities makes full recognition of the United States having killed over 100,000 innocent civilians by dropping bombs on Hiroshima and Nagasaki during World War II (Alperovitz, 1995). The American emphasis upon other nations' destructive potential helps deny its own intramural violence, as well as the fact of its bombing of Vietnam, Cambodia, Laos, and Iraq. Transcultural paranoia hides national depression.

In general though, there is nothing wrong about the notion that prejudice is mostly directed at others. However, this presents an incomplete picture since prejudice can involve attitudes about oneself as well. Thus a Jew can be anti-Semitic, a black person racist against his own group, a colonized individual ashamed of his national origins, and so on. Regardless of the complex etiological roots of such self-loathing (e.g., identification with others' attitudes towards oneself, guilt from various developmental levels being vented in the form of ethnic self-devaluation), the target of prejudice in such instances is clearly the self. Then there is the characterologically narcissistic situation of self-glorification in which a fatal denial of one's blemishes, hostility, and manipulativeness is evident. This, too, constitutes judgment without knowing the facts, though the facts here are mostly intrapsychic ones. On a large group level too, self-glorification occurs as a result of "robbing" a hated group of its good qualities and claiming them for oneself. Also involved here is a negation of the problematic aspects of one's own history. The insistent pride of the United States over its democratic institutions, for instance, can hardly remain unquestioned if one takes into account its long-lasting denial of voting rights to women and blacks, and that whenever a vote goes against the US interest in the world's democracy (i.e., the UN), the United States responds to it by a walkout or a veto. One thing becomes clear in the end: prejudice can be as easily directed at oneself as it is against others. This pertains to both its positive and negative forms, and is applicable to both individuals and groups.

This brief epistemological excursion demonstrates that prejudice can (i) occur in the presence of knowledge, (ii) involve good feelings, and (iii) be directed at oneself. These features exist alongside the customarily recognized facets of prejudice, that is, that prejudice is (i) often based upon ignorance, (ii) derogatory and hostile in content, and (iii) directed at others. Putting these prevalent and the newly proposed components together yields a richer and more comprehensive view of prejudice. According to this view, prejudice is a false-positive or negative assumption regarding oneself and others that is based either upon ignorance or deliberate distortion or denial of available external or intrapsychic information.

Such a broadening of the definition, however, carries with it the risk that the current, meaningful use of the work *prejudice* might get eclipsed. All sorts of erroneous beliefs might be lumped together, and the benefits offered to social science research and policy making by the use of a widely agreed upon and crisp terminology might be lost. On the other hand, a broader definition offers the possibility that hitherto unthought facets of prejudice might be "mentalized" (Fonagy & Target, 1997). The frequent coexistence of self-aggrandization and devaluation of others, for instance, might now attract sharper attention. The same applies to certain forms of ethnic self-loathing that might come under the microscope of those studying the poisonous germs of the prejudice. All in all, an expanded definition is likely to enlarge the field of investigation. The resulting increase in thinking and dialogue might yield newer strategies for prevention and amelioration.

Is prejudice a monolithic phenomenon?

The foregoing attempt at expanding the definition of prejudice leads not only to the possibility that more phenomena might now come under this rubric, but also that prejudice might be found to be of more than one variety; its various constituents might exist in different permutations and combinations, giving rise to phenomenologically and dynamically distinct entities. In fact, to regard all prejudices as similar and all prejudiced individuals as basically alike itself seems prejudiced. Young-Bruehl (1996) is among the most vocal opponents of the "allure of a monolithic idea of prejudice" (p. 67), suggesting that the nature of prejudice varies with the characterological makeup of the prejudiced individual. Others (e.g., Halstead, 1988; Parens, 1998) have also attempted to divide prejudice into subtypes. A number of variables seem to have been utilized in these classifications. Among them, the following are the most prominent ones.

Specific content

Prejudices along the dividing lines of religion, ethnicity, race, region, national identity, political belief, gender, and sexual choice are included here. Terms such as *anti-Semitism*, *racism*, and *homophobia* populate the chamber of this dialogue. While mostly distinct from each other, such prejudices can at times overlap. For instance, the expression of an anti-Israel sentiment can be a clever disguise that sheaths the sharper dagger of anti-Semitism. On the other hand, an accusation of anti-Semitism can be deployed to invalidate an anti-Israel political stance. Thus regional, political, and religious dimensions get all mixed up. In a related example, one notices frequent overlap in the dimensions of race and socioeconomic status when it comes to the US white mainstream's disparaging attitudes about African Americans living in poverty-ridden ghettos.

Societal sanction

Included here are *culturally syntonic* and *culturally dystonic* prejudices. The former represent widely distributed societal norms (e.g., anti-black sentiment in the pre-civil rights South), and the latter representing idiosyncratic biases that are not shared by the majority of the group (e.g., someone in Brooklyn hating the Chinese). Whether prejudices arising out of widely accepted societal biases are any less morbid than those whose origins seem deeply personal is an open question.

Role of cognition

The categories of *prereflective* and *postreflective* prejudices (Halstead, 1988) belong here. The former arise from ignorance of facts and are correctable by educative means. The latter are deeply entrenched in one's emotional life and resistant to change upon confrontation with facts that challenge them. The former are closer to the biases that are ubiquitous in human experience. The latter lie at the core of problematic and hurtful attitudes toward others. To paraphrase Shengold (1995) from another context, these are among the delusions of everyday life.

Experiential familiarity

The concept of *experience-near* and *experience-distant* prejudices arises from classification along this variable. The former refer to the subject having actually rubbed shoulders with a particular outlying group and thus having accumulated a proverbial kernel of truth (even though a distorted truth) in the subject's narrow and biased perception of that group. The latter refer to a prejudiced individual having no real experience whatsoever with a group that the individual presumably hates. Examples of the former are countless and include whites hating blacks, Christians hating Jews, Hindus hating Muslims, and so on. It is the latter type of prejudice that is more curious since it reveals the fundamentally hollow and false nature of prejudice. An example of this prejudice is that of some young Pakistani immigrants to the United States. Never having had any personal dealings with a Jewish person in their life, many of them instantly develop anti-Semitism upon their arrival in this country. This experience-distant anti-Semitism seems to be in the service of forging a pan-Islamic identity, a defensive measure especially needed by those unwilling or unable to assimilate and undergo the slow and painful identity transformation consequent upon immigration (Akhtar, 1999b). Here a prejudice serves as glue to a threatened inner self more than a knife directed at an outer group.

Scope and extent

A close correlation of prejudice with ethnocentrism in early studies of the subject (especially Adorno & Frenkel-Brunswick, 1950) gave rise to the notion that an individual prejudiced against one minority is usually prejudiced against all other minorities as well. Real-life experience does not always bear this out. Some prejudiced individuals hate all those who are different from them. Others do not. A person might hate blacks but not Jews, Muslims but not Latinos, and so on. Thus prejudice can be classified into *diffuse* and *focal* types. But do we really know which one is sicker: hating everyone or hating only a specific group of individuals? And, are the dynamic factors involved in the genesis of diffuse prejudice the same as those in focal prejudice?

Character types

Following Freud's (1931a) early characterology, Young-Bruehl (1996) has divided prejudices into *obsessive*, *hysterical*, and *narcissistic* types. According to Young-Bruehl, obsessional prejudices are marked by their tie to aggression. Obsessional individuals "… purge themselves of polluting thoughts and desires by displacing them onto others, who then are experienced as dirtying and assertively polluting. Their ideal is self-filtered of all impurities, all temptations, and imperturbable, perhaps even saintly self that cannot be attacked" (p. 214). In contrast are hysterical characters who view themselves to be more refined and less sexual than others. It is crucial to them that others appear lower, which means coarse and more sexual. Finally, there are the narcissists who express their prejudices in the realm of mental abilities. They are intellectual elitists who relish exhibiting their cultural and esthetic superiority while considering others stupid and uncultured.

While the foregoing list of categories can be extended along other dimensions (e.g., prejudices of the majority versus prejudices of the minority, handed-down prejudices versus manufactured prejudices, and so on), the point of this exercise is not merely to collect phenomenological curiosities. Classifications of the sort mentioned here are stepping stones for elaborating heuristic explanations and developing protocols for empirical research. Theoretical speculation and observational findings can then benefit each other in a dialectical fashion.

One problem, however, still remains unaddressed. This pertains to the uniformly *one-person* emphasis upon the conceptualization of prejudice in all these classifications. All of them see prejudice as existing merely within one person. This seems questionable since prejudice is a *two-person* phenomenon par excellence. It must therefore be viewed in a relational context. A shift from one-person to two-person psychology would, I believe, alter and enrich the picture. For instance, a benign prejudice (Parens, 1998) might be benign for the one who possesses it, but might not be experienced as benign at all by the one toward whom it is directed. Who is to judge what is benign and what is malignant in the realm of social discrimination? Should it be the possessor of those attitudes or their recipient? Clearly more thought is needed here. One thing though is certain, and it is that any contemporary classification of prejudice must take its relational context into account and pay attention to the associated distortions of *both* the object and self-representations. However, before addressing such nuances, it might be useful to pause for a moment and consider the ever important question about what gives rise to prejudice.

Origins of prejudice

While the causes of prejudice arise out of both external and internal realities, in the end most of these are traceable to the complex vicissitudes of human development. The following six factors are especially important in this regard: (i) development of stranger anxiety, (ii) ambivalence towards the mother, (iii) viewing father as the "invader" of the mother's body, (iv) perceiving the younger sibling as an unwelcome intruder, (v) disownment of pregenital drives, and (vi) creation of "us and them" in the service of identity formation.

The development of stranger anxiety

Beginning from the earliest periods of life, unpleasure generating experiences are repudiated as "not me," that is, the dangerous, frustrating, and unreliable Other. Moreover, the establishment of a *libidinal object* (Spitz, 1946), creating a specific bond of recognition, belonging, and safety with the mother, paradoxically generates the normative *stranger anxiety* (Spitz, 1965). This type of distress:

> ... serves to contain and direct the infant's inborn object-attachment tendency ... away from the non-primary caregiving object. In the average normal child, starting from about the fifth month of life, any encounter with an object the child has not already seen repeatedly will engender helplessness in the infantile ego ... the infant seems to experience the unknown object as a threat to the intrapsychic structuring of the libidinal object, and therewith the infant's attachment to the libidinal object. (Parens, 1999, p. 135)

Stranger anxiety, a normal experiential factor, can become the foundation of later ethnic and racial xenophobia and what Parens (1998) calls "benign prejudice."

In contrast to Parens's receptivity towards Spitz's proposal of "stranger anxiety" is Szekely's (1954) suggestion that there might be an innate or instinctively programmed and hardwired xenophobia in the neonate. The tension between these opposite perspectives can only be resolved if one regards Szekely's idea as representing, at a psychic level, the human body's propensity to reject certain foreign material (e.g., certain types of blood) and Spitz's idea as derived from a purely experiential basis. Even if conceptual space can exist for both these viewpoints, one thing remains clear: the infantile recoil from the unfamiliar is a rudimentary prototype for prejudice, not a sufficient condition for the latter's development.

A novel perspective on "stranger anxiety" has recently been provided by Ad-Dab'bagh (2012). He proposes that it is the gaze of the non-maternal parent that serves the "cultural function" of pulling the child into the membership of a family (and by implication, into that of a larger clan). Ad-Dab'bagh further states that:

> ... this cultural function could develop independently from the extent to which the containment function [of the mother] has developed. The proposed function is a result of imbuing the skin with the quality of being the integument to the self that separates it from whomever is not a member of the shared collective. (p. 30)

And, more pertinent to the issue of stranger anxiety is Ad-Dab'bagh's proposal that:

> ... the development of this "cultural function" is unlikely to be the result of the natural development of stranger anxiety, and may, in

fact, chronologically precede its onset … . Stranger anxiety possibly includes and involves psychological structures and subjective experiences that may include this cultural function of the psychological skin. However, if a link exists between the two phenomena, stranger anxiety and the cultural function, it may be the cultural function that sets the stage for stranger anxiety.[1] (p. 30)

Clearly, Ad-Dab'bagh's ideas differ from those of Spitz as well as Szekely's and further neonatal and child-observational research is needed to confirm or refute them. What does remain refreshingly original here is his proposal of paternal gaze as an early consolidator of "us-them" differences (see more on this issue later in this chapter).

Ambivalence towards the mother

From its earliest days, the growing child experiences both satisfaction and frustration at the hands of his mother. When experiencing pleasure, the child elaborates pleasurable phantasies in which the mother is seen as inexhaustibly bountiful. Parallel to this is an exalted "all-good" view of the self. These self and object representations are organized around a pleasurable affect (Kernberg, 1975; Klein, 1946). In contrast, when frustrated, the child elaborates hostile and destructive phantasies regarding the mother. Accompanying them are ruthless, cannibalistic, and violent self-representations. Such self and object representations are organized around angry and rageful affects (Kernberg, 1975; Klein, 1946). At first, the two sets of self- and object representations exist separately, with the child's mind being swayed in one or the other direction depending upon whether he is experiencing gratification or frustration. With increasing neurophysiological maturation and burgeoning ego capacities for synthesis, it becomes possible to bring the two views together into a composite whole. There now develops a deeper, somewhat ambivalent but more sustained internalized maternal object representation (Mahler, Pine, & Bergman, 1975), libidinal attachment to which does not get seriously compromised by temporary frustrations. In tandem, there is the emergence of a more realistic and less shifting view of the self which suffers minimal fluctuation under drive pressures. Together these achievements result in (and, in a dialectical fashion, are themselves contributed to by) the disposal of aggression toward self and its object by repression rather than by splitting. Capacity for tolerating ambivalence now emerges on the psychic horizon and the child becomes capable of deeper and more complex human relations (Akhtar, 1994; Kramer & Akhtar, 1988).

This normative sequence of events is disrupted if the child's experiences with his mother are predominantly frustrating. Under such circumstances, hurt and "mental pain" (Akhtar, 2000) accumulate, leading to a build up of much unneutralized aggression. Positive images of the self and mother are then safeguarded by splitting this aggression off and keeping the hostile self- and object representations compartmentalized. Splitting predominates over repression and vulnerability to projecting the hate-ridden self images becomes great (Kernberg, 1975). An individual with such a mental set looks for *suitable targets of externalization* (Volkan, 1997) into which the dreaded inferiority of the self and the repudiated hatred of one's mother (and, by displacement, of one's *motherland*) can be deposited. The result is the perpetuation of a holier-than-thou self image and an idealized mother and *motherland* representation on the one side and the "discovery" of a deeply resented external group on the other side. Realistic perception is compromised and prejudice abounds.

Viewing father as the invader of the mother's body

A second ontogenetic source of anger towards others lies in the vicissitudes of the oedipal phase. Beginning around the third or fourth year of life, this developmental period confronts the growing child with some confusing realities of the family life. So far the child has handled his relationship with the two parents somewhat separately with little thought about the relationship they have with each other. Burgeoning ego capacities and a widening circle of reality exploration, however, now force the child to deal with the fact that his parents have a relationship with each other and that he is not privy to all the intricacies of that bond. Feeling excluded, the child intensifies his curiosity and competitiveness on the one hand, and develops a sense of inferiority and hurt on the other hand. While children of both sexes feel it, the sense that one's mother has been co-opted, indeed invaded, by the father is especially intense in the case of a boy (Freud, 1910h, 1912d). Exposure to the primal scene (in actuality or imagination), in the setting of immature ego-functions, and anger at the parents for such "betrayal" further fuels the child's rage. By the mechanism of compartmentalization, mother's active sexual participation is negated and the father is seen as a violent invader of the mother's pristine body. The need to rescue mother is powerfully felt.

While it would be outrageously reductionistic to attribute the ethnic and religious prejudice felt by an adult to such childhood roots, it is also hard to altogether deny a remote echo of the childhood oedipal scenario in the howlings of communal scapegoating. The theme of rescuing the motherland from a group deemed to be descendant of an "invader" (forget that the so-called invasion might have occurred centuries ago) is amply evident in ethnic hatreds. In the Balkan ethnic cleansing, for instance, the Bosnians and ethnic Albanians suddenly found themselves to be the representatives of Turkish invaders of centuries ago; this rendered them as legitimate targets of Serbian plunder and violence. A similar dynamic is discernible in anti-Muslim hatred in India.

Perceiving the younger sibling as an unwelcome intruder

A third source of hatred towards others is constituted by the feelings aroused in a child by the arrival of a younger sibling. The newcomer is experienced as an interloper and one who has come between the older sibling and his mother. To forgive this theft of mother's attention is difficult and requires empathic reassurance that mother's love will continue to be available. Also helpful is parental support of the older child's secondary narcissism vis-à-vis being the more accomplished and wiser of the two children. In the absence of such compensations, and if the older sibling feels completely dropped from the maternal attention, hatred of the younger sibling acquires a pathological and destructive intensity. Associated with this hatred is a fantasy that life before the arrival of the intruder was blissful and would have remained as such *if only* (Akhtar, 1996) it had not been spoiled by this unfortunate event.

Displacement of such affects and fantasies upon societal members unconsciously representing younger siblings (e.g., racial and ethnic minorities) is not uncommon and becomes a factor in the consolidation of prejudicial attitudes towards them.[2] There develops a belief that the hated group is an unwelcome intruder who has disrupted a previously harmonious community. A malignant next step in this logic is that elimination of the hatred group (Hitler's *final solution*; Milosevic's *ethnic cleansing*) can restore the earlier, joyful life.

Disownment of pre-genital drives

Eclipsed by the current emphasis upon the object relations, self-psychological, relational, and intersubjective perspectives in psycho-analysis, the vantage point of *drive psychology* (Pine, 1988) nonetheless remains a powerful explanatory model. Progressive maturation of pregenital erotogenic zones give expression and form to instinctual pressures. These, in turn, are associated with phantasies that get elaborated, content-wise, in the matrix of interpersonal relationships. For instance, during the earliest, oral period, impulses of sucking and biting predominate and phantasies of greedy incorporation and cannibalistic destruction occupy the center stage of the psyche. Subsequently, the anal phase is characterized by impulses to retain and hoard on the one hand, to angrily soil and defile on the other. Temptations of coprophilia and defiant randomness exist side by side with defensive and adaptive constellations of purity and order. Still later, during the phallic-oedipal phase, tendencies towards bodily exhibitionism, voyeurism, refusal to accept generational differences, and insistence upon incestuous object choice collide with the need for restraint and waiting, tolerance of generational boundaries, acceptance of one's exclusion from the primal scene, and establishment of the incest barrier.[3]

If such opposing tendencies of various psychosocial phases do not adequately merge, the ongoing superego pressures lead the drive-based scenarios to undergo projection. Even under the best circumstances, the unmerged residues of such drives are subject to projection. This gives rise to the feeling that someone else, not oneself, is greedy and omnivorous, dirty and hoarding, exhibitionistic and unmindful of the incest barrier. One's own temptations in such directions are transformed into accusations of wrongdoing by others. Pertinent to this connection is Bird's (1957) comment that "The feeling of prejudice is put into force and is used by the oppressing race as a defense against its own temptation to do the very thing it accuses the oppressed race of doing" (p. 501). Additional support to the brittle ejection of the intrapsychic malcontent is then provided by contempt for those who now seem to harbor the disowned tendencies.

Given this, it is not surprising that racial prejudices and religious hatreds from different regions and eras all seem to center upon contempt-laden perceptions of projected pregenital drives that have been projected upon onto others. The despised group is viewed as greedy and gluttonous (oral derivatives), messy and miserly (anal derivatives), edgy and exhibitionistic (phallic derivatives), pansexual and promiscuous in love object choice (oedipal derivatives). To be sure, projection of repressed childhood drives is not the sole determinant of adult social attitudes; the latter are governed by a multiplicity of intrapsychic and reality factors. Yet, drive projection does contribute to the genesis of prejudice. The ubiquitousness of such projections in human life is responsible for the striking resemblance between the supposed rationalizations of prejudice sought by various groups. Anti-Semitic Christians, for instance, hold that Jews are smelly, dirty, and unkempt (Adorno & Frenkel-Brunswick, 1950). The exact same belief is held by ethnocentric Hindus about Muslims in India (Varma, Akhtar, Kulhara, & Kaushal, 1973).

Creation of "us and them" in the service of identity formation

Going down to the elemental levels of protein differentiation, antigen recognition, blood grouping, and antibody formation, there is a somatic inclination for accepting some things as "ours" and belonging to "us" and others as "not ours" and belonging to "them." The distinction, at this level, is existentially necessary if bodily integrity is to be maintained. Extrapolating this biological imperative in the spirit of Freud's (1923b) renowned dictum that "the ego is first and foremost a bodily ego" (p. 26) leads one to assume that a similar "us-them" distinction might be necessary for the human mind as well (Szekely, 1954). And, indeed, this turns out to be the case.

Ongoing psychic development through separation-individuation, oedipal phase, latency, and adolescence provides further nodal points for "us-them" distinctions to evolve. The resolution of the Oedipus complex especially leads to generational filiation and entry into a temporal order of existence. Extension of this sense, in turn, results in a feeling of belonging to a historical community. In Volkan's (1988) words: "By identifying with others in one's own group—parental figures, peer groups, teachers, religious authorities, community and national leaders—one identifies with their investment in religion, ethnicity, nationality, and so on, and shares in the differentiation of those persons unlike the group and inimical to it" (p. 49).

Such ethnic identity is both "positive (*we do this*) and negative (*we do not do what they do*)" (Thomson, Harris, Volkan, & Edwards, 1993, italics in the original). This early ethnic sense might at first border on ethnocentricity. Sadly, transgenerationally transmitted biases and nationalistic pride inculcated in schools have a tendency to embellish such narrow-mindedness. The role of such "educational" measures in the consolidation of prejudice is best captured in a 1949 song from Rodgers and Hammerstein's musical, *South Pacific*: "You've got to be taught/ Before it's too late." The lyrics go on to declare that even before the age of seven or eight, one has to be "instructed" to hate those whom your family disapproves.

Intensification of "us-them" distinction and exaggerated clinging to group identity at the cost of individual authenticity tends to occur during societal crises and regressions (Aviram, 2009; Freud, 1921c). More malignant destructiveness towards others now begins to characterize the group's prejudices.

> Prejudice deals with anxiety generated by the attachment system by using a specific strategy, that is, by creating an identificatory affiliation in the face of difference. The person re-affirms his belonging by exaggerating the lack of shared characteristics with the object of prejudice, while implicitly strengthening his ties to another group, similarly distorting accurate perception by exaggerating the overlap and homogeneity of characteristics. (Fonagy & Higgitt, 2007, p. 71)

Under less turbulent circumstances, the "normal" ethnocentricity of latency gets diluted during adolescence when a certain disidentification with parental mores occurs (Blos, 1967; Jacobson, 1954; Money & Ehrhardt, 1972). The wider interaction with diverse social and ethnic groups that takes place at this time facilitates a diminution of childhood ethnocentricity. In the absence of such dilution, ethnocentricity persists and the need to distinguish oneself by aggressively separating oneself from others remains intense.

Together the six factors outlined above give rise to a universal vulnerability to prejudice. However, more than such ordinary childhood frustrations is needed to turn this potential into actual hatred of others.

Factors including those pertaining to the real world (e.g., economic hardship, excitation by powerful paranoid leaders) and to group psychology (e.g., intensification of affects and lowering of critical judgment, as noted by Freud in his 1921 paper) are required to fuel this hatred and create the inferno of inter-ethnic and inter-religious violence. The factors giving color to a specific prejudice (and, especially those turning it into violence) vary from situation to situation. The factors leading to intrapsychic potential for prejudice are ubiquitous and universal. And this lays the groundwork for returning to phenomenological nuances in this realm, especially as these involve the levels of intensity of prejudice.

Levels of intensity

The manifestations of prejudice are myriad. Some are overt. Others are covert. Some are restricted to the realm of thought. Others spill into the arena of action. Some are direct expressions of a rigidly held bias. Others are defensive attempts to hide that very bias. Some are crass and crude. Others are subtle and sinuous. Indeed, the ways in which ethnic, religious, or racial prejudice (or for that matter, any other prejudice) becomes evident are so variable as to defy an organized presentation. Yet this seems a necessary first step to help sharpen our thinking in this regard. Such a classification might also assist in research planning and deciphering the various factors that play a role in the emergence and sustenance of the various manifestations of prejudice.

It is with this purpose in mind that I offer the following schematic organization of prejudice into six levels (see Table 1). Levels I and II constitute mild prejudice, levels III and IV, moderate prejudice, and levels V and VI, severe prejudice. While it might require fine-tuning in light of a conceptually challenging critique, this outline is distinguished by three characteristics: (1) it places manifestations of prejudice along a hierarchical order of increasing severity; (2) it includes the distortions of both self-view and the view of others, and (3) it opens up the conceptual space to theorize about the factors (e.g., psychological, social, politico-economic, media-based) that lead an individual or a group to move from mild to moderate to severe levels on this diabolical ladder.

Table 1.   Manifestations of prejudice.

Level of prejudice	Views about oneself	Views about others
Mild prejudice		
Level I	Unquestioning self-acceptance; no psycho-logical-mindedness.	Unmentalized xenophobia; benign provincialism.
Level II	Subtle belief in one's moral superiority; ethnocentrism.	Stereotyping; enjoyment of ethnic jokes.
Moderate prejudice		
Level III	Lopsided political ideology; emergence of "villain hunger."	Mistrust of minorities; active avoidance of them.
Level IV	"Propaganda addiction"; narrowing of perception; overt smugness.	Conscious hate of others; glee in their failures.
Severe prejudice		
Level V	Fantasy of the self being in danger; regression to group identity.	"Justified" discrimination; dehumanization of others.
Level VI	Paranoid megalomania; emergence of "messianic sadism."	Organized violence; murder and genocide.

By accomplishing these three tasks, this manner of organizing the symptomatology of prejudice becomes superior to a mere listing of negative attitudes toward others. In emphasizing the distortion of the object representation by the projection of unwanted self-attributes, the prevalent view overlooks that the denial of the object's authenticity (and goodness) leads to a parallel and increasing distortion of the self-representation. This ignored factor is accounted for in the scheme offered here.

The distorted self and object representations inherent in prejudice exist in a rigidly held relational matrix. Davids (2006, 2011), in his delineation of the "internal racist organization," eloquently describes the sequence of events in such interaction:

> 1. A real difference that divides subject and object is identified … . 2. Unwanted aspects of the mind are split off and projected across that divide, [and] … . 3. An organized inner template is set up to govern the relationship between subject, now free of aspects of himself, and object, now containing them. Henceforth, all their interactions must conform to the demands of that organization, i.e. they have to stick to their roles. (2006, pp. 71, 72)

The evolution of such distorted relationship is gradual, however. Things go step-by-step. The first step in this development is passive disinterest in those different from oneself and the existence of significant blind spots in cross-cultural perception. Disagreeable self-attributes are firmly repressed, intrapsychically pulverized, and then exiled into the unconscious "container" (Bion, 1967) of an experience-distant other. Little need to think about oneself or others is felt. The next step involves some "owning" of the tendency toward projection. Enjoyment of ethnic humor and mistrust of minorities now become manifest. In still more advanced forms of prejudice, one can observe a conscious hatred of others and active buttressing of one's hostile views by seeking selective media input. The continuing outward projection of hatred results in paranoid fears of attack by others. This is defended against by heightened narcissism and a regressive fusion of id and superego functions. Moral megalomania is the next step in this course of events.

Matters do not end here. As aggression is displaced outward, others become bad. In a parallel development, their goodness is cannibalized by the self. The latter keeps becoming nobler by the minute. But this repudiation of inner hostility sooner or later boomerangs, causing a sense of self-endangerment. This dread, in turn, is used as a ploy for hating, attacking, and even destroying others, with full moral justification since they appear threatening to the self's survival. Malignant narcissism (Kernberg, 1984), which combines arrogance with hostility and sociopathic behavior, now dominates the psyche. Factors of group regression (Freud, 1921c), revisionist use of history by narcissistic and paranoid leaders (Volkan, 1997), and real or imaginary economic threats to one's group also enter the picture at this stage. The ground is now set for organized violence.

Four novel concepts

Four concepts that make their appearance in this phenomenological spectrum of prejudice (see Table 1) need special mention. These are (1) unmentalized xenophobia, (2) villain hunger, (3) propaganda addiction, and (4) messianic sadism.

Unmentalized xenophobia

The individual at the most preliminary level of prejudice displays a bland lack of interest in those who are culturally, racially, or religiously different from him. He lacks knowledge of them and does not make use of the opportunities that can provide such knowledge. The circle of his socialization is restricted to those of his own group, and his life-style reflects that loyalty. An inevitable correlate of such profound disinterest in those different from oneself is a smug self-acceptance. It is as if one knows all there is to know about oneself and there is nothing further to be discovered. Besides being defensive against inner uncertainty, the effects of the passage of time, and the awareness of death, "… such ordinary simple-mindedness makes life easier, less demanding; and, more important, it makes us less likely to allow into consciousness repressed or suppressed shameful, guilt-ridden, unwanted, and dangerous aspects of our mental picture of ourselves" (Shengold, 1995, p. 145).

The restriction of the ego's social rind to a homocultural in-group buttresses intrapsychic repression. One simply does not think about discordant cultures and people, nor does one pay attention to the inner voices that are discordant from a highly sanitized view of oneself. This is the syndrome of *unmentalized xenophobia*.

Villain hunger

Extending Volkan's (1998) concept of the "need to have enemies," I have elsewhere (Akhtar, 2007b) proposed the term *villain hunger*. This consists of the need to have someone (an individual or a group) to blame for one's problems. Such externalization of aggression blocks awareness of one's own contributions to the hardship being faced; sadness and mourning are thus kept in abeyance. Anger makes one feel strong. Paranoia becomes a psychic vitamin for threatened identity and a powerful anodyne against the pain that results from genuine self-reflection. This is the essential dynamic of villain hunger. And this hunger is readily activated when a large group's identity is threatened by external or internal sources. Most such threats are constituted by economic upheaval, but sometimes the sudden disappearance of a well-known enemy can also destabilize the group. The fall of the Soviet Union, for instance, created a vacuum in American large group dynamics and, in part, led to it finding a new enemy in the form of Islamic fundamentalism (not that these Muslims did not invite such an occurrence themselves).

Propaganda addiction

This refers to the voracious appetite that some prejudiced individuals develop for published or broadcast material that supports their worldview. Such material may be of historical interest and origin, or of current parlance. While books published by reputed (or shall we say disreputed?) presses and renowned leaders (e.g., Hitler's *Mein Kampf*) do figure in this cornucopia of hate, it is more dependent upon agenda-based pamphlets, internet websites, and even musical bands that propagate prejudice. The individual who is spiraling downward into an abyss of rage toward minorities finds material of this sort exalting. It diminishes his inner aloneness and enhances his narcissism. By mirroring his prejudice, it makes his distorted beliefs seems rational, consensual, and even normal. Propaganda can become addictive under these circumstances.

Messianic sadism

As the extreme end of hateful prejudice is approached, the raw aggression of the id begins to flow in the veins of the superego. The individual's psyche is now taken over by "malignant narcissism" (Kernberg, 1984); an idealized self-image and an ego-syntonic, sadistic, self-serving ideology begins to rationalize antisocial behavior. Thinking becomes dangerously stilted and utterly devoid of empathy for others. When such a "fascist state of mind" (Bollas, 1992) receives encouragement from politico-religious exhortations, violence and even murder appear to be divinely sanctioned and guilt-free. Killing others becomes a means of buttressing one's own callous megalomania and also of obtaining and sustaining merger with an idealized deity or leader who embodies an archaic, cruel, and omnipotent superego. This constitutes the stage of *messianic sadism*, which can propel riots, mass killings, and genocide.

Concluding remarks

In this chapter, I have delineated the limitations of the way prejudice has been conventionally defined. I have expanded the purview of this concept and described six levels of its intensity, noting that each level is associated with more and more deformation of self and object representations. Following this, I have discussed the origins of prejudice and demonstrated the complex interplay of ontogenetic, trauma-based, "educational," group regression related, and sociopolitical variables in the consolidation of severe prejudice and the occurrence of ethno-racial violence. Adding to the phenomenology of prejudice, I have introduced the novel concepts of unmentalized xenophobia, villain hunger, propaganda addiction, and messianic sadism.

This foray into the terrain of prejudice's phenomenology, however, remains incomplete since I have left the following areas unaddressed: (1) the overlap between prejudice and bias, (2) the role of language in expression, concealment, and accusation of prejudice, and (3) the anchoring of some of the phenomena mentioned here in the deepest layers of the human psyche, even if such an anchor is in the form of a sequestered and split-off potential. I will now attempt to address these three areas.

Prejudice and bias: Bias, defined as "an inclination of temperament or outlook ... [that is] highly personal" (*Webster's Ninth New Collegiate Dictionary*, 1987, p. 147) is ubiquitous. Such predilections can be positive (e.g., liking football more than baseball) or negative (e.g., disliking sushi). Either way, they are subtle, harmless, and, most important, recognized by the individual as biases. Indeed, people can be playfully proud of their biases and have little reservation in displaying them. Their existence adds spice to life and gives each individual's identity its own characteristic stamp. When they involve the realm of ethics, the individual becomes idiosyncratically moral but not moralistic. All in all, it seems safe to say that a bias resides in what Winnicott (1953) has called the "intermediate area of experience." Prejudice, in contrast, is harmful to others and, insofar as it leads to distortion of the self-representation, to oneself as well. And it "refuses" to be recorded in a register other than that of reality. This distinguishes it from bias, which is a "transitional phenomenon" (ibid.).

Prejudice and language: Language plays multiple roles in the realm of prejudice. To begin with, language is the most frequent medium through which prejudice is expressed. Slurs such as *faggot, kike,* and *nigger* are prime examples of the power of words in giving vent to prejudicial attitudes.[4] This is the language of the perpetrator. In contrast are terms such as *anti-Semitism, racism, homophobia,* and the more recent *Islamophobia,* which have helped identify instances of a particular group's injustice toward another group. They constitute the language of the victim. These terms are potent weapons for societal vigilance and reform. However, they can be overused and abused in order to invalidate legitimate complaints against a particular group. Under such circumstances, these terms lose their lexical honesty and acquire the status of rhetorical ploys. Yet another manner in which language plays a role in matters related to prejudice is the defensive coinage of politically correct phraseology to avoid the appearance of prejudice. All sorts of terms (e.g., *intellectually challenged* instead of *mentally retarded*) thus are coined, though their sanitized luster usually does not last very long. Search for still newer expressions soon begins again.

Prejudice's deepest anchor in the human psyche: It is always tempting to declare some individuals as prejudiced and others—including oneself—as free of prejudice. While at gross levels of the phenomena involved this might be true, the attitude seems itself prejudicial. The tendency to divide human beings into two types results from the negation of the fact that all human beings are, at their core and in their potentials, more or less alike. Keeping this in mind gives rise to the idea that rather than there being prejudiced and non-prejudiced individuals, there might be prejudiced and non-prejudiced parts of the personality in all human beings. The former part contains a potential for omnipotence, arrogance, aversion to knowledge of reality, and hatred of differences. The latter part contains a potential for flexibility, humility, curiosity about self and others, and a fundamentally pleasant though a bit sad attitude in encountering the world at large. It is the proportion of these two parts in the intrapsychic economy (and its evocation by sociopolitical triggers) that ultimately determines whether and to what extent an individual is overtly prejudiced. Klein's (1946, 1975) "paranoid" and "depressive" positions as well as Bion's (1957) "psychotic" and "non-psychotic" parts of the personality are clinical equivalents to what is proposed here in a social context.

All in all, such an enrichment and deepening of our views of prejudice, as offered in this chapter, has the advantage of giving impetus to further theorizing, forming the basis of models in empirical research, and facilitating the development of strategies for the diminution of prejudice. It might also encourage us to take a fearless look at our own inner selves, which is where I believe the problem of prejudice as well as its potential remedies reside.

Notes

1. Ad-Dab'bagh (2012) suggests that if the maternal "containment function" has been well internalized, then attack upon the "cultural function" of psychological skin in the form of prejudicial slurs is experienced as an assault on the group that one belongs to. However, if the "containment function" is not well established within oneself, then the same sort of attack leads to psychic disintegration.

2. Long ago, Sterba (1947), while discussing the anti-black feelings of white people, stated that the former are perceived by them as "unwelcome intruders … (signifying) … younger siblings" (p. 421).

3. The drive determined aspects of the human mind and its motivations are presented here in a thumbnail sketch. On the one hand, having formed the core of psychoanalytic developmental theory for many decades, they do not require citations. On the other hand, the increasing neglect of this perspective in contemporary analytic theorizing necessitated this reminder here.

4. Another common tendency is to refer to the hated others as animals, such as "apes," "pigs," "vermin," "snakes," and so on. For details on such dehumanization of others, see Chapter 6 of this book.

CHAPTER FIVE

The tripod of terrorism

A ny 2017 discourse on terrorism must maintain a tight focus upon the threat posed to world peace by groups like al Qaeda and ISIS. After all, most bloodshed of recent times (e.g., the attacks in London, Paris, Nice, Berlin, San Bernardino, Orlando, Dacca, Istanbul, and Barcelona) can be traced to these groups and to independent operators loosely affiliated or inspired by them. It would be sociopolitically irresponsible and conceptually impoverishing to not try to understand the origins, motives, and aims of these groups. At the same time, we must not permit investigative zeal to condemn us to the very narrow-mindedness we find at the base of their "messianic sadism" (Akhtar, 2007b). Therefore, I begin this contribution to a psychoanalytically informed understanding of terrorism by acknowledging the nosological, geopolitical, and conceptual breadth of this realm and by entering some caveats.

Some caveats

First, even though jettisoned in popular discourse, the word "terrorism" originated in connection with state-sponsored suppression of dissent. The word entered the English lexicon in 1795, when it referred to the governmental suppression of defiance by pumping fear in the arteries of its subjects. The term was derived from the French Revolutionary statesman Maximilien de Robespierre's Reign of Terror (1785–1794). From then on, the world has witnessed many horrific examples of such "terrorism from above," including the purges of Joseph Stalin (1936–1938), the Holocaust of Adolph Hitler (1941–1945), the killing fields of the regime of Pol Pot (1975–1979), and the torture chambers of August Pinochét (1973–1990).[1] On a lesser scale, the assassination of nearly 30,000 Haitians by François Duvalier (1957–1971), the ruthless persecution of ethnic minorities in Uganda by Idi Amin (1971–1979), and the stunning atrocities by Hissène Habrè in Chad during the 1980s can also qualify as "terrorism from above." Yet, both the professional and popular coverage of terrorism gives far more attention to the "terrorism from below," that is, the mayhem let loose by comparably small groups of people who, for real or imaginary reasons, consider themselves humiliated and disenfranchised. This discordance is something to be kept in mind as we proceed with this discourse on terrorism. Another point to remember is that "terrorism from below" is the weapon of the weaker party in the conflict ("weaker" being defined as resource-constrained); it has two choices: either surrender and accept defeat or devise homemade means to fight the enemy. The decision to take the latter route is less ideological and more tactical—maximum benefits to be accrued from minimum resources.

Second, the designation "terrorist" is not a self-earned medal of identity. It is assigned to one by others who might be driven by politico-economic expedience and narrow self-interests. Thus, the British, at different eras in their history, have regarded George Washington (1732–1799), Subhash Chandra Bose (1897–1945), and Menachem Begin (1913–1992) as terrorists, while the respective American, Indian, and Israeli followers of these leaders upheld them to be great freedom fighters. Moreover, someone labelled "terrorist" one day can be celebrated as an "outstanding contributor to world peace the next day. In 1987, the United States held that Nelson Mandela's (1918–2013) African National Congress was one of the world's "most notorious terrorist groups" (Chomsky, 2003, p. 190), but six years later celebrated his receiving the Nobel Peace Prize. The leader of the Palestine Liberation Organization, Yasser Arafat (1929–2004), was long held to be a terrorist by the United States and Israel but later in his political career was awarded the 1994 Nobel Prize for Peace. More recently, Narendra Modi (1950-present), leader of the right-wing Hindu fundamentalist BJP (Bhartiya Janata Party), was barred entry into the United States for being a terrorist. Upon becoming India's prime minister, however, Modi was not only allowed to travel to the United States, but was feted with great fanfare by President Barack Obama in June 2016. Who is and who is not a terrorist (and what is and what is not a terrorist act) thus comes to lie in the proverbial eye of the beholder, and how clear and far-sighted is such eye's vision is not easy to tell.

Third, while most "terrorist attacks" of today are traceable to Muslim groups of this or that stripe, the politico-religious violence subsumed under the label of "terrorism" is not exclusive to any religion. One does not have to invoke the Crusades (the intermittent religious military campaigns from 1096–1291), which Pope Urban II declared to be the will of God, in order to illustrate this point. The warring Protestants and Catholics of Ireland, the Tamil Tigers of Sri Lanka, the Khalistan secessionists and Maoist Naxalites of India, and the Basque separatists of Spain give testimony to the deployment of terrorist tactics by Christians, Hindus, and Sikhs alike. As none other than the Israeli prime minister, Benjamin Netanyahu acknowledged in his September 22, 2016 speech to the United Nations: "There are also acts of terror committed by Jews" (Israelam.com). Moreover, history tells us that the practice of suicidal terrorism—reflexively equated with today's Muslims—goes quite far back and elements of it can be found in the tactics of the first-century Jewish Zealots and Sicarri, the eleventh-century Ismaili Assassins of Northern Iran, and the twentieth-century Japanese kamikazes. Such practices were given the contemporary form of suicide bombing by the Tamil Tigers, a Marxist-Leninist Hindu group of Sri Lanka, and only later adopted by Muslim terrorists of the Middle East. In fact, the prime minister of India, Rajiv Gandhi (1944–1991), was killed by a Hindu woman suicide bomber of this group.

Fourth, the gamut of violence subsumed under "terrorism" varies greatly. It ranges from the savagery of lone actors (e.g., Timothy McVeigh in the Oklahoma City bombing; Nidal Hasan, who killed thirteen and injured thirty people at the Fort Hood, TX, military base; Baruch Goldstein who, in 1994, showered bullets on Muslim Palestinians praying in a mosque, killing twenty-nine worshippers and wounding another 125; and Dylann Roof, the white supremacist who recently killed nine African American people in a mass shooting at a South Carolina Bible study), through the nefarious rampage of gangs (e.g., Baader-Meinhof in Germany) to the mass violence caused by the political right (e.g., Ku Klux Klan in the United States of the 1950s), or the political left (e.g., the Shining Path guerrillas of Peru, the Naxalites of India), or by religious zealots (e.g., Boko Haram of Nigeria). Thus, all "terrorist attacks" are not the same. There are different kinds, different degrees, different motivations, and different results involved here. Any search for a common denominator of group mentality or individual dynamics must not overlook such diversity.

Fifth, a caveat must also be entered about the writing and reading of contributions such as this. From the writing side, the subject lies beyond the clinical realm that is my area of whatever expertise I possess as a psychoanalyst. Reasonably well versed in depth psychology of individuals, I am less adequately equipped to explain matters that involve large groups of people and partake of variables from history, politics, economics, and religion. My tenure on the Group for Advancement of Psychiatry's Committee on International Relations (1996–2001), my work in the area of immigration and cross-cultural dialogue (Akhtar, 1995, 1999b, 2011a; Akhtar & Choi, 2004), my attempt to forge links between Islam and psychoanalysis (Akhtar, 2008a, 2008b), my tenure on the International Psychoanalytical Association's Working Group on Terror and Terrorism (2002–2005), as well as my earlier writings on terrorism (Akhtar, 1999c, 2003), and problems of ethno-racial minorities (Akhtar, 2014) have given me some insights in the realm of sociopolitical turmoil. Nonetheless, the territory is still somewhat unfamiliar to me. Another problem is that a modicum of personal bias is nearly impossible to avoid in this sort of writing. No matter how hard one tries for it not to be the case, the picture one paints ends up receiving colors not only from one's professional discipline, but also from the deepest core of one's identity. This has to be acknowledged. From the reading side too, matters are not simple. Encounter with politically charged essays such as this one can shake up psychological equanimity and neutrality. Feeling validated or invalidated in their own ethno-political convictions and thus becoming narcissistically exalted or injured, readers become vulnerable to regressive simplification and partisanship.

Finally, this discourse on terrorism does not claim to be all encompassing. It does not include some pertinent perspectives on terrorism based upon the evolutionary concept of "male coalitionary violence" (Thomson, 2003), neurophysiology (Prakash & Lo, 2004), monetary funding (Ehrenfeld, 2003; Wissing, 2012), and the role of print and digital media (Freedman & Thussu, 2012; Nacos, 2016). Such matters lie beyond my sphere of knowledge and expertise.

Having entered these important caveats, I am now prepared to elucidate the multifaceted psychosocial dynamics of current radical Muslim's terrorism and to propose some ameliorative strategies to deal with it, not overlooking even for one moment that the understanding and interventions needed here are multidisciplinary and not exclusively based upon the principles of psychoanalysis.[2] Before proceeding with this, however, it seems worthwhile to recount some basic facts about Islam and Muslims. This is important since one often encounters an astounding lack of factual knowledge regarding such matters among Western readers.

Some facts about Islam and Muslims

The information provided below is categorized into that pertaining to Islam and that pertaining to Muslims. The former is a religion with its scriptural canon, moral dictates, social rituals, history, and jurisprudence. The latter is a multitude of individuals who are spread all over the globe and have considerable regional differences among them. The distinction between Islam and Muslims is important to make since not all Muslims act in accordance with Islam, and many features of their lives, including their politics, have little to do with their religion.

Facts about Islam

The word "Islam" is derived from the Arabic *salama*, which means "to submit." It shares the same Arabic root as the word for peace or *salaam*. The religion of Islam thus calls for active submission to the will of God. Its prophet is Mohammad ibn Abdullah, or simply, Mohammad. The two sources of sacred knowledge in Islam are the *Holy Quran* and the Prophet's teachings called the *Sunna*.

Mohammad was born in Mecca, Saudi Arabia, in 570 AD. He was an only child. His father died soon before his birth. His grandfather took him and his mother to live with the family but he too passed away two years later. Mohammad was then sent away to be taken care of by a woman from a nomadic clan. At age six years he was brought back to his mother, only to lose her to death soon afterwards. Relatively little is known about Mohammad as a subsequent child and adolescent except that he was extremely industrious and trustworthy. At twenty-five years of age, he married a wealthy business woman, Khadijah, who was considerably older than he (between fifteen to twenty-two years older, according to different accounts). He fathered two sons and four daughters by her but only one, a daughter, Fatima, survived to adulthood. At the age of forty, Mohammad declared that he had begun to receive messages from God, delivered to him by the angel Gabriel. The recording of these divine utterances comprise the *Quran,* a book of over 500 pages that serves as the sole religious scripture of Islam. Mohammad's wife died when he was forty-eight years old. Soon after Khadijah's death, and due to the increased prejudice against the community of his followers, Mohammad migrated to Medina, a city 200 miles from Mecca. There, he spread his message, gathered a large following, married many women, and returned as a warrior to capture Mecca. By the time of his death in 632 AD, he had become the de facto ruler of nearly all of Arabia.

While central to any discussion of Islam, its Prophet, Mohammad, is not regarded as the author of the *Quran* by the believers. Instead, the *Quran* is viewed as the direct and literal word of God. And, to become and to be a Muslim, one has to abide by the following five "pillars" of Islam:

- *Shahada*: one must declare commitment to the faith by earnestly reciting *La-ilaha-il-lillah, Mohammad-ur-rasul-Allah*. Literally translated, this means, "There is no god but Allah and Mohammad is His messenger." The implication, of course, is that no other form of deity or ideology is worthy of worship and the message relayed by Mohammad is divine.
- *Salat*: one must offer prayers five times a day, with each prayer (including the required ablutions preceding it) taking about twenty-five minutes.
- *Ramadan*: one must fast and abstain from sexual activity from dawn to dusk for this whole month of the Islamic calendar. This pious month ends with the most important festival of Muslims, *Eid-al-Fitr* (the Happy Day of Breaking Fast).
- *Zakat*: one must donate two and a half percent of all assets (not just annual income) each year to the poor, sick, or suffering. This is not viewed as voluntary or charity but as a divine mandate to share wealth received from God.

- *Hajj*: one must travel, if able-bodied, at least once in a lifetime to Mecca, where the Prophet Mohammad was born and first received God's revelation.

These five mandatory requirements form the core of "submission" to the will of God in Islam. In addition, a Muslim is expected to follow the rules of life described in the *Quran*, the exhortations of *Sunnah* (sayings of the Prophet), the encouragements of *Hadith* (tales told about his behavior) to emulate the Prophet and, finally, the conduct delineated in *Shariah* (Islamic law). The latter:

> ... regulates a broad range of Muslim behavior, such as ritual washing to prepare for prayer, valid forms of worship, rights and obligations of spouses, inheritance law, trade, and criminal law. Some of these rules were relegated to the realm of individual observance, whereas others were to be administered by the state. (Hamid, 2008, p. 12)

Two other points need mention. First, Islam does not claim to be an entirely new religion. Instead, it emphasizes that it is a continuation of Abrahamic faith and recognizes the prophets who came before Mohammad, including Moses and Jesus. With slight variations, the tales contained in the Old and New Testaments (e.g., Adam and Eve, Noah's Ark, David and Solomon, Mary and Jesus) are all contained in the *Quran*. Second, like all other religions, Islam has different (and sometimes contradictory) theologies, jurisprudence, mystic orders, and regional idioms. This accounts for the great diversity that exists among the world's Muslims.

Facts about Muslims

In order to understand the Muslim psyche, if such a generalization is ever possible, one needs to know not only their present demographic and cultural characteristics, but their past as well. In this context, it is imperative to recognize that over the few centuries following Mohammad's demise, a vast swath of the globe—ranging from Syria to Spain, and including Turkey as well as significant portions of the Middle East and Africa, came under domination of Muslim rulers. A "golden age of Islam" thus began. Major libraries of sacred texts were established as early as AD 634 at the al-Aqsa Mosque in Jerusalem and in AD 721 at the Umyyad Mosque in Damascus. While focusing on Islamic culture, scholars at these and other similar institutions studied important literary texts from faraway lands as well. A most striking cross-cultural accomplishment of this era was the translation of the great Indian collection of fables, the *Panchtantra*, into Arabic around AD 750. The Hindu discovery of the number zero was transmitted to the Western mathematical world only after its assimilation in the Arabic numerals. The greatest think tank ever seen by the medieval world was established by Caliph al-Mamun in AD 1004 in Baghdad, the capital of the Abbasid Empire. It was called *Bayt al-Hikmah* (the House of Wisdom). Without the translations and research that went on there, much of the Greek, Latin, and Egyptian knowledge would have been lost to the world. By the middle of the thirteenth century, Baghdad alone had thirty-six libraries, and similar enthusiasm about scholarship was evident in Cairo, Aleppo, Timbuktu, and the major cities of Iran and central Asia. The Muslim world produced complex and elaborate fiction, rich parables, and heart-melting poetry of epic proportions. Perhaps the most outstanding among this literature is the *Shah-nama* ("The Book of Kings") that was written in Persia circa AD 1010 by Abdul Qasim Mansur Firdausi (934–1020 AD). It was a poem of 60,000 verses (seven times the length of Homer's *Iliad*), detailing the history of the Persian kings from their legendary beginning to Khusrau II in the seventh century AD. It has remained the great national poem of Iran and is a preeminent literary work of the Muslim world. The great Arabic tale of *Alf Layla wa-Layla*, the old Urdu tract of *Tilism-e-Hoshruba*, and the medieval romantic stories of *Majnun-Layla* (Arabic) and *Shirin-Farhad* (Persian) are among some other immortal contributions of Muslims to world literature.

The glorious days of Islam which had begun in the eighth century AD started to decline in the mid-thirteenth century largely as a result of brutal invasions by Mongols. Soon the Muslim empire of Spain faltered and became a matter of the past by 1492 AD. The advent of gunpowder gave impetus to new Muslim powers, especially the Safavids in Iran, Mughals in India, and Ottoman Turks in Asia Minor, the Balkans, and North Africa. Speaking of the latter, Mikhail (2017) states that:

> The Ottomans held more territory in 16th century Europe than either England or the Netherlands. More Christians lived in the

Ottoman Empire than any other European state. The city with the largest Jewish population in the 16th century world was Ottoman Salonica. (p. 19)

This era of conquest and expansion added much to the world civilization, especially in the realm of fine arts, poetry, calligraphy, and architecture; the majestic Sultan Ahmed Mosque in Istanbul and the breathtaking Taj Mahal in Agra were built between 1609–1616 and 1632–1643 respectively. But by the middle of the seventeenth century, these great empires were crumbling (partly due to internecine conflicts and partly due to the rise of Western powers). With the rise of the Austro-Hungarian Empire, the Ottomans retreated to the South Balkans and their original homeland. The European takeover of erstwhile "Muslim lands" in the East started in the mid-eighteenth century, and reached its zenith in the late nineteenth century. The Muslim world did not produce a reformative line of thinking that, in the West, originated with Martin Luther (1483–1540) and John Calvin (1509–1564) and was polished and transmuted into a firm Church-state separation by John Locke (1632–1704) and Thomas Jefferson (1743–1826). Governmental rule in the Muslim world remained entangled with religion, often at the cost of taking steps towards modernity. As a result, the Muslim world fell behind in industrialization and scientific development, even though pockets of academia continued to be productive here and there. In most places, however, regional conflicts took center stage at the cost of educational and economic progress. Some succumbed to the tyranny of colonialization, and others to tribal warfare. To a certain extent, twentieth-century Turkey became an exception since under the leadership of Mustafa Kemal Ataturk (1881–1938), it made significant strides towards modernization.

Other major events of the twentieth-century history of Muslims include: (i) the carving out of East and West Pakistan from India in 1947 at the insistence of the Muslim separatist Mohammad Ali Jinnah (1876–1948); (ii) the exodus of Palestinians with the creation of Israel in 1948; (iii) the 1952 overthrow of Egypt's King Farouk (1920–1965) and the subsequent tension between the liberal-leaning Gamal Abdel Nasser (1918–1970) who became the nation's president, and the anti-modernity Sayyid Qutb (1906–1966) who became the leading spokesman of the Muslim Brotherhood[3] in the 1950s and 1960s; (iv) the crushing defeat of the armed forces of Egypt, Jordan, and Syria at the hands of Israel in 1967; (v) the breakup of Pakistan and the rise of a secular-leaning Bangladesh from the ashes of East Pakistan in 1971; (vi) the overthrow of the US-supported Mohammad Reza Shah Pahlavi (1918–1980), the king of Persia (Iran), by Ayatollah Ruhollah Khomenei (1902–1989) and the establishment of the isolationist Islamic Republic of Iran in 1979; (vii) the signing of the peace accord in that very year between Egypt's Anwar el-Sadat (1918–1981) and Israel's Menachem Begin (1913–1992); (viii) the Srebrenica massacre where over 8,000 unarmed Muslim boys and men were killed by Serbian forces in a 1995 ethnic cleansing effort and, (ix) the re-emergence of *Mujahadeen* (Afghani warriors whom the US had supported as a bulwark against the Russian invasion of Afghanistan) as the dreaded *Taliban* during the late 1990s, under the influence of Osama bin Laden (1957–2011).

With the advent of a new century came the devastating 9/11 attacks on the Twin Towers of the World Trade Center in New York City, the repercussions of which still linger on. The American pillage of Iraq, the civil war in Syria, the militant fundamentalism in the form of ISIS—the Islamic State of Iraq and Syria—and its nostalgic and brutal ambition for establishing an Islamic caliphate worldwide, and the failed "Arab spring" (student uprisings in Cairo and Istanbul) complete the picture so far.

This brings us to today's Muslims, who are spread all over the globe and hardly represent a culturally monolithic group. In most major realms of their daily existence (e.g., nationality, language, cuisine, rituals, literature, art, music, and politics) they differ considerably from each other (Esposito & Mogahed, 2007; Mamdani, 2005). It is illuminating and psycho-politically useful to know such facts, especially for those inclined to interact and intervene with or hypothesize about this large and diverse group of people. The following realities are especially important to keep in mind.

- There are 1.4 billion Muslims in the world and, in fifty-seven of the 196 UN recognized countries, they constitute the majority of the population.
- Not all Muslims are Arabs and not all Arabs are Muslims. In fact, Arabs constitute only 20 percent of the world's Muslim population.
- The country with the largest Muslim population in the world is Indonesia. India, Pakistan, and Bangladesh are second, third, and fourth, respectively, in this context.

- Nearly 85 percent of the world's Muslims are *Sunni,* and most of the remaining are *Shia*; a small proportion belongs to other minor sects of Islam. *Shias* constitute a majority only in Iran, Iraq, and Bahrain.

- Muslims speak many languages. These include (in alphabetical order) Arabic, Bahasa, Bengali, Bosnian, Chinese, Danish, Dutch, English, French, German, Gujarati, Hindi, Kashmiri, Malayalam, Orya, Persian, Punjabi, Pushto, Russian, Serbo-Croatian, Spanish, Swahili, Tamil, Telugu, Turkish, and Urdu.

- Muslim women's status in society varies greatly. In some places (e.g., Saudi Arabia, Yemen), they are segregated, disenfranchised, barred from the social arena, and "silenced" (Fivush, 2010). They lag behind men in literacy and have little control over their life trajectories. However, the situation of women is different in other Muslim societies. In the United Arab Emirates and Iran, for instance, women constitute the majority of university students (Esposito & Mogahed, 2007) and in Jordan and Pakistan, they are heavily represented in the legal and medical professions, respectively. Even more impressive than this is the fact that women have held the highest elected office in five Muslim majority nations: Benazir Bhutto (prime minister of Pakistan, 1988–1990; 1993–1996), Tansu Ciller (prime minister of Turkey, 1993–1996), Sheikh Hasina Wajid (prime minister of Bangladesh, 1996–2000), Begum Khalida Zia (prime minister of Bangladesh, 1991–1996; 2001–2006), and Megawati Sukarnoputri (president of Indonesia, 2001–2004).

- Muslims live in economic conditions that are vastly different across nations. The oil-rich Saudi Arabia and the Persian Gulf states, like Qatar and United Arab Emirates, are strikingly distinct from the poor African nations like Mali or the somewhat less poor Bangladesh.

- The four countries with the largest Muslim populations (Indonesia, India, Pakistan, and Bangladesh) have democratically elected constitutional governments. Muslims living in these countries are not suppressed. They have a political voice and are regularly elected to high offices. Most Arab nations (e.g., Saudi Arabia, Yemen, Kuwait), however, are ruled by autocrats, monarchs, or self-appointed "presidents." Such governments limit civic opposition and curtail access of non-governmental organizations (NGOs) to international media and political affairs.

- Belief-wise too, the world's Muslims vary greatly. Just like Christians in the United States, most believe in the basic tenets of their religion and try to abide by its dictates; only few truly live in accordance with all of Islam's "rules." Most believers are "moderate" in their socio-political views. Then, there are Muslims who are agnostics and athe-ists; many of them think of themselves as "culturally Muslim." Then again, there is a whole world of Sufi Muslims, given to mysticism. Still others turn "Islamists" and devote themselves to social services that provide educational, legal, and medical services to Muslims liv-ing in slums, refugee camps, and other poor communities. Finally, there is the militant fringe which reflects what is now popularly dubbed "Islamic radicalism." Constituting a very small faction of the global Muslim population, these violent individuals (and the nefari-ous groups they form) have become a threat to both the West and to the Muslim world itself.
- In the Muslim majority nations, the proportion of Muslims who believe that *Shariah* laws should be applied to the entire popula-tion varies greatly. In Afghanistan, Iraq, and Pakistan, 99 percent, 91 percent, and 84 percent of Muslims subscribe to this view, respec-tively. The percentages are strikingly lower in Azerbaijan (8 percent), Turkey (12 percent), and Lebanon (29 percent).
- On an average, 18 percent of the population in Muslim majority nations believe that other religions also lead to eternal salvation. For American Muslims, this figure jumps up to 56 percent.[4]
- The widely prevalent narrative of Muslim-Jewish, Muslim-Hindu, Muslim-Christian acrimony seems one-sided. There is ample evi-dence that Muslims have lived peacefully with Jews (Montville, 2008), Christians (Kayatekin, 2008), and Hindus (Akhtar, 2005b) alike, in various times and in various parts of the world. The mention of such consilience and amity brings to mind that six Muslims have been awarded the Nobel Peace Prize over the past forty years: Anwar Sadat (1978), Yasser Arafat (1994), Shirin Ebadi (2003), Mohammad El Baradei (2005), Mohammed Yunus (2006), and Malala Yusufzai (2014).

With such facts about Islam and Muslims to hand, and keeping in mind the caveats entered earlier in this discourse, we are prepared to delve into the possible origins of the current wave of terrorism by radical Muslims.

A trio of causes

Let us begin this section with the official US government definition which declares it to be "the calculated use of violence or threat of violence to attain goals that are political, religious, or ideological in nature, through intimidation, coercion, or instilling fear" (cited in Chomsky, 2003, p. 188). The British government's definition is similar. It states that "terrorism is the use, or threat, of action which is violent, damaging, or disrupting, and is intended to influence the government or intimidate the public and is for the purpose of advancing a political, religious, or ideological cause" (cited in Curtis, 2003, p. 93). These definitions seem to make sense. However, they also pose two problems. One, these definitions do not help differentiate between terrorism and legitimate acts of resistance. Two, they apply equally to the acts of "sub-state" organizations (e.g., al Qaeda) and to those of nation states; in other words, they fail to distinguish between "terrorism from below" and "terrorism from above," or between "terrorism" and the so-called "counter-terrorism."

This brings up the tight, if subterranean, relationship that frequently exists between the two kinds of terrorism. Vedantam (2003) underscores this link and provides many illustrations of such an axis of intimidation and violence. And, I take the liberty of quoting him at length.

> Some sub-state terrorist groups, like the Ku Klux Klan (KKK) in the American South, once held close ties to the corridors of political power. In some cases, politicians and police officers donned the dreaded white mask and cape at night to terrorize black people, creating a seamless link between officials of the state and sub-state terrorists. In Haiti, "President for Life" Papa Doc Duvalier set up the dreaded Tontons Macoutes, a paramilitary organization that combined voodoo superstition with the latest techniques of torture to suppress all opponents, spread terror, and strengthen his grip on power (Nash, 1998). In early 2002, Hindu fundamentalists in India—informally allied with the state and federal Hindu nationalist governments—killed between 800 and 2,000 Muslims in what has been widely termed as a pogrom: various human rights groups charged that state officials were complicit in the terror, in that they did not intervene to stop the bloodshed. Like the links between the KKK and white segregationist politicians, the links between state officials and those who perpetrated the terror fall into a grey

area that makes it impossible to separate one from the other. In Sri Lanka, the Tamil Tiger separatist movement has simultaneously conducted terrorist strikes in the south while playing administrator in northern areas under its control, where it has collected taxes and provided civic services. Along front-lines where neither side was fully in control, the Sri Lankan government and the Tigers have exchanged state power on a daily basis—some localities have been under government control during the day and under the control of the Tigers at night. The terror practised by the Tigers cannot be neatly described as sub-state or state-sponsored violence. More recently, several states have used terrorism and terrorists to strike at other nations in lieu of waging war—U.S. support for holy Muslim warriors to end the Soviet occupation of Afghanistan in the 1980s, the Taliban's subsequent sponsorship of global terror networks around the world, and Pakistan's widely reported support for terrorism in Kashmir being but a few examples. (pp. 20–21)

The observation that "terrorism from above" and "terrorism from below" are often interlinked lays the groundwork for the search of etiological factors leading to the current political violence unleashed by Muslim groups like al Qaeda, ISIS, and their various and sundry offshoots. In the view being proposed here, the so-called "radical Islamic terrorism" is a phenomenon that has been cocreated by Europe, the United States, and the Muslim majority nations. Even the prefix "Islamic" in this context is a collusive concoction of convenience; Muslim zealots wish to justify their violence by handing it a religious banner, and the West, expressing its own prejudices and need for exoticization, accepts such conflation of Islam and violence without question. Replacing the term "radical Islamic terrorism" by the "terrorism of radical Muslims" or, even better, by "radical un-Islamic terrorism" de-links acts of violence from Islam per se, the majority of whose followers are peaceful citizens of the world. Designating some of Islam's followers as "radical Muslims" is a reminder that there are "non-radical" Muslims as well and the term "radical un-Islamic terrorism" serves the useful purpose of isolating the violent fringe of Muslims from the rest of the Islamic world. It has the benefit of diminishing an en-bloc condemnation of Muslims and reducing what has come to be known as "Islamaphobia." With that being said, I now turn to the contributions by Europe, the

United States, and the Muslim world to the emergence and sustenance of the current "terrorism by radical Muslims."

European contributions

The seeds of today's global unrest were, in part, sown during the "glorious" days of European colonialism. Vast swaths of Africa, the Middle East, and Southeast Asia were turned into the outposts of British, French, Dutch, Portuguese, Belgian, Spanish, and Italian imperialism. The results were mixed. On the positive side, the colonized nations saw infrastructural growth (e.g., roads, railways), betterment of educational systems, and the import of post-Industrial Revolution know-how.[5] On the negative side, the colonizers dominated, exploited and, at times, slaughtered the "natives." The following three examples from the history of British colonization should drive this point home.

- During the Second Boer War (1899–1902), the British placed nearly one sixth of the Boer population in concentration camps. Of the more than 100,000 people interned, about 28,000 Boers died and so did countless black Africans.
- British soldiers, under the orders of Brigadier Reginald Dyer, shot nearly 500 unarmed, nonviolent protestors in the walled Jallianwala Bagh in Amritsar, India in 1919.
- The British Army raped and tortured Kenyan civilians during the Mau Mau Uprising (1951–1960), and estimates of people brutally murdered range from 20,000 to 100,000.

Corresponding examples from the history of French colonization include the following:

- The words of French Lieutenant-Colonel Lucien de Montagnac (1885, p. 153) stationed in Algeria, speak volumes about the colonizers' attitude of hatred towards their subjects: "This is how, my dear friend, we must make war against Arabs: kill all men over the age of 15, take all their women and children, load them onto naval vessels, send them to the Marquesas Islands or elsewhere. In one word, annihilate all who will not crawl beneath our feet like dogs" (letter to a friend dated March 15, 1843).

- After the defeat of the Japanese in the Pacific War, the French ruling class was determined to reestablish its control over Vietnam. In 1946, the French prime minister ordered the shelling of Haiphong, killing 6,000 Vietnamese.
- Another example is France's Rwandan *Operation Turquoise* (circa 1994) which assisted in the fully armed escape of the French-backed and equipped perpetrators who initiated the Hutu-Tutsi genocide that eventually claimed 800,000 lives. The French government also provided sanctuary for Agathe Kanziga (wife of the Rwandan dictator) and her entourage that were fully involved in the governmentally instigated genocide.

It is in response to such atrocities by the British, French, and other colonial powers *and* in the context of post-World War II vulnerability of European colonialism that a number of groups emerged which used terrorist strategies to win freedom for their people. Of the numerous examples, three stand out: (i) Menachem Begin's Zionist *Irgun Zvai Leumi* (National Military Organization) was one of the first to systematically target Britain's "oppressive rule of Palestine" (Hoffman, 1998, p. 50), (ii) Subhash Chandra Bose's *Azad Hind Fauj* (Free Indian Army) which attempted to forcibly overthrow the British government in India during the 1930s, and (iii) the Algerian *Front de Libération Nationale* (FLN), whose fiery spokesman, Frantz Fanon (1925–1961), declared that colonialism "is violence in its natural state, and it will only yield when confronted with greater violence" (1963, p. 61).

Worse, when politico-economic benefits dimmed, the colonizers left and abandoned their subjects. The last-mentioned action was sometimes a response to local freedom movements and at other times the result of waning economic interests of the colonizing nations themselves. Not infrequently, their departure was correlated with the hitherto governed nations being sliced into two or three "meta-nations." New and untenable geopolitical entities were carved out by the "divide and rule" politicians and by geo-culturally ignorant cartographers enlisted by the colonizing powers. Such divisions resulted in bitterness and grudges that festered (and, continue to fester) long after the lands' "rulers" were gone. The still unresolved consequences of the 1916 Sykes-Picot Agreement (a secret pact between England and France which planned to divide the Arab East into smaller colonies) and the 1917 Balfour Declaration (which committed Britain to a pivotal role in the creation of Israel) as well as the continuing acrimony between India and Pakistan (partitioned in 1947) are among many such examples. A different sort of problem also arose with colonialism's demise. This was comprised of the migration of the colonized people to their erstwhile masters' original homelands, a trend especially marked among those who were born around the time of their nation's gaining freedom—the "Midnight's Children" in Salman Rushdie's (1980) terms. Thus, Belgium, England, France, and Holland, for instance, witnessed a large influx of Indo-Pakistani, North African, and Middle Eastern immigrants. Still under the awe of their white rulers of yesterday, these immigrants gladly suffered discrimination and marginality in order to gain economic advantages. Their consciously held idealization of the erstwhile masters served as a salve against the wound of geo-cultural dislocation. Their unconsciously held hatred of the erstwhile masters was trans-generationally transmitted to their children who were less likely to be wide-eyed admirers of the West. The members of this new generation faced an additional dilemma. They were born in European countries but yet they were not regarded as "truly" European by their peers. Thus kids whose parents had come to England from Pakistan or whose parents had come to France from Algeria were not regarded as "British enough" or "French enough" by their white-skinned neighbors and schoolmates. To make matters worse, these kids were not felt to be "Pakistani enough" or "Algerian enough" by their parents. A gap thus appeared in their identity, one that unfortunately was often filled with "meta-nationalistic" ideological exhortations by narcissistic-paranoid orators in their homo-ethnic enclaves. As a result, such youth became "agents of the large group identity" (Volkan, 2014, p. 115) and were no longer under the influence of their own individual psychology; charismatic "trainers" could then cultivate a sense of noble martyrdom in them, turning them into potential or actual suicide bombers (Atran, 2003; Volkan, 2014). Mockery of their religious beliefs and their Prophet, Mohammad, in the form of scathing documentaries and cartoons[6] produced and relished by their nation's majority further fuelled the sense of disenfranchisement and "justified" the paranoid rage felt by these marginalized individuals. They were now ready for *Jihad* against the West.[7]

On an entirely different level, the influx of African (and, to a lesser extent, Asian) immigrants was felt as a threat to the "purity" of white European identities. While liberal voices continued to welcome diversity (or, at least, bear it graciously), a significant block of European citizens took a sharp turn to the political right and found refuge in xenophobic nationalism. Anti-immigrant (translate: anti-African, anti-Arab, anti-Muslim) sentiment rapidly grew. Leaders like France's Jean-Marie Le Pen and his fiery daughter, Marine Le Pen, Greece's Nikolaos Michaloliakos, Holland's Geert Wilders, and Poland's Jaroslav Kaczynski have become the most vociferous spokesmen of this virulent trend. Under the guise of their respective nationalist agendas, they advocate social strategies of hate and racism.[8] As a result, a dialectical loop evolved whereby the rhetoric spewed by such fanatics fuelled the immigrants' sense of isolation and rage and that, in turn, "justified" the right wings' disdain. One could smell blood in the air.

American contributions

The United States, though not a colonizer of African, Middle Eastern, and Asian nations, has also played a role in fuelling the violent passions underlying the terrorism of radical Muslims. It has done so in the following four ways: *First*, the United States has unleashed crushing violence itself against certain Muslim majority nations. Foremost among these is Iraq. Ostensibly responding to the 9/11 terrorist attack by al Qaeda, this unwarranted pillage of a country that had nothing to do with the collapse of the World Trade Center's Twin Towers in New York, resulted in between 112,000 and 123,000 civilian deaths (Steele, 2010; Tirman, 2011) directly attributed to the "coalition forces" led by the United States.[9] The disproportionality (3,200 killed in the 9/11 attack vs. 200,000 killed in Iraq) would be shocking in itself but the horror is intensified when one takes into account that the "rationale" for attacking Iraq was entirely fabricated (Clarke, 2004; Woodward, 2004). Moreover, destruction was not limited to military casualties but extended to civilian casualties and led to a ravaged nation which subsequently became a haven for al Qaeda operatives. The armed intervention by the United States left Iraqis devastated and shocked; millions were dislocated and became refugees. It should surprise no one if their hurt and rage gets deposited in the hearts and minds of their next generations. Iraq is, however, not the only Muslim majority nation that has received blows from American military might. Afghanistan and Pakistan are others. The former has especially been the target of fiery US bombing intended to eradicate al Qaeda and the Taliban; this, presumably, has been a "just war," an American Jihad, so to speak. However, none of the criteria for considering a war as "just" (e.g., protecting innocents, right intentions, last resort; see Elshtain, 1992) applied to the US attacks on Afghanistan which resulted in nearly 3,000 civilians being killed on an annual basis and thousands more injured, dislocated, and made homeless. Worse than all this is the lasting grief of parents who have lost children and children who have lost parents. It should also be remembered that the American military interventions with disastrous consequences are still continuing; since 2014, US Air Force has dropped about 40,000 bombs in Iraq and Syria and an additional 1,200 bombs in Afghanistan (Sullivan, 2016). Add to this the military "errors" which have led drone attacks both in Afghanistan and in the Western frontier provinces of Pakistan that bombed schools, hospitals, and wedding processions, and the devastating portrait of human tragedy becomes clear.[10] As shock settles and before mourning can occur, rage accrues. In this context, the following finding of the Chicago Project on Suicide Terrorism is highly pertinent.

> Examination of *al-Qaeda's* pool of suicide terrorists—the seventy-one individuals who actually killed themselves on missions for *al-Qaeda* from 1995 to 2003 shows that the presence of American military forces for combat operations on the homeland territory of the suicide terrorists is stronger than Islamic fundamentalism in predicting whether individuals from that country will become *al-Qaeda* suicide terrorists … *al-Qaeda* suicide terrorists are ten times more likely to come from Muslim countries where there is an American military presence for combat operations than from other Muslim countries. (Pape, 2005, pp. 103–104)

This suggests that suicide bombing is a reaction to helplessness and humiliation. While this might be true, other pathways to such self-destruction also exist. At a pragmatic level, suicide bombing is merely a poor man's weapon delivery system. At a psychological level, it represents what Freud (1910g) called the ego's renunciation of "its self preservation for its own egoistic motives" (p. 232) and what Winnicott (1960a) regarded as a form of giving up on the total self rather than giving up on only the true self. Seen this way, some suicide bombers are killing themselves for ideological reasons and because a life of inauthenticity has become utterly unbearable. A few others might do so because they are already psychically dead and feel that they have little to lose by being actually dead as well. Thus, suicide bombing can express rage, altruism, a denunciation of indignity, and the actualization of a pre-existing intrapsychic state.

Second, the "democracy-hypocrisy" of the United States on the international stage is a source of greater frustration to the Muslim world. Presenting itself as a lover of democracy and its great proponent, the United States does not come across as democratic at all to the rest of the world.[11] The record of the United States over the last half century or so speaks for itself.

> Parliamentary governments were barred or overthrown, with US support and sometimes direct intervention, in Iran in 1953, in Guatemala in 1954 (and in 1963, when Kennedy backed a military coup to prevent the threat of a return to democracy), in the Dominican Republic in 1963 and 1965, in Brazil in 1964, in Chile in 1973, and often elsewhere. Our policies have been very much the same in El Salvador and many other places across the globe. The methods are not very pretty. What the US-run Contra forces did in Nicaragua or what our terrorist proxies do in El Salvador or Guatemala isn't ordinary killing. A major element is brutal, sadistic torture—beating infants against rocks, hanging women by their feet with their breasts cut off and the skin of their faces peeled back so that they will bleed to death, chopping heads off and putting them on stakes. The point is to crush independent nationalism and popular forces that might bring about meaningful democracy. (Chomsky, 1992, p. 20)

American installation of dictatorships (e.g., Chile) and kings (e.g., Iran), alliances with monarchs (e.g., Saudi Arabia), and restrictions on who can and cannot seek office in an open, national election (e.g., stopping Yasser Arafat from running in the 2006 elections for the Second Palestinian Legislative Council) complete the anti-democratic posture experienced by others. The fact that the United States sides with Israel—often being the only nation on its side—when a majority of UN nations vote against the latter also diminishes the US claim for respecting democracy.[12]

Third, the insistent one-sidedness in the United States' stance on the Israeli-Palestinian conflict is yet another source of helplessness and frustration in the Muslim world. To be sure, the United States agrees that the ever-increasing Jewish settlements in the West Bank are illegal under international law but it does little to stop them. The American position on other regional conflicts in the Middle East is also found distressing by Muslims of the world. For instance, the American outrage at Iran's nuclear aspirations stands in sharp contrast to its silence regarding Israel's massive nuclear stockpiles. Indeed, Israel is the world's only country whose "unverified" nuclear facilities have never been inspected by IAEA (International Atomic Energy Agency). The United States says nothing about this.

Finally, the strident xenophobia of some current American politicians and the right-leaning "nationalist" groups (and their media outlets) project negative stereotypes of Muslims which portrayal in turn is used by the Muslim zealots to "justify" their hatred of American might and hegemony. The recently attempted "Muslim ban" on travel to the United States and blockage of Syrian refugees from entering the country also did not help. Acting in unison, these factors (e.g., military invasions, toppling democracies, supporting dictators and monarchs, bias in the Israel-Palestine territorial conflict, and anti-Muslim rants of some leaders) contribute to the Muslim rage against the United States.

Muslim world's contributions

The European and American contributions outlined above exacerbate the trouble that has already been brewing in the Muslim world. Some of this "trouble" is specific to—or, at least more marked in—the Arab section of this cosmos while other aspects of discontent are pervasive, being anchored in the very nature of Islam. The problem that exists in the Arab world is that the vast majority of its nation states are under the rule of kings, monarchs, self-appointed dictators, and power-hungry despots. Many, if not most, such heads of state are self-serving, corrupt, and oppressive of the masses. Tyranny prevails and citizens' dissent is not permitted. People are "silenced" (Fivush, 2010) but underneath the fearful compliance lurk bitterness and anger. Given the slightest plausible excuse, this rage gets displaced from the national authorities to international agencies. The suppressed and repressed hostility toward one's own king then takes on a new life as the hatred of Western powers.

A more nuanced trajectory of rage involves the psyche of women who—in most, though not all, Muslim majority nations—constitute a severely disenfranchised minority. The unconscious and/or unmentalized pain of these women is deposited in their offspring, especially their sons, who are seen as the potential avengers of the social injustice dished out to their mothers on a daily basis. This "deposited" anger is also ready to be shifted from its original targets (e.g., paternal authority at home, political leadership of the nation at large) to the "decadent permissiveness" of the West.

In addition to the *suppressed rage* directed at their despotic heads of state and the *deposited rage* on behalf of their mothers, Arab youth also have to contend with the *reactive rage* mobilized by American military excesses and by frequent witnessing of paternal humiliation at the hands of occupying forces (e.g., in the Israeli-occupied territories of Palestine). Yet another tributary adding to this river of anger is the *defensive rage* that is an instinctual response to sexual deprivation; intermingling of sexes is not allowed and homosexuality is despised in most Muslim nations. This leaves violence as the only game in town, so to speak.

The cauldron of fury receives input from other sources as well. The number of college-educated youth in the Arab world who cannot find employment is staggering; the resulting helplessness fuels resentment and rage. Access provided by the internet to actually seeing the economic inequity across the globe (e.g., how people live in the USA vs. how they live, say, in Nigeria, Morocco, rural Iran, or South Sudan) causes envy and rage, too. Exposure to the Western ways of living (via internet, movies, songs, television) threatens regional Muslim cultures. The exhortative oratory of narcissistic-paranoid leaders constantly evokes the threat globalization poses to Islamic values. All this mobilizes annihilation anxiety (Hurvich, 2003; Klein, 1932, 1948; Winnicott, 1962); rage becomes the loyal lieutenant of efforts to ward off such anxiety. Hating Western nations and their ways of life becomes a salve for the lacerations in the Muslim cultural identity. What might have been personally ego-dystonic (e.g., committing violence) now turns "ethno-syntonic" (Erikson, 1954).

A pause is needed here and also a flashback to the 1950s when the Muslim hatred of Western civilization began to be solidified in the writings of the Egyptian activist, Sayyid Qutb (1906–1966). Having spent two years in the United States, Qutb returned to his native country harboring intense criticism of what he had seen: materialism, individualism, superficiality, racism, lack of interest in art and poetry, sexual freedom, and strong support for the new state of Israel. Qutb began putting his dislike for these "values" in writing and rapidly acquired sociopolitical prominence that threatened the nation's President Gamal Abdel Nasser. Efforts at reconciliation between them failed and in 1966 Qutb was convicted of plotting Nasser's assassination and was executed by hanging. His message did not die with him, however. The Pulitzer Prize-winning author Lawrence Wright (2006) declares that Qutb:

> ... intended to show that Islam and modernity were completely incompatible. His extraordinary project, which was still emerging, was to take apart the entire political and philosophical structure of modernity and return Islam to its unpolluted origins. For him, that was a state of divine oneness, the complete unity of God and humanity. Separation of the sacred and the secular, state and religion, science and theology, mind and spirit—these were the hallmarks of modernity, which had captured the West. But Islam could not abide such divisions. In Islam, he believed, divinity could not be diminished without being destroyed. Islam was total and uncompromising. It was God's final word. Muslims had forgotten this in their enchantment with the West. Only by restoring Islam to the center of their lives, their laws, and their government could Muslims hope to recapture their rightful place as the dominant culture in the world. (p. 28)

Qutb's message gained its commanding power from two lesser-known but highly important facts. The first fact refers to his repeatedly calling the Western people and even the followers of his rival, Nasser, *Jahilyya*. This meant "the ignorant ones" and was a term used by Islam's prophet, Mohammad, for the pre-Islamic people of his region. Qutb's choice of this label gave implicit permission to conservative Muslims to destroy and kill people who disagree with them and act as *Jahilyya*. The second fact involves the way he died. While it is true that he was executed by hanging, a well-documented account (Wright, 2006) of events surrounding his hanging reveal that two days before his execution, Qutb had been offered clemency, which he declined. He declared that he would be more valuable to his cause by being hanged. In effect, he committed suicide (J. Anderson Thomson, Jr., personal communication, March 15, 2017) and thus became a martyr. These two facts laid the groundwork for killing and being killed in the name of radical Islam, "elevating" Qutb to be the father of Messianic sadomasochism of the radical fringe of Muslims.

Qutb's grandiloquent and sadomasochistic ideology became an inspiration for Ayman al-Zawahiri and Osama bin-Laden, the progenitors of the current violent groups such as al Qaeda and ISIS. They (and via "trickle-down" effect, their widespread followers, including the instructors at some *madrasas* for the children of poor and conservative Muslims) demonize the West and follow Qutb's order to "plant the seeds of hatred, disgust, and revenge in the souls of [our] children [and to] teach children from the time their nails are soft that the white man is the enemy of humanity, and that they should destroy him at the first opportunity" (cited in Wright, 2006, pp. 27–28). These icons of religious zealotry constantly evoke the "chosen glories" and "chosen traumas" (Volkan, 2004, 2006) of the Muslim world.[13] Prominent among the former is the Muslim rule over not only vast swaths of Africa and Asia but in parts of Europe as well. Prominent among the latter are the Crusades, and the *Naqba* (the exodus of Palestinians around the time of the creation of modern-day Israel). The evocation of the "chosen glory" mobilizes nostalgia for a lost paradise, and the evocation of the "chosen trauma" stirs up a sense of victimhood. The combination of these two feelings pushes for a search for grandeur and revenge. In Bohleber's (2003) words:

> Aggression and violence can grow even further when unbearable, weak, despised, and helpless parts of the self, emotions, and fears, are projected upon the external, ideologically distorted object, which are then to be purged by attacking the victim. If this form of violent self-constitution does not cease, then [one] is in danger of completely losing all inner contact to those projected parts of the self that [one] finds to be weak, helpless, and shameful. The inner emptiness that results is then filled by ideological clichés, culled from politically or religiously radical ideologies. (p. 126)

To all these anger-producing variables (see above),[14] something far more potent is added from the deepest layers of the Muslim psyche. This is a risky matter to bring up but avoiding it would bypass an important variable. What I have in mind here is that there is something inherent to the religion of Islam that fills its followers with the potential of explosive anger. The *font origio* of this *basic rage* does not reside in the Quran's exhortations to destroy the non-believers and apostates, as popular media and lazy anti-Islamic theorizing would have us believe; such "encouragements" to vanquish those who differ in belief can be readily found in both the Old and New Testaments of the Bible. Thomson (2003) makes a highly pertinent observation in this context:

> While one is quick to point the finger at Islam, most Christians want to pretend that Christianity was not imposed by the sword. The cross has accompanied the sword everywhere. The Torah contains instructions on stealing from, enslaving, and murdering outsiders (Hartung, 1995). Parts of the Old Testament are a blueprint for murder and genocide. In the Bible, Deuteronomy (20:16) instructs the Jews entering the cities promised to them by God to "leave alive nothing that breatheth." (p. 83)

This sort of rhetoric is present in the Quran as well. However, it is my assertion that the basic "Islamic rage" arises not from such dictates but from the fact that this religion requires so much from its followers (e.g., five times a day prayer, thirty-day fasting, annual donation of 2½ percent of one's total assets). These are not suggestions or recommendations or advisable actions; these are requirements for being Muslim. And, very few Muslims abide by them.[15] In other words, the majority of Muslims live in silent noncompliance with their faith and this, I believe, floods the basement of their psyche with unconscious guilt. This guilt carries the potential of being transformed into irritability and blaming others. Paranoia, as we know, can serve as a defense against depressive anxieties. Contrition is turned into anger at others. Here the elucidation of the relationship between guilt and hate, by Ernest Jones (1929), becomes highly pertinent.

> Hatred for someone implies that the other person, through his cruelty or unkindness, is the cause of one's suffering, that the latter are not self-imposed or in any way one's own fault. All the responsibility for the misery produced by unconscious guilt is thus displaced onto the other, supposedly cruel, person, who is therefore heartily hated. (p. 384)

All in all, the Muslim world contributes heavily to the problem of terrorism. Major sections of this world are filled with frustration and anger that has diverse origins: (i) being silenced, (ii) being economically deprived, (iii) being sexually frustrated, (iv) being the containers of mother's unconscious rage, (v) being the avengers of father's humiliation by colonizers and occupying forces, (vi) being encouraged by inflammatory speeches of provincial militants, and, above all, (vii) being unconsciously guilty over their religious noncompliance. The last-mentioned is an irreducible burden indeed since the Quran is held literally to be God's word and is immutable. However, if all other causes of anger are controlled, then the transformation of unconscious guilt into rage might become avoidable.

A trio of solutions

The tri-factorial model of terrorism's etiology proposed above dictates that the search for possible solutions involve the same three regions of the world. In other words, in order to eliminate, or at least sharply reduce, terrorism, ideological and strategic changes in the sociopolitical climate of Europe, the United States, and the Muslim world need to be implemented. Some of these changes might occur independently of each other, though not without influencing other parties and other variables, while some will require conjoint efforts and collaborative safeguarding of what has been put into place. Interdisciplinary theorizing and inter-institutional (e.g., judiciary, intelligence community, pertinent NGOs, police) collaboration will certainly be needed. Punishment of perpetrators of violence must be swift and condign but the temptation of extra-judicial retribution should be resisted.[16] And, it must be acknowledged that changes in one venue (for instance, Europe) alone will provide limited benefits. Success in overcoming the plague of political violence will come only as a result of changes occurring in all three theaters of operation. With this in mind, let us turn to what each region needs to do in order to diminish the threat of terrorism.

What Europe needs to do

Europe can help curtail terrorism in the following four ways. *First and foremost*, its citizens who truly believe in democracy, its liberal politicians, its literary intelligentsia, and its scientists and academicians-at-large have to stand firmly against the rise of the anti-immigrant, anti-Muslim, anti-African, racist political right. Through words and actions, through op-ed pages and documentary films, and through electoral and judicial reform, the good-hearted and the wise in Europe must block hate-mongers like France's Marine Le Pen, Holland's Geert Wilders, Poland's Jaroslav Kaczynski, and Greece's Nikolaos Michaloliakos from acquiring political power. These leaders carry the dagger of anti-refugee, anti-Semitic, anti-Muslim, and anti-African prejudice under the seemingly honorable cloak of nationalism. They seek to stir up the basest of emotions in the masses and create an environment ripe with anti-minority violence.

A *second* task on the part of European governments is to introduce middle and high school level courses on the history of their colonizing African and Asian nations. Such courses must include not only the benefits their rule bestowed upon the colonies but also the abuses and harms they inflicted upon their colonized subjects. Acknowledgement of this sort resembles Germany's coming to terms with its Nazi past and with the work of South Africa's Truth and Reconciliation Commission. By owning up to crimes against humanity in their former colonies, European nations would develop a modicum of useful remorse as well as a deeper regard for the humanity of immigrants who now show up at their threshold.

A related *third* task for European nations is to somehow come to the painful but ultimately salutary recognition that a fundamental change in their very nature is underway. Unlike the United States, which has historically been a nation of immigrants, most European countries have had relatively monolithic cultural and ethnic identities. Who was legitimately French and Dutch, for instance, had till recently been self-evident and clear. This is no longer the case. Some European nations (e.g., the UK) have become more or less resigned, if not genuinely accepting, of such transformation; the election of the first generation Pakistani-British, Sadiq Khan (1970-present), to be Mayor of London is a stunning illustration of the shift. Other nations are hurting in the process and find it difficult to emotionally accord true equality to those who have arrived from their erstwhile colonies, or have sought residence there for economic reasons, or have ended up there as refugees flung out by regional wars in African and Middle Eastern countries. All sorts of questions arise as a result: can Surinamese living for a couple of generations in Holland call themselves Dutch? Might one call oneself Turkish-German? Can offspring of early twentieth-century French-Algerians move to Paris and produce a generation of Algerian-French?

Matters might be more complex in Scandinavian countries since their record of colonialism is old, thin, and pale (compared to Great Britain and France, for instance), and who have, for humanitarian reasons, accepted culturally diverse immigrants and refugees. Their national identity, though for now "safe," owing to the small numbers of such newcomers, will sooner or later also be threatened. A major revision is thus required in the definition of national identity in Europe. The accompanying mourning[17] will not be easy but the pain has to be borne for a genuine move from today to tomorrow, and for solid grounding in reality.

A *fourth* task involves accepting that the "melting pot" model, advocated in the United States by political conservatives like Patrick Buchanan (1992, cited in Fukuyama, 1994), Peggy Noonan (1994), Lawrence Auster (1990), and Irving Kristol (1995), actually denigrates newcomers to the land. The "melting pot" model suggests—in fact, insists—that immigrants and refugees renounce their cultures and try their best to assimilate and adopt the culture of their new country; it implicitly upholds the latter as superior. Instead of accepting the moral validity of all cultures and people's right to express, celebrate, and live according to their religious and cultural preferences, such self-appointed guardians of the "superior" and invariably white culture regard allowing fresh cultural traditions to be a death knell for Western civilization. The model of "multiculturalism," in contrast, permits diverse ethnic cultures to exist in parallel and with equal respect, knowing full well that such allowance would result in "assimilation" that is slow, painless, and bidirectional. The culture of the immigrants' adopted country would be internalized by the following generations *and* portions of culture brought by the immigrants would seep into the culture-at-large. Note in this latter regard, British fondness for Indian *chicken tikka masala*!

The *fifth*, and perhaps most important measure, is the social uplifting of ethnic minorities. This is easier said than done. It requires multiple steps, each of which depends upon the cooperation between governmental agencies, the electorate, and the political representatives it puts in power. I have discussed the various strategies involved in a true uplifting of ethnic, racial, and religious minorities in Chapter Three of this book. Here, I offer only a brief outline. In essence, the required steps include: (i) providing access to or restoring full civil rights, including those of voting, religious freedom, and travel, (ii) acknowledging the majority's role in the minority's problems (by remembering and reminding oneself that, for instance, if Moroccans and Algerians are in France today, it is because the French were in their communities yesterday), (iii) accepting the minority's culture (discussed above), and (iv) including minorities in social iconography (e.g., naming streets after, and erecting statues of their revered figures). Additionally, it might be a great help if an afternoon each week in elementary schools was devoted to a class co-taught by a teacher belonging to a minority and another belonging to the majority, with each upholding the contributions of the other's culture. For instance, if a white, French-born "real" French teacher tells little African-origin children in Paris about the goodness of African ancestral traditions while an immigrant teacher of African origin (perhaps from Algeria, Morocco, Congo, or Tunisia) instructs them into the beauty of French culture, the chances of healing the bifurcation in the identities of such children stands a great chance.[18] And, the resulting sense of their comfortably belonging to France, in this instance, would increase the capacity to bear ambivalence. Less aggression and less paranoia would thus accrue in the heart.

What America needs to do

Reversing what has been delineated as its etiologic contribution to the current wave of terrorism would necessitate the United States undertaking the following steps. *First*, its leaders would need to curtail their "villain hunger" (Akhtar, 2007b) and to stop inducing fear of powerful enemies about to destroy the nation. The collapse of the Soviet Union led to a gap that American politicians quickly filled with all sorts of nefarious characters. Commenting upon this in 1992, Chomsky wrote: "So the threat to our existence has been Qaddafi and his hordes of international terrorists, Grenada and its ominous air base, Sandanistas marching on Texas, Hispanic narco-traffickers led by arch-maniac Noriega, and crazed Arabs generally" (p. 57). This last group constitutes America's favorite villains today. The names keep changing from Moammar Ghaddafi (1942–2011) to Saddam Hussein (1937–2006) to Osama bin Laden (1957–2011) to Ayman al-Zawahiri (1951-present) to Abu Bakr al-Baghdadi (1971-present) but the lament never loses its consistency. The chant goes on: "they hate us," "they want to destroy us," "they are out to vanquish our civilization." An ill-fitting pastiche of contradiction (e.g., American support for Saudi Arabia and UAE from where most of the 9/11 attackers originated), ignorance, prejudice, and "dehumanization"[19] (Akhtar, 2003) sustains the demeaning caricature of Muslims in general and Arabs in particular. This has to be strenuously discarded if any progress is desired in the US-Muslim world relationship and for any true gains to be made in American efforts at reducing terrorism. Hated and mocked people hate and mock in return; people who feel respected and understood, respect and empathize with others in return. Needless to add, that a drastic reduction, if not total cessation, of American military interventions in Muslim nations would constitute a loud and visible step in the right direction.

Second, a balanced, "two-nation" approach to resolving the Israeli-Palestinian conflict is needed. Equally forceful denunciation of the Palestinian terrorist activities and the Israeli atrocities in the occupied territories is required. America needs to explicitly recognize that the number of Palestinians killed by Israelis exceeds by many thousands the numbers of Israelis killed by Palestinians; in the 2008–2009 Gaza war alone, the Israeli casualties stood at thirteen and the Palestinian casualties at 1,166. The secret tunnels made by Hamas and the illegal settlements made by Israel both need to be stopped by forceful American diplomacy. The formation of an independent and autonomous Palestinian state which respects Israel's right to exist would heal a festering wound in the Middle East. This, in turn, would preclude one major source of "Arab rage."

Third, the United States has to clearly demonstrate its love of democracy to Muslim nations if it wants them to adopt this form of government. This would require that the US stop supporting kings and monarchs in the Muslim world (e.g., Saudi Arabia, Kuwait), behave in a manner consistent with democracy in the United Nations even if it involves voting against Israel, and "permit" Muslim nations to have open and free elections and not restrict who can run for office and who can not.

Finally, the United States has to assure that its people know some facts about Islam and Muslims, including their history and their contributions to human civilization (elaborated in an earlier section of this chapter). To dispel ignorance of this realm, didactic courses might be introduced in middle and high schools. The public would also benefit by an encounter with the broad canvas of Islamic art, including glazed ceramics, miniature paintings depicting historical scenes, illustrated manuscripts, intricately weaved prayer rugs, and ornately inscribed Holy Qurans. The Museum of Modern Art in New York, the Brooklyn

Museum, and the Freer and Sackler Galleries of the Smithsonian Institution in Washington, DC, contain collections of such items from as far back as the ninth century AD. And, the Doris Duke Foundation is doing a yeoman job in enhancing American awareness of fine arts from the Muslim world.

Working in unison, reduction of "villain hunger" and cessation of military interventions in Muslim majority nations, demonstration of genuine respect for democracy, fast resolution of the Israel-Palestine conflict, and educational advances that assure the transmission of a balanced portrait of Islam and Muslims to the American populace, especially to those in their formative years, would go a long way in presenting America as a benevolent, empathic, respectful, and fair nation. Seeing America in such light would greatly diminish worldwide Muslim rage and help curtail evil embodiments like al Qaeda and ISIS.

What the Muslim world needs to do

The foregoing delineation of needed reforms in the sociopolitical fabric of Europe and the United States must not eclipse the fact that a major contribution to reducing terrorism is to be made by the Muslim world itself. The sort of changes this requires are bound to be difficult, slow to achieve, and are certain to meet enormous resistance. Long-held traditions would be put under the microscope of logic and reality testing. Regional identities would be threatened and widespread beliefs questioned. With such reservations in mind, I suggest the following blueprint for tempering the bubbling rage in the Muslim world.

First and foremost, well-placed representatives of the global Muslim community should take it upon themselves to publicize the fact that a large number of Muslim organizations have harshly condemned the violence perpetrated by fanatic and "radicalized" Muslims. With the help of television ads and full-page announcements in major newspapers of the world (e.g., *The New York Times*, *The Washington Post*, *The Guardian*, *The Times*, *Le Monde*), the Muslim leaders should bring greater public awareness to the following facts: (i) US Muslims widely condemned the 9/11 terrorist attacks, (ii) a survey conducted by the British newspaper *The Daily Telegraph* published two weeks after the July 2005 bombings of the London Underground showed that 88 percent of British Muslims opposed such acts, (iii) in 2010, Mohammed Tahir-ul-Qadri issued a *fatwa* against terrorism which was endorsed by the prestigious Al-Azhar University in Cairo, (iv) a coalition of leading US Muslim organizations came out strongly against the November 2015 terrorist attack in Paris, (v) Sunni clerics in Uttar Pradesh, a northern state in India, issued a *fatwa* against Muslim terrorism in 2015, (vi) recently, a group of more than forty French Muslim lawyers, doctors, and other professionals decried the younger generation of Muslims becoming "the prey of Jihadi Islam idealogues" (Ganley, 2016, A-12) and (vii) Herra Hashmi, a nineteen-year-old Muslim American student at the University of Colorado, has recently put together a 712 page list of Muslims condemning terrorist violence (Mahdawi, 2017). All this is good but more needs to be done in this regard. The keepers of holy Islamic sites (e.g., the king of Saudi Arabia) and prominent heads of Muslim nations (e.g., the highest ayatollah of Iran, the emirs of Kuwait and UAE, the prime ministers of Turkey and Pakistan) need to issue official statements that ramming airplanes into American skyscrapers and killing hardworking civilians, knifing innocent bystanders in Israel, and mauling unsuspecting vacationers under a truck in France or Sweden, are despicable, unacceptable, and un-Islamic acts.

Second, more and more Muslim majority nations need to move towards a democratic form of government. To what extent such democracies shall concurrently be theocracies remains to be seen. The current situation is this: societies with a significant proportion of liberal and secular voices (e.g., Bangladesh, Turkey[20]) lean more towards democracy without theocracy while others (e.g., Pakistan, Iran) do so to a lesser extent. Regardless of the permutation that becomes acceptable, the gradual replacement of monarchy and of transfer of power along intergenerational imperial lines by elected government officials would permit the masses to feel heard; it will diminish their sense of being helpless and trapped. This, in turn, would diminish the endemic rage in such societies.

Third, the Muslim world needs to ensure that its populace recognizes and appreciates the goodness of Europe and the United States. Besides making public the enormous benefits of the foreign aid provided by the West to them, Muslim countries have the responsibility for teaching, in schools and colleges, the remarkable and universally beneficial achievements of Western civilization. Here the emphasis ought not to be upon the great Western works of literature, art, and music, since this could backfire and mobilize competitiveness and envy. The emphasis should stress the scientific achievements of the West that have made daily life easy for all the citizens of the world, including the Muslims: the inventions of trains, cars, airplanes, phones, email, and so on. Conveyed tactfully, "reminders" of how the world's Muslims are drawing daily benefits from Western ingenuity, have the potential of kindling gratitude and softening a hardened stance of resentment.

Fourth, the Muslim world might need to "titrate" the flow of internet-based information into its veins. Too much and too rapid exposure to the economic inequities rampant across nations and, more important, too intense an encounter with the more "free" ways of Western living might puncture the societal "protective shield" (Freud, 1950a) and cause traumatic rebellion or retreat. Conceptually solid and empirically grounded research needs to be undertaken to evaluate the risk-benefit ratio of open access to internet pornography, snuff movies, suicide instruction sites, and apps touting paraphernalia for drug use. In essence, internet-caused globalization must not be permitted to become cultural "gobble-ization." Let me hasten to add that far from absolute censorship, such judicious regulation of the information flow is meant to permit the resultant cultural shifts to evolve on a slower basis.

Fifth, something has to be done about empowering women. To be sure, in some Muslim majority nations, women have access to voting, education, financial enterprise, and electoral representation. But there are many Muslim societies which are lagging behind in this regard. This needs rectification. However, simpleminded attempts directed at vestimentary transformation (e.g., women giving up the hijab or burqa) are not the key here. The key is education, freedom of speech, voting privileges, legal equality, release from bondage to male hegemony, and the open ability to achieve elected offices. Documented accounts of Muslim women—especially those from Arab nations—who have made remarkable achievements and stood up for their rights (Shaheed & Shaheed, 2011; Zoepf, 2017)[21] should be translated into regional languages and widely disseminated through the Muslim world. Such societal transformation promises to benefit many fronts: (i) happier, more self-actualized women will be more fulfilled mothers raising more satisfied children (who will grow up to be less angry adults), (ii) such women will draw respect from their less fortunate sisters and will become regional role models for the latter to emulate, and (iii) women's increased presence in educational institutions and at workplaces would allow greater intermingling of the sexes and diminish the reservoir of pent-up erotic drives (which, by "drive-vs-drive" defense tend to fuel male aggression in these societies).

Sixth, the Muslim world also needs to generate and support narratives that underscore Muslim–Christian, Muslim–Jewish, and Muslim–Hindu harmony. Support needs to be provided for playwrights, filmmakers, poets, and litterateurs who produce such works. Within the specific context of Israeli–Palestinian acrimony, effort should be made to publicize real life stories of reconciliation and forgiveness. People need to be made aware of books that recount how a New York-based rabbi forgave the Palestinian youth who shot him during his visit to Israel and even made friends with him (Blumenfeld, 2002) and how a Toronto-based Palestinian physician, whose three daughters were killed in an Israeli bombing of Gaza, established a foundation for promoting camaraderie between Jewish and Palestinian girls (Abuelaish, 2010). Also significant is the book titled, *The Faith Club* by Idliby, Oliver, and Warner (2016), which details the search for mutual understanding on the part of a Muslim, a Christian, and a Jewish woman. Antithetical to "propaganda addition" (Akhtar, 2007b) that demonizes the West, such cultural input would kindle historically based, and imaginatively provoke, good internal self-object representations (see the important work of Joseph Montville, 1987, 1991, in this regard). A related, though slightly different, approach to redirecting aggression is to emphasize sports and athletics in schools.[22]

Finally, there is the issue of Islam itself. As stated in earlier parts of this discourse, Islam is a demanding religion. And, most of its followers do not follow all the requirements to be proper Muslims. Consequently, they live lives of perpetual unconscious guilt (which, as also noted before, can have a propensity to turn into externalized rage). Now, to think that some of the "requirements" of Islam can or should be changed into "recommendations" is naïve and foolhardy. The *Quran* is considered to be the word of God himself. The chances of changing its dictates are as likely as the Catholic Church denouncing the notion of Immaculate Conception, Hindus announcing that their deities are fictitious, and world Jewry declaring the Holocaust is a myth. In other words, the requirements enunciated in the *Quran* are immutable; the guilt attendant upon not following the recommendations is irreducible and can at best be transformed into the more humane attributes of gratitude and reparation towards the human and nonhuman environment. Muslim religious leaders can play a significant role in facilitating this turn by promoting the kinder aspects of their religion.

The highly significant work of University of Virginia professors Jerry White and Peter Ochs enters the picture right at this juncture. White, a 2007 Nobel Prize for Peace winner and a former US diplomat, has joined forces with Ochs, a theologian and respected contributor to *Modern Judaic Studies*, to create an organization called the Global Covenant of Religions (Gates, 2015). The goal of this organization is to make sure that religion is not left out of efforts to curtail terrorism and to assure collaboration between religious leaders (who delegitimize justification for violence), governments, and regional community networks. The organization seeks to create interreligious dialogue and to promote the humanitarian aspects of Judaism, Christianity, Islam, and Hinduism. White says that the numbers are on the side of peace.

> The majority of the world are religiously affiliated. And the majority of those don't want to kill. Even if they regard someone as the enemy, they don't want to kill in the name of God. Most people aren't ISIS and would never want to join ISIS. The fringe—the criminal, terror fringe—remains just that, something to contain or criminalize or punish appropriately. But it's not the majority of the story. (cited in Gates, 2015, p. 44)

White recognizes the scale of the challenges but exhorts us to keep faith and reminds us of the Apostle Paul's formulation of faith in Hebrews: "confidence in things unseen."

Concluding remarks

The terrorism of radical Muslims has been the central concern of this discourse, although with the understanding that violent political tactics of such sort and the ideology that propels them are not restricted to Muslims. A complex interplay between wide-ranging sociopolitical variables is responsible for the emergence of such terrorism. These variables include (i) the protracted aftermath of European colonialism, (ii) the massive loss of civilian lives and destruction of societal infrastructure caused by American interventions, (iii) the threat posed by Western cultural hegemony to the regional identities in Muslim nations, (iv) the cracks that have appeared in monolithic European identities (e.g., French, British) by the influx of African, Arab, and Southeast Asian immigrants, (v) the suppressed rage among citizens of Muslim nations governed by autocratic rulers, (vi) the anger and hostility derived from the unfair policies of the United States in the context of the Israeli-Palestinian conflict, (vii) the rage of dislocated or oppressed Muslim parents that is deposited in their offspring, (viii) the reactive intensification of aggressive drive owing to lack of discharge of libidinal erotic drives, and (ix) the potential transformation of unconscious guilt among Muslims into a tendency to blame others. It is the admixture of such powerful forces, alongside mindless submission to inflammatory hate speech and fundamentalist propaganda that propels radicalization and violence. What can not be overemphasized here is that the problem exists on both sides of the East-West divide. The East, especially the Middle East, is feeling threatened by the cultural juggernaut of the globalized economy, the American military hegemony, inter-ethnic strife, and domestic uprisings against their governments. The West is feeling threatened by the influx of Asian, African, and Muslim immigrants and refugees (see Chapter Two for details) and the multiculturalism this brings in its fold. Regional identities are thus threatened in both East and West. As a result, both regions are witnessing a rise of conservatism: romanticizing the past, resisting change, and ostracizing those who support change as traitors and apostates. Both East and West are suffused with anxiety, xenophobia, and defensive rage.

Given this complex etiology, the "treatment" of terrorism is far from simple. A three-pronged approach is essential. On the European front, the social uplifting of minorities (especially of the immigrants and refugees from African and Asian nations) is of central importance; this will also necessitate a painful shift in the European monolithic identities themselves. On the American front, cessation of bombings and killings, evenhandedness vis-à-vis Israel and Palestine, a truly democratic attitude in the affairs of the United Nations, respect of Muslim regional democracies, and withdrawal of support from kings and monarchs are measures that would be beneficial. On the Muslim world's front, an unequivocal, repeated, and loud denunciation of violent groups (e.g., ISIS, al Qaeda, and Boko Haram), explicit upholding of the West's great contributions to the common civilization of this world, liberation of women, sexual desegregation, establishing democratic forms of government, and promoting the softer sides of Islam (that can diminish

THE TRIPOD OF TERRORISM

unconscious guilt in its followers) are the methods to reduce frustration and rage.

Working in unison, these three sets of actions can lead to marked diminution of terrorist acts by radical Muslims. Such a rosy picture must, however, be tempered by acknowledging that such changes will be very hard to bring about and the forces of provincialism, economic self-interest, and rigid belief systems will obstruct progress at each step of the way. Psychoanalytically derived understanding and advice can play a role here but the ultimate work will require multidiscipli-nary perspectives, including those of politics, diplomacy, religion, history, economics, ecology, and negotiation practices. Even with all this, whether full eradication of terrorism will be possible or not is hard to say. Three things are certain though: (i) it is preferable to be optimistic than to be cynical regarding such matters; (ii) "war against terrorism" will not result in peace; it will fuel "terrorism against war," and (iii) dia-logue among warring factions is the only sensible path to take. Only by knowing the Other, experiencing empathy for the Other, and respecting the Other can the path to peace be created. In this context, the views of the eminent Jewish philosopher, Emmanuel Levinas (1906–1995) are pertinent. Briefly put, Levinas proposes that ethical relatedness to the Other is the foundation stone of the psychic self and requires recognition of difference. Erasing self-other distinction leads to totalization and sets the stage for domination and control. Commitment to dialogue, in contrast, endorses a relation between self and Other while accepting the autonomy of both parties. Closer to "home"—both in terms of the United States and psychoanalysis—Calvin Settlage (1992), a North American child psychoanalyst, declared that "predominance of love is the glue of a unified self-representation" (p. 352). While made in the context of individual personality development, this comment also applies to the "unification" of the conflictual agendas threatening to rip the world apart.

Notes

1. Arguably, the illegitimate and brutal invasion of Iraq by George W. Bush (1946-present) can also form an example of "terrorism from above."
2. At the same time, all my "etiologic" and "therapeutic" proposals are undergirded by psychoanalytic concepts. Without explicitly bringing

them up, I will rely heavily upon notions such as the human need for enemies and allies (Freud, 1900a; Volkan, 1988), the sacrifice of individual superego at the altar of group regression (Freud, 1921c), the "principle of multiple function" (Waelder, 1936), paranoid and depressive positions (Klein, 1940), narcissistic rage (Kohut, 1972), transgenerational transmission of trauma (Brenner, 2004; Faimberg, 2005; Kestenberg & Brenner, 1996; Kogan, 1995; Krystal, 1968), societal stress-induced retreat into large-group identity (Volkan, 2004, 2014), and so on.

3. Even though the Brotherhood was founded in 1928 by Hasan al-Banna (1906–1949), Qutb acquired far greater prominence as its interlocutor. Author, educator, poet, and Islamist theorist, Qutb is best known for his magnum opus, *Fi Zilal al-Quran* (In the Shade of the Quran), a thirty-volume commentary on the holy book and for his book, *Ma'alim Fi al-Tariq* (Milestones), a powerful delineation of the sociopolitical role of Islam in the world. The role of Qutb's ideology in inspiring al-Qaeda is discussed later in this essay.

4. The figures mentioned in this and the preceding bullet point are taken from the 2011 Pew Research Center study of Muslims in thirty-nine countries (cited in Lipka, 2017).

5. The short-lasting French campaign in Egypt and Syria (1798–1801) was especially noticeable in this regard.

6. Elsewhere (2016), I have raised three objections to the publication of *Charlie Hebdo* cartoons of Mohammad: (i) the staff of the paper is all white while French Muslims are predominantly African-born, non-white individuals; (ii) the paper and its readership is mostly white French majority while French Muslims are a post-colonial immigrant minority, and (iii) France is among the fourteen European countries where Holocaust denial is punishable by law; for it to mock religious feelings of Muslims smacks of unfairness and prejudice.

7. While deficiency in the sense of personal identity and subjective experiences of social marginalization can facilitate attraction to radical ideologies, most research studies (Alderdice, 2018; Borum, 2004; Fried, 1982; Sagerman, 2004) do not support the notion of a "terrorism-prone personality" (Atran, 2003); these investigations suggest that there are many different pathways and different psychosocial agendas that lead to vulnerability to committing such violence.

8. In this emphasis upon the regional rise of hyper-nationalism, one should not overlook the role of Russia, which is trying to promote populist forces in Western Europe for its own vested interests.

9. One pre-publication reader of this essay, Dr. Mitchell Cohen, responded to my mention of "disproportionality" with the following statement: "Proportionality of terror/horror is more than body counts. The fact

that fewer died in the fall of the Twin Towers vs. the ravaging of Iraq is disproportionate in numbers, but not so much in impact. All victims of the Twin Towers were civilians. The organization, precision, infiltration of flight schools, happening right under American noses, gave the tragedy its impact, along with startling optics. Terrorism likes but does not require large body counts. Terror thrives on optics. The number of people who died in Nazi camps was staggering, but again more chilling were the organization, secrecy, stealth planning and horrific optics" (personal communication, April 6, 2017).

10. The most recent example of such bombing "errors" is the March 2017 US airstrike against ISIS in the Iraqi city of Mosul, which led to the deaths of more than 100 civilians (Ryan, 2017).

11. Even within its own confines, the United States seeks only to create "a form of top-down democracy that leaves traditional structures of power—basically corporations and their allies—in effective control. Any form of democracy that leaves the traditional structures essentially unchallenged is admissible. Any form that undermines their power is as intolerable as ever" (President Clinton's National Security Advisor, Anthony Lake, paraphrased in Chomsky, 1994, p. 136).

12. Two recent exceptions to such bias are the following: the outgoing US ambassador to Israel, Daniel Shapiro, explicitly declared that "Too many attacks on Palestinians lack a vigorous investigation or response by Israeli authorities; too much vigilantism goes unchecked; and at times, there seems to be two standards to the rule of law: one for Israelis and another for Palestinians" (cited in Booth, 2016, p. A-2); and, the United States' December 2016 refusal to veto a UN Security Council resolution condemning Israeli settlements in the occupied territories.

13. For the frequent admixture of fantasy and reality in history and for varied sociopolitical uses of historical narratives, see Loewenberg (1995).

14. Awad (2003) traces the roots of Arab anger against the West to Qutb's Islamist ideology but adds the variables of colonialism, the loss of the 1967 war to Israel, American economic sanctions against Iraq, and the continuing presence of US troops and military bases in the Middle East.

15. I recently conducted an informal survey of more than twenty Muslims to assess the percentage of believers who observe all the "rules" of Islam. Their answers varied from 5 to 20 percent, depending upon whether the respondents themselves were liberal or conservative.

16. Compare in this context the 1962 'civilized execution' (i.e., with a proper trial and with physical and legal protection offered to the defendant) of Adolph Eichmann (1906–1962) by Israel and the 2011 extra-judicial assassination of Osama bin-Laden by the United States.

17. Freud (1917e) explicitly declared mourning to be a reaction not only to the loss of a loved person but, at times, also to "the loss of some abstraction which has taken the place of one, such as one's country, liberty, an ideal, and so on" (p. 243).

18. In responding to the terrorist attack in Belgium, Yves Goldstein, the cabinet chief to the Brussels regional president, emphasized the role of conflicted identity in the nation's Muslim youth and asserted that educational and experiential interventions with children from age seven to twelve are essential to prevent their future radicalization (Rubin, 2016).

19. See the US soldiers' degrading behavior (e.g., soldiers urinating on prisoners, forcing naked prisoners to walk on their hands and knees) towards their captives in Iraq's Abu Ghraib prison, for instance.

20. Unfortunately, current political developments in Turkey do not bode well for its sustaining the instruments of democracy, especially a free press.

21. Also pertinent in this context are the writings of Ahmed (1992), Akhtar (2015), Lambert-Hurley & Sharma (2010), Sheikh (2015), Shukla (2015), and Tschalaer (2017).

22. A remarkable example of the friendship-enhancing potential of sports is evident in the American nonprofit agency, *Soccer for Peace*, which organizes soccer camps for Israeli and Palestinian teenagers. Play and peaceful dialogue readily evolves between these customarily contentious parties in such a setting.

CHAPTER SIX

The ultimate abyss of dehumanization

We take the experience of being human for granted. The safety and integrity of our bodies, the unperturbed flow of our psychic subjectivity, and a comfortable locus within the context of historical and current group processes provide us with the foundation of this mostly acknowledged privilege. A commendable by-product of such "humanity" is that it aligns us with our fellow human beings in very fundamental ways. Apart from the obvious sharing of physiognomy and anatomy, we find ourselves motivated by psychological needs that are common to all members of our species. These include the need for biological dignity, the need for identity and affirmation, the need for intrapsychic and interpersonal boundaries, the need to know the causes of events, the need for the optimal emotional availability of significant others, and the need for self-expression and generativity. While they seek their gratification through wishes that are experience-bound and hence individually and culturally variable, the needs themselves are ubiquitous and universal in their distribution (for an explication of the need-wish distinction and for further discussion of the ubiquitous human psychic needs, see Akhtar, 1999a). In addition to this shared motivational substrate, there exist other features that are common to the human experience, including the capacity for thought

151

and thinking, the acquisition of language, barriers against murder and incest, group affiliation, and the elaboration of myths and rituals.

Definition

These shared structural and dynamic characteristics lie at the heart of feeling and being human. That all this depends, at least in part, upon the individual's existing in an "average expectable environment" (Hartmann, 1939) goes without saying. A logical extension of this last postulate is that when the environment—formative or current—shifts dramatically in a direction away from "average" and "expectable," the resulting psychic turmoil can be of such proportions as to destabilize the core of one's humanity. "Hardwired" constitutional vulnerabilities can also contribute to this occurrence in individual instances. Regardless of the etiology, this constitutes the state of "dehumanization"—in other words, "dehumanization" refers to that state of mind where the structural and dynamic features central to being human are seriously interfered with, often to the extent that the individual stops feeling, and behaving, like a human being.

Let me hasten to deflect the criticism of circular reasoning in what I have just written by describing what I actually mean by "dehumanization." This state, to my mind, is characterized by a variable combination of callous disregard for one's body, focal or pervasive mindlessness, the inability to contain affects and fantasies by symbolization, a horrifying disaffiliation from others and a profound lack of empathy with them, grotesque reduction or exaggeration of one or more basic psychological needs mentioned above, non-renunciation of infantile omnipotence, thanatophilia, poverty of language as a dominant vehicle of communication, and the collapse of the barriers erected by civilization against incest and murder. Such a state of affairs can remain confined within the afflicted individual's mind, or he or she can violently project it into others to make them feel dehumanized. Yesterday's victim thus becomes today's perpetrator.

My goal in bringing attention to such phenomena is to shed light upon certain aspects of the politically motivated violence associated with terrorism. Incidents of this sort often demonstrate a striking disregard of the humanity of those maimed and killed in the pursuit of a political agenda. The stunning indifference that the perpetrators often show towards their own bodily selves also defies comprehension.

Deeper exploration of "dehumanization" could therefore help in unraveling the sociopolitical mystery that has come to acquire the designation "terrorism." At the same time, it is useful to differentiate between various types of dehumanization, especially if insights regarding dehumanization associated with terrorism are to yield remedial strategies in that realm. It is in this spirit that I describe five types—deficiency-based, defect-based, regression-based, identification-based, and strategy-based—of dehumanization and offer some guidelines for the remediation of dehumanization associated with terrorism. Efforts at "rehumanization" along these lines might constitute one aspect of the multipronged approach needed to address the problem of terrorism.

Deficiency-based dehumanization: feral children

Though in the foregoing passages, I mentioned the function of "average expectable environment" in sustaining the essential core of humanity, I failed to emphasize the imperative role of such external input in helping evolve and consolidate the human psychological experience in the first place. I also did not specify what constitutes this "average expectable environment." These gaps need to be filled as I consider states of dehumanization arising out of environmental input that is far too deficient for the purposes of psychic structuralization.

Clearly, it is impractical to summarize the voluminous empirical and conjectural observations on how the socially hapless and psychically inchoate infant gradually acquires a recognizably "human" mentation and behavior. A psychoanalytic aphorism and the title of a significant text on child development fortunately come to my rescue. The former refers to the statement by the British pediatrician-turned-psychoanalyst, Donald Winnicott, that "there is no such thing as an infant" (1960b, p. 39).[1] The latter refers to *The Psychological Birth of the Human Infant* by the renowned child psychoanalyst Margaret Mahler and her colleagues (Mahler, Pine, & Bergman, 1975). Both convey, in a pithy manner, the fact that a human infant never exists in isolation and that a certain amount, type, and duration of human—at first, mainly maternal—care is essential for the infant's unstable and scattered inner experience to cohere into a recognizable human psychosocial existence. Without such human care, the unfolding and maturation of "human" instincts does not take place. The body might survive, but the mind certainly fails to develop.

Nowhere is such a malady more evident than in the case of feral children. Starting from ancient myths through the writings of Linnaeus (1707–1778), the originator of the present-day system of naming and classifying animals, to the clinical reports by the distinguished eighteenth- and nineteenth-century "alienists," such as Arbuthnot, Pinel, and Itard, there exist striking accounts of children raised by animals. Similar cases have been reported in recent times as well, especially from Africa (see Newton, 2002) and the Indian subcontinent (see Singh and Zingg, 1939). Cared for, from their birth onwards, by wolves, bears, and, in one instance, sheep, such children grow up entirely dehumanized, or, to put it more accurately, "nonhumanized." They display some or all of the following features: walking on all four limbs, eating raw vegetables and meat, nudity, the absence of a social smile and other gestures of affiliation, non-acquisition of human speech, living in bushes and caves, gaze abnormalities, and propensity to withdraw into solitary places. In a compensation for such deficits, as it were, there is often an exquisite sharpness of the senses of hearing and smell.

A less stark but essentially similar picture is seen in children raised by human beings under situations of intense social deprivation. The most celebrated clinical history in this context is that of Kaspar Hauser (Von Feuerbach, 1832), a seventeen-year-old German youth found wandering the streets of Nuremberg in 1830. Imprisoned in a dungeon for all his life, he had had no human contact except for an occasional glimpse of his jailer. His conduct seemed to befit a two or three year old. He could not walk properly, and he lacked all human emotions. Similar features have been noted in children raised in profound isolation during recent times, including a seven-year-old Texan girl born in 1995 and raised in a tiny closet for most of her life by her severely paranoid mother (Emily, 2002). Such cases attest to the fact that becoming psychosocially human depends upon being lovingly cared for by other human beings.

Defect-based dehumanization: infantile autism and Asperger's syndrome

Children with early infantile autism and, to a lesser extent, its phenomenological cousin, Asperger's syndrome, also show an absence of "human" qualities (DSM-IV, 1994, pp. 66–71, 75–77). They display marked interpersonal disaffiliation, gaze abnormalities, indifference or aversion to cuddling, occasional cruelty towards others, poor acquisition of language, and an overall attitude of psychic withdrawal and solipsism. They do not view other people as having thoughts or feelings. Unable to seek out adults or peers for emotional gratification, they fail to engage in social or imaginative play. Preferring stereotyped activities and involvement with a limited range of physical objects, they react to any environmental change with extreme distress.

Originally thought to be the result of unempathic and cold parenting (the "frigidaire environment"), infantile autism is now viewed as a manifestation of subtle but intense intrauterine insult to the central nervous system of the baby. Maternal rubella during pregnancy, fragile-X syndrome, and developmental hypoplasia of certain areas of the brain or its hyper-masculinization are among the factors held responsible for the disorder.

In essence, whether it is a feral child (who did not receive adequate and proper human input), or one suffering from autism (who did not have a sufficiently intact inner apparatus to accrue and utilize the human input offered), what becomes clear is that having a human body does not necessarily mean having a human mind. When this state of affairs exists from the beginning of life, the results are truly uncanny. Only slightly less striking is the loss of human quality of mind once it has been achieved.

Regression-based dehumanization: schizophrenia, lycanthropy, and other psychotic states

True to the well-regarded psychiatric aphorism, the schizophrenic has lost what the infant is yet to achieve. While the two etiological vectors of deficient—or at least disordered—human input and its defective internalization do play a role in the genesis of schizophrenia, more striking is the fact that most afflicted individuals grow up to be reasonably "human" until they reach a stage of drastic regression at the onset of young adulthood. With this biochemically mediated reversal of development, the unusually imaginative turns bizarre, and idiosyncrasy is replaced by autism. Metaphor deteriorates into neologism, and uncanniness replaces the familiarity of the mundane.

One manifestation of all this is the schizophrenic's confusion about what is alive and what is not. Feelings that one is dead, is made of cardboard, or has turned into stone lose their "as-if" quality and become literal. In severe catatonia, such beliefs render motility difficult, if not impossible. The patient, regarding himself to be inanimate, sits vacantly staring into space for hours. Like a piece of furniture, he can be moved, but only in response to another's volition. In other instances, the individual feels that he has turned not into a thing but into an animal. Delusions of lycanthropy (turning into a wolf) and other forms of zoophilic metamorphosis associated with remote subcultures typify such bizarre states of "dehumanization".[2] Prominent among the latter are the delusions of being pregnant by or of becoming a baboon in the African syndrome of *amafufanyane,* mimicking birds or snakes in the Indonesian cultural psychosis *latah,* and running naked through the snow imitating the cry of some animal or bird among the Eskimos affected by "Arctic hysteria" or *piblokto.*

Less dramatic manifestations of regressive dehumanization include the sense that a particular body part is dead, alien, or machine-like and hence something that needs removal. Many self-amputations by schizophrenics emanate from such delusions. On the other hand, blurring of the animate-inanimate distinction in schizophrenia can result in experiences of merger with nature, accompanied by feelings of bliss awe (similarly blissful dehumanization of the self can at times be seen in religious mendicants and ascetics of the East). Moreover, the confusion between animate and inanimate is not restricted to the self-experience. Significant individuals in one's environment can also be felt to have undergone a diabolical transformation and have become automatons or robots.

Schizophrenic regression also rekindles the infantile, magical quality of the inanimate world. Physical objects appear to possess all sorts of power. They seem to offer protection against imagined dangers, help maintain psychic boundaries, and enhance dwindling narcissism. Underlying the resultant clinging to physical objects (e.g., self-protective layers of clothing, grotesque self-decoration, hoarding) is a desperate effort at maintaining a tie with external reality and through that with the gravely endangered psychic core of humanity within oneself. Such animate-inanimate confusion indicates a partial return to early infantile states of nondistinction with the universe, and gross dehumanization under such circumstances represents psychic death.

Identification-based dehumanization: serial killers

In sharp contrast to the above-mentioned tragic form of dehumanization is the situation where an inwardly dehumanized self becomes a highly charged but sequestered psychic structure that is violently projected into others. Rather than fragmentation and confusion, this scenario is dominated by malignant triumph and sadistic glee. The individual does not feel a dread of "falling apart"; instead, he or she has a perverse mental clarity, a pathway out of chronic boredom and nothingness. Through serendipity, mimicry of others, or "guidance" from a more powerful but psycho-structurally similar individual, the dehumanized person finds that killing others gives relief from the anhedonia and meaninglessness of life. The exhilarating effect of committing murder is great, and it fuels the need to find more and more victims. Features of sexual perversion, addiction, and psychotic-like thinking become gradually intermingled in the resulting syndrome of serial killing. The central element, however, remains cruelty towards someone else's body and soul.

Serial killing typically involves male perpetrators and female victims. The former attests to the biopsychosocial fact that male is more often discharged in the form of outward destructiveness. The latter hints at real, imagined, and displaced scenarios of hate, envy, and violence towards the mother, mother-substitutes, and, subsequently, women in general. This is hardly surprising, since most serial killers come from a background of profound neglect and dreadful physical, sexual, and emotional abuse. To be sure, not all children abused in this manner grow up to be serial killers. Some constitutional propensity towards sadism also seems to contribute to such an outcome. Nonetheless, the fact remains that all serial killers have been mercilessly humiliated during their formative years. In Sue Grand's (2000) terms, they have frequently experienced "catastrophic aloneness" or been subjected to "soul murder" (Shengold, 1989), which has destroyed their capacity for rational thought and robbed them of a reason to live. They feel hollow, dehumanized, and dead. Parts of them have become identified with their parents, who, at the time of beating them, seemed to have lost all human qualities and have turned into "beating machines." Other parts have succumbed to their parents' treatment of them as non-living objects. Either way, major sectors of their psyche have become dehumanized, and it is the "instinctualized" (i.e., psychosomatically anchored, tension-reducing, cyclical, and repetitive) extrusion of this dehumanized core via its induction in others that forms the central dynamics of serial murder.

The act of turning another human being into a terrified, helpless victim of violence, physical torture, and mutilation is charged with high sadomasochistic drama. The actual moment of murder itself bears a resemblance to sexual orgasm and serves as a trophy for the killer's megalomania. Unfortunately, this poisonous reversal of dehumanizing/dehumanized parties from one's childhood does not offer the perpetrator a chance of becoming human. While providing a momentary rush of malignant narcissism, it leaves the killer once again to face his uncanniness, wordless despair, and the internal abyss of isolation.

Strategy-based dehumanization: terrorism

The dehumanization of victims in the carnage of terrorism is quite different. To be sure, blowing up a bus carrying schoolchildren or bombing a night club filled with merry adolescents is hardly regarding them as distinct human beings with a right to life and dreams of growth. The terrorist's indifference towards them and lack of concern for their devastated families borders on being inhuman. The callous disregard some terrorists show towards their own lives is also beyond ordinary human comprehension. Does a ISIS -inspired suicide bomber not fear his or her own bodily destruction? How did Mohamed Atta remain poised, during the 9/11 attacks, while guiding a plane into the World Trade Center building, knowing that in a few minutes not only would he kill a large number of strangers but his own body would be blown to bits? Clearly, there is dehumanization of others as well as of oneself here. The phenomenon, however, is quite distinct from serial killing.

Five differences exist: (1) serial killing is personally motivated, while terrorism is politically motivated; (2) serial killing is usually the act of a loner, whereas terrorism is usually the act of an organized group; (3) in serial killing, murder is the end point, while in terrorism it is a device to influence an adverse political situation; (4) in serial killing, the target and victim of hatred are one and the same, whereas in terrorism, the victim is not the target and the target is not the victim; and (5) unlike a serial killer who takes pleasure in torturing his victim, the terrorist has little emotional involvement in the suffering of those he kills. He might revel in the "glory" of his act and its impact upon his opponents, but he is indifferent to the anguished wails of his victims.

To put it bluntly, dehumanization in terrorist violence is largely a matter of strategy. It is a Janus-faced defensive maneuver of the terrorist's ego. In the external reality, killing innocent bystanders in order to influence their political rulers is made easy for him because he views them as mere pawns in the game. In the internal reality, dehumanizing others protects him from the dread of empathy (which would prevent his hurting innocent people). Dehumanization of his own self, spurred by the adrenaline-pumping exhortations of a religious or social nature, is also essentially strategic. A demonized self has greater immunity against fears of bodily harm and less sadness over a wasted life. It is useful as a weapon. Here is a thought experiment I devised not long after the nefarious 9/11 attacks.

> Imagine for a moment that you are Mohamed Atta, the ring-leader of the September 11 terrorists who rammed planes into the World Trade Center and the Pentagon. You walk up to the check-in counter, show your ticket, and ask for an aisle seat. All this time, you know what you're up to but you keep it to yourself and appear entirely composed. You get your boarding pass, thank the check-in agent, and walk towards the security clearance. You are fully aware that your intention is to kill thousands of people within the next half an hour or so. You also know that you, yourself, are going to die along with them. Yet, you are peaceful and walk onto the plane like any other person. You take your seat, buckle the seat belt, say hello to the person sitting next to you, and leisurely leaf through the in-flight magazine. The plane takes off. You look around. There is a bald man in the row to your left. A blonde woman who has a bandage on her wrist. Two boys of eight and ten talking loudly to each other. An elderly woman who is already fast asleep. And there are so many others. You know that that you're going to kill all of them in a matter of minutes, yet you remain calm. You also know that the fireball that the plane is soon to become will engulf your body as well, burning and charring it beyond recognition. But somehow the awareness does not bother you. Or, perhaps you no longer register such "minor inconveniences." You have a job to do and that is all there is to it. No empathy for anybody. No concern for yourself. No recognition that someone's husband or wife or son

or daughter or mother or father might be waiting for him or her to arrive. No wish and no dream for your own future. No thoughts of your parents, your siblings, and your children. The work has to be done. Everybody has to be killed, including yourself. You do not care about anything else. You are a walking machine, a human bomb. In fact, you are not human at all. (Akhtar, 2005c, pp. 193–194)

Now, I know that most of us would have difficulty putting ourselves in the scenario described above. We would be unable to become so utterly indifferent to the lives of others and certainly that of ourselves. We would be scared, filled with anticipatory remorse, and therefore become incapable of the callousness required of a terrorist. We are simply too human; we care about ourselves and about others. Mr Atta, I presume, had become something other than human. Perhaps, a machine. He regarded others as inanimate objects ("things") too. In other words both his own self and those of others around him were completely dehumanized.

The notion that a terrorist's dehumanization of others is a defensive device finds support from the fact that he is prone to experience horrible remorse upon being confronted with the three-dimensional actuality of his victim's life. This theme is explicated in two literary works, one of fiction, the other of nonfiction: the play *Kya Chahti Hai Shivani?* by Achala Sharma (2000), the former chief of BBC Radio's Hindi Service in London, and the other the highly personal memoir *Revenge* by the *Washington Post* staffer Laura Blumenfeld (2002). Sharma's play is set in New Delhi and depicts the aftermath of a fictional bomb blast by regional separatists in India; its heroine, Shivani, locates the terrorist leader who ordered the attack and confronts him with her physician husband's life history, with all its depth and humanity. Blumenfeld's book reports her encounter with the Palestinian militant who had shot and wounded her father, a New York rabbi; in her own words (cited in Sachs, 2002, p. B-9), one of her goals was "to see if I could make my father human in the gunman's eyes, because I think terrorism is not so much about killing people as about dehumanizing them to make a political point" (i.e., punishing a terrorist by showing his victim's humanity). Written independently of each other, the two texts show the terrorist beginning to have empathy for his victim and remorse over his actions once he learns about the real life of his victim. Both the radio play and the real-life "drama," therefore, reveal that the dehumanizing shield of the terrorist, once penetrated, yields to the hitherto suppressed, ordinary capacity for mutuality and concern.

The hypothesis that dehumanization in terrorist violence is essentially strategic also finds common-sense support. After all, the ordinary terrorist has meager means of undertaking a head-on combat with his oppressors; the latter are all too often well protected and beyond the terrorist's actual reach. The only way he can force them to hear his story is via indirect means, which frequently turn violent. Wounded by territorial disenfranchisement and ethnic humiliation, the terrorist seethes with retributive rage. This is compounded by anger displaced from the corrupt authorities of his own group. Envious destructiveness stirred up by uneven distribution of wealth across nations of the world also contributes to the ensuing hatred. Pent-up sexual frustration, more marked among the terrorists from sexually segregated societies, adds fuel to all this (for more details on the psychosocial dynamics of terrorism, see Chapter 5 of this book).

Bringing a modicum of personal psychopathology, subject to an intensely stifling social milieu, and encouraged by charismatic leaders, the terrorist finds violence not only legitimate but also deeply gratifying. With each act of "revenge," he feels that an abscess has been lanced If such diminution of inner suffering warrants the "sacrifice" of a few innocent bystanders, this seems no more than an unpleasant necessity. The goal is the main thing, not the road that leads to it.

The same logic applies when it comes to the terrorist's own self. While the dehumanization of others permits violence against them, the dehumanization of the self enhances the capacity to carry out such violence. Moreover, it helps to sacrifice the total self rather than the true self alone when conditions for the latter's safety cannot be found. The suicide bomber, from his perspective, does what Donald Winnicott had described nearly fifty years ago. In his words, when conditions for an authentic existence cannot be found, "… suicide is the destruction for the total self in avoidance of annihilation of the True Self" (Winnicott, 1960a, p. 143). A dignified death is thus preferred over living in shame.

Some caveats

The five types of dehumanization described above are not exclusive of each other. At the etiological level, for instance, the deficiency and defeat models frequently overlap. Deficient environmental input can result in peculiarities of neural pathways in the neonate's brain, and genetically determined neural disharmonies can confound the environmental input. In fact, defect, deficiency, regression, identification with malevolent caretakers, and strategy play a variably synergistic role in all forms of dehumanization. The unspeakable and, at times, bizarre acts of cruelty perpetrated by Hitler's lieutenants (e.g., making lampshades and purses out of the skins of Jewish camp inmates), for instance, showed a terrifying mix of sadistic pleasure, regressive thinking, and identification with a malignantly paranoid leader. Spine-chilling degrees of dehumanization of others were also witnessed during other large-group conflicts, including the 1947 Hindu-Muslim riots during India's partition into India and Pakistan, the twenty-year-long Vietnam War (1955–1975), and the 1995 Serbian massacre of Albanian and Kosovar Muslims.

At the phenomenological level, too, one comes across hybrid forms. The 2002 Washington, DC area "sniper" killings illustrate this point. They were unlike any other serial killings insofar as the perpetrator acted from a long distance and had little emotional involvement with the victim. In their effect upon the general population too, these murders resembled terrorist violence more than serial killing. The fact that the seventeen-year-old Lee Boyd Malvo, alleged to be the main "shooter," committed this violence largely to win the affection of the much older John Allen Mohammed is also akin to the dynamics of terrorist violence committed at the behest of a powerful leader. Yet the political ingredient characteristic of terrorism was absent from the mix. The picture was therefore a hybrid of terrorism and serial killing.

Among other such admixtures are the violent acts of ethnopolitical outrage committed by single individuals. Timothy McVeigh's bombing of the Murrah Building in Oklahoma City, Baruch Goldstein's spraying with bullets of Palestinian Muslims praying in a mosque, and Ted Kaczynski's stealthy campaign against technological modernity are thus generally viewed as outbursts of deranged minds and not "true" terrorist acts. Assassinations of heads of state—such as Anwar al-Sadat of Egypt, Yitzhak Rabin of Israel, Indira Gandhi and Rajiv Gandhi of India—by fanatical political opponents also do not fit the ordinary pattern of violence associated with terrorism.

There are still other conceptual fine points. Some forms of dehumanization emanate from individual problems (be it deficiency, defect, regression, or identification), whereas others (e.g., terrorism) are end-products of large-group dynamics. In the former, genetic predispositions, vicissitudes of child rearing, and neurotransmitter abnormalities play a central role. In the latter, sociopolitical, economic, religious, and historical forces dictate the unfolding of events. Moreover, some forms of dehumanization (e.g., autism, schizophrenia) are relatively "self contained," while others (e.g., serial killing, terrorist violence) not only affect the population at large but also thrive upon attention from the media. Notoriety achieved through such public attention serves a powerful mirroring function for the perpetrator's narcissism.

Finally, it should be noted that both the tendency to dehumanize others and the potential for losing one's own "human" qualities might have deep and universal foundations. Freud's (1923b) designation of the cauldron of instincts as the "it" (later changed to the "id" by his translator, James Strachey) hinted at this cold-blooded substrate in human beings. Donald Winnicott's (1963) description of the infant's "ruthlessness" and Melanie Klein's (1940) speculations about the child's violent "phantasies" towards the mother also support the possibility that the capacity for dehumanizing others lies dormant in all of us. The other pole of this spectrum—namely, dehumanizing the self—is addressed by Heinz Lichtenstein (1961, 1963) in his seminal writings on the genesis of identity. According to him, human life exists in an oscillation between the two forces of living out an "identity theme" and undergoing "metamorphosis" by giving up the human quality of identity altogether. Abandonment of identity produces confusion and anguish. However, it can also be experienced as liberation and ecstasy;[3] this is often evidenced in states of meditation, in martyrdom, during periods of intense intellectual work or physical exercise, and during sexual orgasm. While this might be true, the fact remains that the ubiquitous "seeds" of dehumanization lie mostly dormant and psychically "calcified," so to speak. Much biopsychosocial stress is required to activate the inner potential and turn it into overt phenomenology of any significance.

Returning to such "symptomatology," it seems that there is much overlap in the dynamic and descriptive characteristics of the five types of dehumanization described here. To a greater or lesser extent, the substrate of each is biopsychosocial. Each affects the individual, and each has an impact on others around him. Even though one or the other pole might be more evident in a given situation, dehumanization of the self and the other are, in the end, inseparable. One cannot be addressed in isolation of the other.

Is "rehumanization" possible?

In light of the etiological complexities in this realm and the other cave-ats mentioned above, it is clear that ameliorative attempts directed at dehumanization need to be multipronged and specifically tailored to the context at hand. Setting aside the medical, rehabilitative, and judi-cial interventions for "treating" dehumanization in feral and autistic children, schizophrenics, and serial killers, I will focus upon the ways to curtail the dehumanization associated with terrorism. It is my feel-ing that since terrorism is a multiply determined phenomenon, the "treatment" of dehumanization associated with it should approach the issue from multiple vantage points that, in the end, form a harmonious gestalt of purpose. Three major goals of such intervention should be: (1) to enhance the capacity of thinking in "oppressed" people, (2) to diminish their rage, and (3) to create and enhance empathy in them towards their "oppressors."

In order to accomplish the first goal, the physical safety and psy-chosocial dignity of the "oppressed" must be restored. Reasonable mentation requires what Joseph Sandler (1960) called a "background of safety." An individual or a group threatened with violence, curfews, deprivation of food, lack of medical supplies, poverty, overcrowding, and squalor can hardly be expected to think rationally about matters of political and religious difference. Attention must therefore be paid to rectifying or, at least, improving these situations. Moreover, earnest efforts must be made to meet the basic psychological needs of human beings, as mentioned above. To recapitulate, these were the needs for affirmation and identity, optimal responsiveness from others, knowing the causes of events, maintaining personal and social boundaries, and self-expression and generativity. Clearly, minimizing the group's sense of humiliation at the hands of others, providing forums for the group to voice its grievances, and ensuring the political and religious freedom of its members are of paramount importance in meeting these needs. The empowerment of women, sexual desegregation, and the safeguarding—or establishing—of democratic forms of government are among other important measures in this context. To be sure, this sounds like a tall order, but any appeal for rationality is likely to fall on deaf ears if these steps are not taken.

The second goal should be to diminish the hatred felt by the "oppressed" and the "disenfranchised." In this connection, it is important to remember that hatred, at its base, is invariably rooted in feelings of hurt and shame. To diminish hatred, one must first minimize what underlies it. The "hateful" group must be allowed to vent its outrage in private and public meetings until the feelings of hurt and shame emerge at the surface. The real or imagined causes of such feelings must be empathically explored and, as much as possible, rectified. Far from utopian promises, such relief must be anchored in reality, as assessed by a neutral third party. Steps should also be taken to diminish inter-group jealousy by ensuring that opposing parties get equal support from the powerful nations of the world.

Finally, there is the matter of creating—and/or enhancing—empathy between the opposing factions in a terrorism situation. Each side must be prodded to learn about the other. Each must be persuaded to know the other's point of view, historical lores and laments, and transgenerationally transmitted grudges and glories.[4] Such knowledge should be dispersed via "detoxified" books that teach history to schoolchildren, via simple but pithy statements on billboards (e.g., "Not all Arabs are terrorists" and "Not all terrorists are Arabs"), and radio and television programs with positive images of the "enemy." The depiction of friendly and cooperative relations between the opposing factions (drawn either from their earlier history or from some exceptional moments during the current crisis) can pave the way to mutual regard (This idea was mentioned to me by Joseph Montville during an informal conversation circa 2000; see also Montville, 1987, 1991). Sponsorship of sports, exchange opportunities for members of one group to live in the homes of the other and vice versa, and other role-playing exercises (whereby one tries to adopt the perspective of the other) also go a long way towards facilitating mutuality and empathy between the two groups. Needless to say, unofficial, "track II diplomacy" (Volkan, Montville, & Julius, 1991) might play a highly significant role in making such exchanges possible. The groups that meet to carry on a dialogue of this sort should not be restricted to psychoanalysts and the civic representatives of opposing factions. They should gradually expand to include security officers, schoolteachers, economists, health-care personnel, and even creative artists; including moviemakers, playwrights, and poets of the two groups in such interactions can catalyze the process, often in unexpected ways.

Concluding remarks

In this contribution, I have identified the following features as being central to the phenomenon of dehumanization: (i) utter mindlessness, (ii) profound disaffiliation with others, (iii) total absence of empathy, (iv) disregard of one's body, (v) poverty of language, (vi) collapse of barriers against incest and murder, and (vii) pervasive thanatophilia. I have then described various conditions that can result in this syndrome and have especially focused upon politically motivated dehumanization of self and others. Following this, I have delineated the biopsychosocial strategies to reverse the last-mentioned type of dehumanization which, sadly, has become rampant in these troubling times.

I have suggested that the synergistic steps taken to: (i) facilitate rational thinking, (ii) diminish hatred, and (iii) enhance empathy between opposing factions should greatly diminish the dehumanization of self and others associated with terrorist violence. This is not to deny that intractable resistances would not be erected in the pathway to peace by personal and large-group interests of power, money, narcissism, and history-making. However, there is little choice but to try. In any case, one thing is certain: the problem of terrorism cannot be solved by violent means. The answer to Osama bin Laden is not George W. Bush. The current "war against terrorism" is not metaphorical absurdity if not a recipe for ongoing bloodshed across the world. In the words of Ralph Johnson Bunche (1903–1971), the African American winner of the 1950 Nobel Peace Prize,

> To suggest that war can prevent war is a base play on words and a despicable form of war-mongering. The objective of any who sincerely believe in peace clearly must be to exhaust every honorable recourse in the effort to save the peace. The world has had ample evidence that war begets only conditions that beget further war. (1950, cited in Henry, 1996, p. 165)

Notes

1. Mentioning it in print in 1960, Winnicott recalled that he had first made this statement in a discussion, circa 1940, at a scientific meeting of the British Psychoanalytical Society in London. He added that what he

meant by it was "that whenever one finds an infant one finds maternal care, and without maternal care there would be no infant" (p. 39).

2. For details regarding psychiatric syndromes where individuals feel that they have turned into animals, see Akhtar & Brown (2003).

3. See in the context my delineation of a "good death instinct" (Akhtar, 2011b, pp. 87–122).

4. For an understanding of the elaboration and mythologizing of trans-generationally transmitted traumas and triumphs of a group, see Volkan (1997).

EPILOGUE

CHAPTER SEVEN

Psychoanalysis and culture: education and training

The shift from "psychoanalytic anthropology" to "anthropological psychoanalysis" (see Chapter 1) and the gradual accrual of newer, dialectically constructed data in the field of psychoanalysis and the pertinent disciplines of the humanities (e.g., sociology, literary studies) need to be reflected in how psychoanalysis is taught and how the skills of its therapeutic craft are imparted to young trainees. Such culturally anchored psychoanalytic education will better prepare candidates to function as clinicians with analysands of different racial and cultural backgrounds. And, it will open their eyes to the fact that the "average expectable environment" (Hartmann, 1939) necessary for the development and sustenance of a coherent psychic structure cannot be taken for granted; it varies from culture to culture and is not restricted to parental care but involves variables that are ecological, politico-economic, and "cultural" in nature.

This concluding chapter of my book is devoted to matters in this realm. I will divide my discussion of how issues pertaining to culture can and should be integrated within the framework of psychoanalytic training and education into five categories: (i) introducing courses on culture in the didactic curriculum, (ii) using cultural means to impart psychoanalytic knowledge, (iii) paying special attention to minority candidates, (iv) tailoring the program for the so-called academic candidates, and (v) assuring an interdisciplinary and international flavor to the "scientific sessions"[1] sponsored by psychoanalytic societies.

Introducing courses on culture in the didactic curriculum

From a culturally anchored viewpoint, the record of psychoanalytic education has been dismal. To be sure, the perspectives of psychoanalytic metapsychology (e.g., topographic, dynamic, economic, genetic) are universally applicable and require little cultural "adjustment" but this is not true of psychoanalytic hypotheses regarding personality development. And yet, with rare exceptions, psychoanalytic developmental theory is taught with the implicit assumption that its Eurocentric and white vantage point is normative and ubiquitous. While the early phallocentrism of Freud has been tempered and the pathologizing trend towards homosexuality has been reversed, matters of socioeconomic class, race, religion, nationality, politics, and ethnicity remain largely unaddressed in psychoanalytic training programs. Note the following observation by Wyche (2012), an African American psychoanalyst, in this context.

> There were no classes that directly addressed the issue of race relations or racial identity, that included something about the black experience in America. For that matter, the white experience in America was not highlighted either, but most of the time it was understood that we were talking about non-blacks. There were no classes on child development that addressed racial identity issues as they differ in the black community … . Everything we discussed in class had to do with what it was like to be a boy or a girl or a male or a female, and often enough it included what it was like to be a Jewish boy or a Jewish girl. (pp. 332–333)

My own experience of going through the didactic coursework during my analytic training (1979–1986) is similar. No instructor ever asked me what it was like for an Indian child to face this or that intrapsychic or interpersonal challenge, what to say of anyone asking me to bring some literature from my cultural background for the group's reading. A similar experience is recounted by a Chinese American candidate from a Midwestern psychoanalytic institute, even though it occurred in a setting where the training program seemed to pay attention to cultural differences.

> In the didactic courses during my analytic training, a single session was devoted to the topic of racism. We spent the allotted 90 minutes talking about black-white relations in America   historic and current, our own biases and assumptions in relating to people of color and ways in which these might manifest in the psychoanalytic treatment of a patient. The discussion, to which I listened silently, was enlightening and useful. Nevertheless, I found myself getting irritated listening to this "lovely" discourse. A thought ran through my mind: "What about me?" I thought that maybe there was no room for someone who was neither white nor black. We Asians are a "privileged" minority in this country so there is no need to talk about us, I rationalized. I tried, in retrospect, to make myself invisible, quiet and not a problem, inviting others—the facilitator, and my classmates, to buy into the stereotype, to not see me in plain sight and therefore make no room for me to speak. At the end of the class, the instructor put his hand on my arm (I was seated next to him), and asked if I had something to say. I said, "I have a lot to say" but I didn't say what I had been thinking: that one class wasn't enough to talk about such things, that there is more to the experience of other-ness than black and white, that I bought into and sold almost as much of the Asian stereotype as those around me, and that you need to see me, and not just as a goddamn guilty afterthought. Instead, I mentioned a case I had of a black patient and how he and I spoke about being treated by a Chinese-American woman. (personal communication, April 25, 2017)

I am comforted that the "cultural rejuvenation of psychoanalysis" (Akhtar, 1998) has now gone a bit further and that many institutes now include a multi-session didactic seminar on the interface between psychoanalysis and culture. However, some training programs still pay only cursory attention to this realm of human experience while others have no course on culture in their roster of required didactic courses. This needs correction.

In my opinion, all psychoanalytic institutes must include courses on culture in their curricula. Such courses should highlight the myriad ways in which socioeconomic, racial, ethnic, linguistic, and religious differences affect the unfolding of early infantile attachment, pre-oedipal and oedipal development, adolescent struggles of identity formation, and the psychosocial challenges consequent upon the "consolidation of adulthood" (Wolman & Thompson, 1998). Such courses might be restricted to didactic seminars or might include experiential workshops. Admittedly, one is training psychoanalysts and not social anthropologists but it does remain important that analytic candidates acquire sensitivity to various facets of cultural diversity. Taylor (1989) offers a formidable list of what one needs to know in this regard:

> Family structure. Important events in the life cycle. Roles of individual members. Rules of interpersonal interactions. Communication and linguistic rules. Rules of decorum and discipline. Religious beliefs. Standards of health and hygiene. Food preferences. Dress and personal appearance. History and traditions. Holidays and celebrations. Education and teaching methods. Perceptions of work and play. Perceptions of time and space. Explanations of natural phenomena. Attitudes toward pets and animals. Artistic and musical values and tastes. Life expectations and aspirations. (pp. 18–19)

Even if such an idealistic agenda cannot be met, effort must be made to help the candidates-in-training become able to examine their own biases and blind spots and move toward a position of "cultural neutrality" (Akhtar, 1999b), that is, the capacity to remain equidistant from the values, ideals, and social mores of the patient's culture and those of their own. In this context, the reader might benefit by knowing that in 1997, the American Psychoanalytic Association, under the far-sighted stewardship of Marvin Margolis, asked the eminent African American psychoanalyst, Enrico Jones (1948–2003) and myself to prepare a model bibliography for a course on culture in American psychoanalytic institutes. This "officially" approved document (reproduced below in its entirety) languished in the association's archives, even though it constituted a suitable blueprint for introducing cultural awareness in psychoanalytic candidates.

Table I.   A model course on cultural, racial, and ethnic diversity.
Enrico E. Jones & Salman Akhtar (1997)

*Session 1: The cultural specificity of psychoanalytic theory
and practice*

1. Devereux, G. (1953). Cultural factors in psychoanalytic theory. *Journal of the American Psychoanalytic Association* 1: 629–655.

2. Kakar, S. (1985). Psychoanalysis and non-Western cultures. *International Review of Psychoanalysis* 12: 441–450.

3. Roland, A. (1996). How universal is the psychoanalytic self? In: *Reaching Across Boundaries of Culture and Class: Widening the Scope of Psychotherapy*, ed. R.P. Foster, M. Moskovitz, and R.A. Javier, pp. 71–90. Northvale, NJ: Jason Aronson.

Session 2: Transcultural and subcultural variations in childhood development

4. DeVos, G. (1982). Adaptive strategies in US minorities. In: *Minority Mental Health*, eds. E.E. Jones and S.J. Korchin, pp. 74–177. New York: Praeger.

5. Kirshner, S. R. (1990). The assenting echo: Anglo-American values in contemporary psychoanalytic developmental psychology. *Social Research* 57: 821–857.

6. Roland, A. (1994). Identity, self, and individualism in a multicultural perspective. In: *Race, Ethnicity, and Self: Identity in Multicultural Perspective*, eds. E.P. Salett and D.R. Koslow, pp. 11–23. Washington, DC: National Multicultural Institute.

Session 3: African-American identity and its psychosocial context

7. DuBois, W. E. B. (1903). Of our spiritual strivings. In: *The Souls of Black Folk*, pp. 3–12. New York: Penguin Books, 1989.

8. Erikson, E. H. (1968). Race and the wider identity. In: *Identity, Youth, and Crisis*, pp. 295–320. New York: W.W. Norton.

9. Apprey, M. (1993). The African-American experience: forced immigration and the transgenerational trauma. *Mind and Human Interaction* 4: 70–75.

Session 4: Biracial and bicultural childhood and adolescence

10. Wilson, A. (1987). *Mixed Race Children*, pp. 38–63, 174–200. London: Allen and Unwin.

Continued

Table I. (Continued)

Enrico E. Jones & Salman Akhtar (1997)

11. Cauce, A. M., Hiraga, Y., Mason, C., Aguilar, T., Ordonez, N., and Gonzalez, N. (1992). Between a rock and a hard place: social adjustment of biracial youth. In: *Racially Mixed People in America*, ed. P. P. Root, pp. 207–238. Newbury Park, CA: Sage Publications.

12. Miller, R. L., and Rotherman-Borus, M. I. (1994). Growing biracial in the United States. In: *Race, Ethnicity, and Self: Identity in Multicultural Perspective*, eds. E. P. Salett and D.R. Koslow, pp. 143–169. Washington, DC: National Multicultural Institute.

Session 5: The psychology of ethnic and racial prejudice

13. Freud, S. (1921). Group psychology and the analysis of the ego. *Standard Edition* 16: 65–143.

14. Bird, B. (1957). A consideration of the etiology of prejudice. *Journal of the American Psychoanalytic Association* 5: 490–513.

15. Volkan, V. D. (1988). *The Need to Have Enemies and Allies: From Clinical to International Relationships*, pp. 17–34, 74–98. Northvale, NJ: Jason Aronson.

Session 6: Cultural, racial, and ethnic difference between the analyst and the analysand

16. Jones, E. E. (1985). Psychotherapy and counselling with black clients. In: *Handbook for Cross-Cultural Counseling and Therapy*, ed. P. Pederson, pp. 137–179. Westport, CT: Greenwood Press.

17. Leary, K. (1995). Interpreting in the dark: race and ethnicity in psychoanalytic psychotherapy. *Psycho-analytic Psychology* 12: 127–140.

18. Thompson, C.L. (1995). Self-definition by opposition: a consequence of minority status. *Psychoanalytic Psychology* 12: 533–545.

Session 7: Cultural, racial, and ethnic difference between the analyst and the analysand (continued).

19. Shapiro, E. T., and Pinsker, H. (1973). Shared ethnic scotoma. *American Journal of Psychiatry* 130: 1338–1341.

20. Taylor, O. L. (1992). The effect of cultural assumptions on cross-cultural communications. In: *Crossing in Mental Health*, ed. D. R. Koslow and E. P. Salett, pp. 18–27. Washington, DC: SIETAR International.

Continued

Table I. (Continued)

Enrico E. Jones & Salman Akhtar (1997)

21. Jones, E. E. (1998). Psychoanalysis and African-Americans. In: *African-American Mental Health: Theory, Research, and Intervention*, ed. R. L. Jones, pp. 471–477. Hampton, VA: Cobb and Henry.

Session 8: Interracial analyses

22. Fischer, N. (1971). An interracial analysis: transference and counter-transference significance. *Journal of the American Psychoanalytic Association* 19: 736–745.

23. Goldberg, E., Myers, W., and Zeifman, I. (1974). Some observations on three interracial analyses. *International Journal of Psychoanalysis* 55: 495–500.

24. Holmes, D. E. (1992). Race and transference in psychoanalysis and psychotherapy. *International Journal of Psychoanalysis* 73: 1–11.

Session 9: The issue of polylingualism and polyglottism

25. Flegenhimer, F. (1989). Languages and psychoanalysis: the polyglot patient and the polyglot analyst. *International Review of Psycho-Analysis* 16: 377–383.

26. Amati-Mehler, J., Argentieri, S., and Cansestri, J. (1993). *The Babel of the Unconscious: Mother Tongue and Foreign Languages in the Psychoanalytic Dimension*, pp. 19–66. Madison, CT: International Universities Press.

27. Potamianou, A. (1993). In exile from the mother tongue. *Canadian Journal of Psychoanalysis* 1: 47–59.

Session 10: Immigration and the analytic process

28. Garza-Guerrero, C. (1974). Culture shock: its mourning and the vicissitudes of identity. *Journal of the American Psychoanalytic Association* 22: 408–429.

29. Grinberg, L., and Grinberg, R. (1989). *Psychoanalytic Perspectives on Migration and Exile*, pp. 67–73. New Haven, CT: Yale University Press.

30. Akhtar, S. (1995). A third individuation: immigration, identity, and the psychoanalytic process. *Journal of the American Psychoanalytic Association* 43: 1051–1084.

To be sure, this 1997 Jones-Akhtar bibliography needs updating. Perhaps another "official committee"—with a stronger voice—can undertake the task of such a revision. Or, perhaps, it is better that each psychoanalytic institute take this bibliography as a starting point and then evolve its own version for a course on psychoanalysis and culture. To the extent my recommendations matter, I propose the following twelve essays for inclusion in the updated Jones-Akhtar reference list. Chronologically arranged, these are as follows:

1. Altman, N. (1993). Psychoanalysis and the urban poor. *Psychoanalytic Dialogues* 3: 29–49.
2. Derrida, J. (1998). Geopsychoanalysis: "… and the rest of the world". In: *The Psychoanalysis of Race*, ed. C. Lane, pp. 65–90. New York: Columbia University Press.
3. Miles, C. (1998). Mothers and others: bonding, separation-individuation, and resultant ego development in different African-American cultures. In: *The Colors of Childhood: Separation-Individuation Across Cross-Cultural, Racial, and Ethnic Differences*, eds. S. Akhtar and S. Kramer, pp. 79–112. Lanham, MD: Jason Aronson.
4. Akhtar, S. (2006). Technical challenges faced by the immigration analyst. *Psychoanalytic Quarterly* 75: 21–43.
5. Gu, M.D. (2006). The filial piety complex: variations on the Oedipus theme in Chinese literature and culture. *Psychoanalytic Quarterly* 75: 163–196.
6. Hamer, F. (2007). Anti-black racism and the conception of whiteness. In: *The Future of Prejudice: Psychoanalysis and Prevention of Prejudice,* eds. H. Parens, A. Mahfouz, S. Twemlow, and D. Scharff, pp. 131–140. Lanham, MD: Jason Aronson.
7. Akhtar, S. (2008). Muslims in the psychoanalytic world. In: *The Crescent and the Couch: Cross-Currents between Islam and Psychoanalysis,* ed. S. Akhtar, pp. 315–334. Lanham, MD: Jason Aronson.
8. Choi-Kain, L. (2009). Second generation Korean Americans. In: *Freud and the Far East: Psychoanalytic Perspectives on the People and Culture of China, Japan, and Korea,* ed. S. Akhtar, pp. 215–233. Lanham, MD: Jason Aronson.
9. Powell, D. (2012). Psychoanalysis and African Americans: past, present, and future. In: *The African American Experience: Psychoanalytic Perspectives,* ed. S. Akhtar, pp. 59–84. Lanham, MD: Jason Aronson.

10. Bullón, A., and Alfonso, C.A. (2015). Latino ethnic identity. In: *The American Latino: Psychodynamic Perspectives on Culture and Mental Health Issues*, eds. S. Akhtar and S.M. Bertoglia, pp. 43–61. Lanham, MD: Rowman & Littlefield.

11. Holmes, D.E. (2016). Come hither, American psychoanalysis: our complex multicultural America needs what we have to offer. *Journal of the American Psychoanalytic Association* 64: 569–586.

12. Tummala-Narra, P. (2016). A historical overview and critique of the psychoanalytic approach to culture and context. In: *Psychoanalytic Theory and Cultural Competence in Psychotherapy*, pp. 7–29. Washington, DC: American Psychological Association.

A course based upon the blending of the 1997 Jones-Akhtar bibliography and some, if not all, of the aforementioned essays, if taught in a sensitive, interactive, and "mentalization" (Fonagy & Target, 1997) enhancing seminar, can be of considerable assistance in helping psychoanalytic candidates evolve "cultural neutrality" (Akhtar, 1999b, pp. 113–116), though a thorough personal analysis and genuinely cosmopolitan lifestyle are perhaps of comparable value in this context.

Using cultural means to impart psychoanalytic knowledge

The founder of psychoanalysis, Sigmund Freud, exemplified the virtue of broad-based scholarship. He derived knowledge about human affairs from all sorts of sources, including myths, history, fiction, folklore, literary classics, and even jokes. He concluded his lecture on femininity by saying to his audience, "If you want to know more, enquire from your own experiences of life, or turn to the poets, or wait until silence can give you deeper and more coherent information" (1933a, p. 135). In his paper on constructions in psychoanalysis, Freud (1937d) declared that the poet can always discern the method in madness. Far more impressive than these remarks is Freud's "confession" that "Everywhere I go, I find a poet has been there before me" (cited in Nin, 1976, p. 14). And yet, the curricula in today's psychoanalytic institutes are noticeably devoid of "poetry." To be sure, there is that lonely nightingale of psychoanalysis, Allen Wheelis, who teaches us in the voice of a wise poet. Take a look at the following passage about love, sex, instincts, sublimation, promiscuity, and inconsolability.

> Love is created anew by each generation from lust and loneliness.
> For this to come about, primary needs may not be primarily spent,
> must be accumulated. But the promiscuous accumulate nothing.
> They wander about improvidently paying out the common need in
> a common and recurrent coupling, never bringing together enough
> of the elemental drives, never subjecting them to sufficient pres-
> sure, to ignite them into love. What eventually becomes reality
> appears first as illusion. The hope attached to illusion sustains life
> when all else is lost. (1975, p. 37)

And now consider these lines about the anxiety of separateness, the
lure of merger, the imperative of identity, and the ever-present footsteps
of mortality.

> Being human starts with the consciousness of a unique self. To
> affirm one's self is to affirm this uniqueness. And if I do not affirm
> myself I cannot meaningfully affirm anything. But uniqueness
> entails the awareness of boundaries between self and not self; so
> to affirm self is to accept alienation. Alienation brings into life the
> experience of death; so the affirmation of self entails the affirmation
> of death. This is the trap: to cling to life drives one towards death,
> and there is no way to avoid anything of death without giving up
> something of life. (1975, pp. 91–92)

Wheelis is even more eloquent regarding matters of eroticism, repeti-
tion, problematic but "destined" object choices, and the dark pleasure
of sadomasochism.

> The large wide-open eyes contain a hint of reproach. The gaze sinks
> deeply into me. She plays a fallen woman, the victim of a need for
> love that leads her repeatedly to villainous men who will use her
> and forsake her. She is stuck with her vulnerability, her hidden
> masochism, and I am stuck with my secret sadism. Across that gulf
> our glances meet, we recognize each other. We are a pair. (1994,
> p. 86)

While the passages cited above illustrate how psychoanalytic ideas can
be conveyed in a poetic manner, two bitter facts remain: (i) Wheelis
is truly an exception among psychoanalytic writers, and (ii) psycho-

analytic literature is not the sole source of knowledge about grief, about erotic passion, about suicidal despair, about rage and revenge, about perversion, about schizoid futility, about desperate longing for a beautiful face, about sleepless nights, and about yearning to recapture infantile omnipotence. We psychoanalysts know this fact but somehow fail to incorporate it into designing the course outlines of our training programs. Just imagine how the appreciation of psychoanalytic proposals can be enriched by the inclusion of pertinent pieces of fiction, poetry, and movies. Understanding thus derived would be at an intuitive and sensual level—more convincing than that obtained only from reading psychoanalytic papers and therefore, in the end, more useful. Take a look at the following possibilities.

- A didactic course on Oedipus complex, for instance, might come fully alive if, alongside the seminal psychoanalytic papers on the topic (Chasseguet-Smirgel, 1984; Freud, 1908c, 1924d; Gitelson, 1952; Neubauer, 1960; Searles, 1959), the students also read the Sophocles (429 BC) play, *Oedipus Rex,* as well. Candidates will also benefit by seeing certain movies together that illustrate different constellations and outcomes of the oedipal conflict: *The Picture of Dorian Gray* (1945) for a masochistic outcome, *Top Gun* (1986) for a perverse outcome, *Back to the Future* (1985) for a neurotic/successful resolution, and *My Girl* (1991) for a motherless girl's struggle toward oedipal consolidation.
- A didactic course on narcissistic character pathology would be greatly enhanced if the candidates were required to read a few relevant pieces of fiction. These might include the urbane *The Custom of the Country* by Edith Wharton (1913), *The Great Gatsby* by F. Scott Fitzgerald (1925), and *The Man Who Was Late* by Louis Begley (1993) as well as the more disturbing *The American Psycho* by Bret Ellis (1991) and *We Need to Talk About Kevin* by Lionel Shriver (2003). Trainees studying pathological narcissism might also benefit by watching movies like *Citizen Kane* (1941), *All That Jazz* (1979), and *Young Adult* (2011), and *Listen Up, Philip* (2014).
- A similar course on borderline personality would benefit by the inclusion of movies like *Taxi Driver* (1976), *Frances* (1982), and *Thirteen* (2003).
- The inclusion of movies such as *The Great Santini* (1979), *Shine* (1996), *Beginners* (2010), and *The Judge* (2014) can deepen psycho-

analytic candidates' understanding of father-son relationships, and watching *Paper Moon* (1973), *Father of the Bride* (1991), *Imaginary Crimes* (1994), and *Trouble with the Curve* (2012) can accomplish the same regarding father-daughter relationships. The impact of father's absence on family dynamics, especially a growing son's erotic longings towards his mother, is well-depicted in *Spanking the Monkey* (1994) and *Mommy* (2014).

- Similar "cultural reinforcements" can be made to a course on grief. Candidates might be required to extend their reading beyond the seminal *Mourning and Melancholia* (Freud, 1917e) and other psychoanalytic classics (e.g., Furman, 1974; Klein, 1929, 1940; Pollock, 1970, 1972, 1976; Volkan, 1981 on the topic. They should be encouraged to take a look at *A Remembrance of Things Past* by Marcel Proust (1913) and *A Grief Observed* by C. S. Lewis (1961), as well as the more recent *The Year of Magical Thinking* by Joan Didion (2006), *Mourning Diary* by Roland Barthes (2010), and *Wave* by Sonali Deraniyagala (2013). Screening of movies like *Ordinary People* (1980), *Blue* (1993), *Ponette* (1996), and *Still Walking* (2008) can also bring much-needed poignancy to the topic and enhance the budding analyst's empathy with individuals who are struggling with loss.

- Teaching of dissociative disorders would be greatly enriched by extending it beyond the "must read" psychoanalytic papers (e.g., Brenner, 2001; Kluft, 1985, 1993) to include novels like *The Strange Case of Dr Jekyll and Mr Hyde* (Stevenson, 1886) and *Sybil* (Schreiber, 1973). In addition, the candidates and the faculty might together watch movies like *Three Faces of Eve* (1957), *Raising Cain* (1992), and *Me, Myself, and Irene* (2000).

- A course on listening should not be restricted to the psychoanalytic literature on the subject but should also include Fred Griffin's (2016) book, *Creative Listening and the Psychoanalytic Process*, which highlights the links between meaningful reading of fiction and proper analytic attunement to patients.

More examples of this sort should be drawn from the minority candidates' own culture and attempts should be made to include English translations of Asian, African, Australian, and Latin-American literary pieces in the curriculum. My point is basically this: psychoanalytic knowledge should be imparted not only in the way it was gathered (i.e., by seeing patients and from discussion of clinical cases) and by reading psychoanalytic texts but also from diverse sources that extend beyond the field's own literature. While I have noted above the role that watching movies and reading fiction can play here, the importance of familiarizing, if not immersing, oneself in poetry can hardly be over-emphasized. This is because deep linkages exist between understanding poetry and psychoanalytic listening (Akhtar, 2000, 2008c, 2012; Ogden, 1997, 1998, 1999).

Paying special attention to minority candidates

Candidates for psychoanalytic training who belong to one or the other minority group (e.g., racial, religious, ethnic) often face special challenges. To recount such occurrences might be akin to washing one's dirty laundry in public but failure to acknowledge and document them can perpetuate the profession's denial of bias and its deleterious impact. The fact is that minority candidates experience subtle and sometimes not-so-subtle discrimination; this can occur during the admission process, classroom participation, and individual supervision. Afaf Mahfouz, an Egyptian-born Muslim psychoanalyst, recalls what happened when she applied for psychoanalytic training during the 1980s:

> One of my interviewers asked, "How come you came from that kind of place (implying that it was backward and primitive) and achieved what you achieved?" I did not know how to answer but I came up with the polite answer: "I guess it was due to the love of my mother." I don't really know how she received it but she ended up accepting me for the training despite my "backward and primitive" background. A second interviewer tried to convince me that psychoanalytic training was not for me because I would be with mostly Jewish people and might find it difficult and awkward. I told him that I was accustomed to Jewish people and thought I would learn from them and they would learn from me. His answer was: "You don't realize but it is going to be hell for you; you are not even Christian!" Even though I was accepted to the institute, these encounters did shake me up a bit. (personal communication, January 22, 2017)

Lest one think that what happened forty years ago does not happen any longer, I cite the following 2009 experience of a white, Christian, applicant to a psychoanalytic institute:

During my application process for psychoanalytic training, I attended an open house event at the psychoanalytic institute. I was wearing a necklace with a pendant, which was only partially visible under my suit jacket collar. A senior analyst spotted it while talking to me, reached out to touch it, and ask, with what appeared to be a concerned expression on his face, "It's not a cross, is it?" It was not, but I have never stopped wondering what if it was. What would have or would have not happened? (Anonymous, personal communication, March 20, 2017)

This sort of thing does not stop at the gate, so to speak. Candidates who belong to a minority are often treated as invisible during the didactic classes, making them feel like pariahs. Allow me to recount a personal anecdote. The incident I am about to report happened thirty years ago.

I was a candidate in psychoanalytic training and was in a class where some developmental issues were being discussed. The instructor was Jewish and so were all my classmates. As the discussion proceeded, the group's attention gradually shifted to Jewish customs and rituals that were pertinent to the developmental issues we were talking about. In its voluble enthusiasm, the group lost contact with me and I with it. They either "forgot" that I was not Jewish or were simply uncomfortable in reminding themselves of our ethnic difference. I, on my part, did little to rectify the situation. I sat forlorn and was incapable or hesitant to mentalize my sense of marginalization. When the class ended and we were walking towards the institute's parking lot, one classmate of mine, Dr. Marc Lipschutz, came up to me, put his arm around my shoulder and said, "You know, I think we owe an apology to you. We all got carried away talking about Jewish customs, stuff that would not have made any sense to you. We did not stop and ask you if something akin to what we were discussing occurred in your ethnic and national background or not." Now, the significant thing to note here is that when I was being treated, as it were, like a white Jewish boy, I felt completely invisible and excluded. But when my brave and tender colleague reflected our difference, I felt vitalized and very included.

My purpose in recounting this anecdote is to not only demonstrate the power of human empathy but also to underscore how candidates who represent ethnic and racial minorities get ignored in their individual veracity during classes and how this precludes potentially enriching input from a diverse perspective. The following observation by Samuel Wyche (2012), an African American analyst, about the way didactic seminars are conducted in psychoanalytic institutes confirms my assertion:

> Everything we discussed in class had to do with what it was like to be a boy or a girl or a male or a female, and often enough, it included what it was like to be a Jewish boy or a Jewish girl, etc. The so-called "cultural rejuvenation of psychoanalysis" (Akhtar, 1998) had not arrived on the scene while I was training to become a psychoanalyst. Most case presentations were of Jewish ancestry and/or European immigrants and indeed, they were discussed with much sensitivity. It was obvious to me that this discussion was something that could easily be done because of the support and invested interest of the participating members who could easily identify with the patient and analyst in ways that were mentioned in class and ways that were not mentioned but unique and familiar to them .... As such, this would not emerge as being out of the ordinary for those who live in the white side of the Black–White experience. While this was something observed from afar by me, this was not something that I could easily address in such an environment as an outsider (i.e., the only Black person in the group). No matter how caring or nurturing the individual participants might have been to me personally, there existed a collective denial of racial differences within the group. A room full of psychoanalysts (and psychoanalytic trainees) was the last place I expected to be overlooked or ignored in my veracity. (p. 333)

The following vignette provided by a white, practicing Christian psychoanalytic candidate tells the same story from a slightly different angle:

> While I was a candidate in the middle years of my didactic courses, during a class, the instructor told a joke that pictured Jesus as a

castrated man. I was offended. "Yeah," I thought, "you hope!," matching his hostility with my own, and pointing to unconscious (and wishful) reasons to believe in the absence of God, just as analysts have so often pointed to unconscious (and wishful) reasons to believe in the existence of God.

My experience as a Christian candidate in analytic training was that belief in the absence of God is regarded as normal, requiring no explanation, while belief in God requires explanation. Even more remarkable, in personal conversations, I found most analytic instructors unable to even pretend about a relationship with God, unable to "play" in the realm of the supernatural. Such a lost opportunity for creativity! (Anonymous, personal communication, April 5, 2017)

A word of clarification is needed here. Since Jewish people represent the majority in the field of psychoanalysis, my expression "minority candidates" refers to those who are Christian, Muslim, Hindu, African American, Iranian, Arab, Indian, Pakistani, Turkish, Korean, Chinese, or Japanese in origin. These candidates, I believe, need extra attention during the didactic course work and clinical supervision (and, of course, during their training analyses).

Instructors and supervisors should make an effort to actively engage such candidates in reflecting on how their ethno-racial backgrounds impact upon the developmental notions being discussed or upon the events in the transference-countertransference axis unfolding in front of them. Done in a dignified manner and without making the trainee feel odd or inferior, such curiosity can enhance mutual respect and enrich clinical and theoretical understanding. The importance of such discourse is greater during supervision of "control" cases. And yet, this happens all too infrequently in reality. Wyche (2012), who has been quoted above, has poignantly described this situation.

> Throughout my analytic training, I have had at least seven supervisors for "control" cases. Most of them were attentive, supportive, engaging, insightful, knowledgeable, and critical in a humane way. But only one was sensitive to my Black ethnicity and asked (without my bringing it up) how, if, and in what way it affected the treatment process and how that impact was understood by me and my patient. Such inquiry was music to my ears as I expected this to be

a prevalent part of any therapeutic process, especially an analysis. (p. 331)

Wyche's experience says it loud and clear: ignoring and denying racial and cultural differences between the analyst and analysand, during supervision, can deplete the learning experience of the candidate and, worse, leave deep pockets of resentment in the minds of trainees. A North American psychoanalyst of Middle Eastern origins, who prefers to remain anonymous, has the following to say about his experience in the didactic portion of psychoanalytic training.

> In none of my classes was the issue of culture raised. Once it did surface, but in an insidious manner. The instructor teaching a 6-session course on analyzability said to the class that we ought to look for a robust case (i.e. one that lacked impulsivity and could form deep object relations), adding "that is good for the Jews." I could not understand why he said that but felt a bit intimidated and remained quiet. In fact, this instructor treated the class as if all that mattered was his Jewish affiliation and that psychoanalysis is essentially a Jewish endeavor. I felt bad since I was not Jewish and felt excluded from the tight knit group in the class. Years later, the only other non-Jew, a Latin American, revealed feeling along the same lines as I did during that particular course. (personal communication, March 5, 2013)

Didactic courses on "culture," while useful, are not a substitute for ongoing, personal engagement with such issues. Dionne Powell (2012), a New York-based African American psychoanalyst, emphatically declares that:

> Trying to promote "culture competence" is now a part of every psychiatry residency or psychology graduate program. However, a seminar or lecture series on cross-cultural "sensitivity" is woefully inadequate without on-going dialogue about race within individual supervision and one's own analysis. (p. 76)

The last-mentioned point cannot be overemphasized. Candidates who belong to ethnic, racial, and religious minorities are more often than not unable to find a "homo-ethnic" training analyst, an unnoticed comfort available to their "majority" counterparts. This must be kept in mind by their analysts and might even need to be actively brought up for associative elaboration. Training analysts, who have "minority candidates" in treatment, should familiarize themselves with the burgeoning literature on bicultural analytic dyads (Akhtar, 1999b, 2011a; Holmes, 1992, 1999, 2006, 2016; Leary, 1995, 1997, 2000; Thompson, 1996). Neglecting the ethnic, racial, or religious difference within the dyad injures the analysand's healthy narcissism and consequently diminishes her "faith" in such work. Clearly, personal beliefs of candidates should be kept in mind when topics of faith, religion, and spirituality are broached during didactic courses or clinical discussions. Supervisors would also benefit by learning about the special technical challenges faced by analysts who are immigrants or who belong to racial and religious minorities. These include racialized experiences in the transference-countertransference axis, value system differences, variability in the sense of time, problems of bilingualism, and so on (Akhtar, 2006). Similar difficulties are experienced by minority candidates. These need to be explored during their supervision. However, for this to occur in a meaningful way, the supervisor must first help the candidate become comfortable in talking about the racial or religious difference existing in the clinical dyad and also in the supervisory dyad. The first step in this direction is constituted by the supervisor's display of respectful and nonintrusive curiosity about the candidate's background. A supervisor who shows no interest in his African American, Indian, Iranian, or Arab candidate's culture implicitly discourages candor and can preclude the entry of useful clinical information into the supervisory discourse. Worse than this is letting assumptions based upon superficial cultural knowledge be transposed upon the candidate's clinical struggles. Doing so can hurt the candidate badly and derail the supervision. Sripada (1999), a Chicago-based Hindu psychoanalyst of Indian origin, describes such an occurrence in disturbing detail:

> Dr. A brought a *New York Times* article to a supervisory session. It described the traditional elevated status of Brahmins in India. He summarized it, telling me that he was willing to bet that I was not a Brahmin. He asked if I was. When I said I was, he was surprised and told me that I did not have Brahmin characteristics. I attempted a joke and said that even he may be mistaken. I told

him that although I appreciated his candor, I found supervision with him to be extremely painful. (p. 229)

Sripada (1999) reports that he ultimately sought supervision from someone else, and that experience was personally congenial and clinically useful. Mishaps of the sort he narrates are not restricted to the supervisory encounter, however. At times, a visiting analyst can display cultural scotoma in dealing with candidates-in-training and end up hurting their feelings. Shahrzad Siassi, a Los Angeles-based psychoanalyst of Iranian origin, recounts the following experience to attest to such distress:

> It was in the early nineties and I was a very proud third year candidate in the full training psychoanalytic program at our Institute. I was not a newcomer to psychoanalysis, as I had had years of informal training and had received glowing evaluations from my instructors. One particular day, a guest speaker who was a very well known, perhaps world renowned psychoanalyst, gave a lecture on Lacan to our class. At that time, Lacan was not well known and his writings were more of a novelty in psychoanalytic circles. For the first time in my analytic training, I ran aground as I tried to make sense of Lacan's paper.
>
> During the discussion, in my frustration, I commented, "Lacan is the most narcissistic writer I have ever come across. He is unempathic with his readers and expects them to follow his trail of free association instead of communicating with them." The instructor was clearly upset by my remark and started questioning me, not in terms of my perspective, but of my worldliness, implying that my comment reflected my ignorance of Europe and European thinking. He further challenged me, saying if I had ever tried to write anything difficult, I would know how painfully hard it is to put complicated, abstract concepts into words.
>
> I felt personally attacked for expressing my opinion, which after all was not an unusual take on Lacan. I decided to wait until the end of the session to confront him. Then, I asked what made him think I was not familiar with Europe or European thinking. He did not respond to my question, but proceeded to accuse me of being glib and flippant in my reaction to Lacan. He was upset that

I was unappreciative of Lacan's amazingly unique contribution to psychoanalysis. It was becoming clear to me that this man's own strong transference to Lacan had turned me into an insensitive aggressor of his idol or perhaps of himself. I responded that he was criticizing my background and was pigeonholing me as an unsophisticated foreigner. I added that my knowledge of Europe and especially of French was beyond what he could imagine and explained that my fluency in French went back to my childhood. As a result, I could read *Ecrits* better in French than in English, and with French as a college minor, I was extensively exposed to 17th, 18th, 19th and especially 20th century French literature. Furthermore, with the exception of two or three countries, I had seen the whole of Europe. Thus, if exposure to Europe and European thinking was the prerequisite to making sense of Lacan, I had met it and stood by my response to Lacan's writing. He was clearly taken aback and apologized for his reaction. (personal communication, April 2, 2017)

This and the other brief vignettes provided above demonstrate that "unmentalized xenophobia" (Akhtar, 2007b) and even outright prejudice towards minority candidates can exist in the setting of psychoanalytic education. Fortunately, this is not always the case. Yasser Ad-Dab'bagh, a psychoanalyst born and raised in Saudi Arabia and trained at the Canadian Institute of Psychoanalysis (Quebec-English Branch) recounts the following:

I fail to find a single memory of being disrespected or marginalized during my analytic training. It was quite the opposite, really. I think I was such a novel entity for everyone involved that there was a great interest in accommodating me and, perhaps, in exploring through me the cultural background I came from. Genuine interest and curiosity, along with warm, welcoming feelings, were what I received from most people in the Institute. Moreover, this wasn't experienced by them as "walking on eggshells" or being "politically correct." (personal communication, May 8, 2017)

While it is a relief to note such large-hearted cordiality, in light of the many other vignettes presented above, the negative and discriminatory attitude towards minority candidates seems to be endemic. This needs to be recognized and candidates need to be encouraged to report such occurrences, with the assurance of confidentiality and remedial action.

Tailoring the program for the so-called academic candidates

The designation "academic candidates" is of recent origin and is reserved for individuals who join psychoanalytic training with the explicit declaration that they would not practice clinical psychoanalysis.[2] Sprinkled in small numbers throughout institutes for psychoanalytic training, such individuals come from diverse professional backgrounds. Priests, historians, budding novelists, lawyers, and businessmen are often represented in these groups. Uninterested in clinical work, these individuals seek psychoanalytic training for intellectual purposes, though emotional undercurrents of a personal nature often underlie their pursuit. Generally speaking, they are "good" students. They read all the assigned papers and raise interesting questions, often bringing a fresh perspective to matters under consideration. All goes well till they come across the requirement to attend and participate in seminars on clinical technique and in continuous case conferences. Now, a feeling of discontent sets in. They find themselves in a quandary. If they refuse to go along, they can be viewed as lacking interest in psychoanalysis but if they do attend the clinical seminars, they feel coerced and find the learning useless for their specific purposes.

A way to negotiate this impasse is to assure that the "academic candidates" take only those classes with the "regular" (i.e., clinical candidates) which focus upon metapsychology, principles of mental functioning, development, and psychopathology. Perhaps, this could be accomplished in the first two years of the didactic curriculum. Perhaps, not. In either case, after the basic courses of the sort mentioned above, the education of "academic candidates" should proceed separately from that of the clinical candidates. The "academic candidates" should be offered courses in the interface between psychoanalysis and other disciplines and professions such as law, business, theology, philosophy, fine arts, music, theatre, cinema, architecture, photography, and so on. This would meaningfully address their needs, diminish their discontent, and elicit positive input from them towards the functioning of the institute in general and towards the didactic curriculum in particular. Upon graduation from the program, they might serve as instructors in the "academic track" and also become important sources of referrals for the institute clinic and candidate pool. Objections to such a proposal usually center upon resources of time, money, and manpower. And, here, Kernberg's (2012) persistent reminder that psychoanalytic institutes need to develop greater ties with a university comes to our rescue. He suggests that psychoanalytic institutes regularly

> invite chairpersons of university departments in the behavioral sciences and humanities to lecture and teach at your psychoanalytic institute and society, as part of an effort to relate psychoanalysis to its boundary disciplines and sciences. Establish working relationships both with academics who are sympathetic to psychoanalysis and with those who are sharply critical, inviting the latter for lectures, informal discussions, and joint seminars. (p. 708)

Armed with greater financial reserves and human resources, a university can more readily fill the gap that exists in our way of handling the needs of "academic candidates." A compendium of psychoanalytically informed essays on a broad range of "bordering" disciplines should also be of great help for the psychoanalytic training of "academic candidates." I, along with my colleague, Stuart Twemlow, have recently prepared such a *Textbook of Applied Psychoanalysis* (Akhtar & Twemlow, 2018) which contains thirty-five essays divided into the following six sections: (i) psychoanalysis and cultural understanding of mind, (ii) psychoanalysis, biology, and the human body, (iii) psychoanalysis and societal turbulence, (iv) psychoanalysis and social praxis, (v) psychoanalysis and fine arts, and (vi) psychoanalysis and performing arts. This encyclopedic volume addresses fields as diverse as anthropology and photography, philosophy and sports, religion and health policy, poetry and architecture, and so on. Each of its thirty-five chapters can form the topic of discussion for a didactic session run by a psychoanalyst and a representative of the particular discipline under consideration. Doing so would provide an attractive pathway for psychoanalysts to collaborate with specialists in other fields while producing more satisfied and better trained academic candidates.

Assuring an interdisciplinary and international flavor to scientific programs of psychoanalytic societies

The scientific" programs of psychoanalytic societies refers to the six to eight evening meetings per year where an invited psychoanalyst (usually from out of town) presents his ideas to the group. More often this consists of the presenter literally reading his paper and then a local discussant reading a prepared response to it. An admixture of tempered cordiality and affectionate respect prevails at such gatherings, and the presenter-audience interaction remains formal. At times, the discussions are enlightening and useful. At other times, the proceedings can turn out to be ponderous. The novice in the audience benefits, even if due more to the "awe-full" identification with the distinguished presenter than to genuinely understanding what he or she has to offer. The more experienced participants come to "pay their dues," rekindle old connections, and appear loyal to the parent organization. With time, they can almost predict what are the presenters' views on a particular topic; they learn little from such meetings.

An important and "culturally attuned" way to improve things is to have most, if not all, such meetings as interdisciplinary conferences. The Psychoanalytic Center of Philadelphia has started a Freud and Franklin Series (under the able chairmanship of Dr. Lawrence Blum) which invariably brings psychoanalysts together with high level academics in order to discuss a particular topic (e.g., incest, racism, children's literature, privacy). The result is almost always refreshing and informative. However, this program (and its counterparts elsewhere) is not part of the main series of "scientific sessions" of the PCOP; it is like a stepchild. This needs rectification. I believe that, barring presentations on special issues of technique, all scientific programs ought to be interdisciplinary. That this is good for psychoanalysis and for psychoanalysts is amply confirmed by the popularity of conferences sponsored by the Freud Museum in London. Under the stewardship of Ivan Ward, its educational director, the Freud Museum has sponsored engaging and productive discourses on topics as diverse as psychoanalysis and architecture, psychoanalysis and sports, psychoanalysis and physical objects, and so on.

Yet another way to culturally enliven the scientific program of psychoanalytic societies is to assure that at least one visiting analyst per year is from outside the country. Monetary hurdles to sponsoring such a visit can be overcome by (i) reducing the number of scientific sessions, (ii) naming the lecture series after a wealthy patron of the institute who would support the program, or (iii) by pooling resources with a psychoanalytic institute in a neighboring city. The advantages of a visit by a "foreign" analyst are manifold. He or she would bring a fresh voice and help the local analysts see things in a new and challenging way. Interacting with him would also open up the "geopolitical space" (Wolman, 2005) of the psychoanalytic society, making it more inclusive not only of the xenophobically avoided Other but also its own collectively repudiated aspects. And, new rituals of clinical practice (e.g., shaking hands, greater or lesser frequency of sessions) and supervision (e.g., silent supervisory sessions, held in the Norwegian Psychoanalytic Society, as described by Sletvold, 2014) become available for consideration.

Concluding remarks

Psychoanalysis is at a crossroads. On the one hand, the field is receiving valuable heuristic nourishment from neurophysiology, neonatal observational research, ethological observations, and, paradoxically, also from linguistics, hermeneutics, and social constructivism. On the other hand, insurance reimbursements for clinical work have all but evaporated, the candidate pool for psychoanalytic training has shrunk, and intra-group warfare on all sorts of issues (e.g., power-related, conceptual, technical) has become rampant. The splits that were characteristic of local and regional societies (see Kirsner, 2000, for details) are now threatening national organizations. What then is to be done in order to save psychoanalysis from psychoanalysts?[3]

The renowned psychoanalyst and a former president of the International Psychoanalytical Association, Otto Kernberg, has recently delineated measures that can prevent the profession from self-destruction. These include: (i) establishing a lifeline with local universities, (ii) developing psychoanalytically oriented psychotherapy programs, (iii) injecting research orientation into organized psychoanalysis, (iv) presenting a realistic public image of the achievements of psychoanalysis and its pertinence to the community, (v) finding innovative ways to impart psychoanalytic education, and (vi) overcoming resistances to the acceptance of the foregoing strategies. To this highly respectable list, I wish to add the need for a "cultural awakening" on the part of psychoanalysis. In this book, I have sought to illustrate how psychoanalysis can evolve beneficial dialectical ties with major areas of cultural concern. Far from the restricted interest in art, literature, and biography, psychoanalysis has an opportunity—more than ever before—to get involved in the realpolitik of ethnic conflict, prejudice, school bullying, gun violence, politics, and terrorism. This shift does not have to be at the cost of its clinical enterprise; it is meant to be additive. However, to produce culturally sensitive and culturally relevant psychoanalysts, we have to enlarge our candidate pool beyond individuals from only a few ethnicities and only certain social strata. We have to evolve curricula and scientific programs that appeal to a wider section of society-at-large: Christians, Muslims, Hindus, and, very important, the greatest victims of psychoanalytic neglect—African Americans and the people of Asian communities. It is only by such demographic inclusiveness and open-hearted and bilateral exchange of information that psychoanalysis can grow, become, and remain, culturally relevant. The great discoveries of Dr. Freud deserve no less.

Notes

1. The designation "scientific sessions" betrays a tendency in psychoanalysis to align itself with science in a desperate quest for legitimacy. The fact is that psychoanalysis, in my opinion, is a hybrid discipline that has overlaps with ethology, neuroscience, and evolutionary studies on the one hand, and anthropology, fiction, poetry, and sociology on the other hand.
2. At times, some "academic candidates" do change their mind and shift towards training to become psychoanalytic clinicians.
3. Rudnytsky's (2011) wry book, *Rescuing Psychoanalysis from Freud*, details the "prehistory" of the potentially deleterious effect of charismatic leaders in the psychoanalytic field upon furtherance of the discipline.

REFERENCES

Abbasi, A. (1998). Speaking the unspeakable. In: A. Helmreich & P. Marcus (Eds.), *Blacks and Jews on the Couch: Psychoanalytic Reflections on Black-Jewish Conflict* (pp. 133–147). Westport, CT: Praeger.

Abbasi, A. (2008). Whose side are you on?: Muslim analysts analyzing non-Muslim patients. In: S. Akhtar (Ed.), *The Crescent and the Couch: Cross-currents between Islam and Psychoanalysis* (pp. 335–350). New York: Other Press.

Abraham, K. (1912). Amenhotop IV: a psychoanalytical contribution towards the understanding of his personality and of the monotheistic cult of Aton. In: *Clinical Papers and Essays on Psycho-analysis* (pp. 262–290). New York: Brunner-Mazel, 1955.

Abuelaish, I. (2010). *I Shall Not Hate: A Gaza Doctor's Journey on the Road to Peace and Human Dignity*. New York: Walker.

Ad-Dab'bagh, Y. (2012). Puncturing the skin of the self: a psychoanalytic perspective on why prejudice hurts. *International Journal of Applied Psychoanalytic Studies*, 9: 23–34.

Adorno, T. (1951). *Minima Moralia: Reflections from Damaged Life*. London: Verso Press, 1978.

Adorno, T. (1956). *Against Epistemology: A Metacritique; Studies in Husserl and the Phenomenological Antinomies*. New York: Polity Press, 2013.

Adorno, T., & Frenkel-Brunswick, E. (1950). *The Authoritarian Personality*. New York: W. W. Norton.

Adorno, T., & Horkheimer, M. (1944). *Dialectic of Enlightenment*. Frankfurt am Main: Verlag GmbH.

Ahmed, L. (1992). *Women and Gender in Islam: Historical Roots of a Modern Debate*. New Haven, CT: Yale University Press.

Akhtar, S. (1994). Object constancy and adult psychopathology. *International Journal of Psychoanalysis, 75*: 441–455.

Akhtar, S. (1995). A third individuation: immigration, identity, and the psychoanalytic process. *Journal of the American Psychoanalytic Association, 43*: 1051–1084.

Akhtar, S. (1996). "Someday … " and "if only … " fantasies: pathological optimism and inordinate nostalgia as related forms of idealization. *Journal of the American Psychoanalytic Association, 44*: 723–753.

Akhtar, S. (1997). The psychodynamic dimension of terrorism. *Psychiatric Annals, 29*: 350–355.

Akhtar, S. (1998). From simplicity through contradiction to paradox: the evolving psychic reality of the borderline patient in treatment. *International Journal of Psychoanalysis, 79*: 241–252.

Akhtar, S. (1999a). The distinction between needs and wishes: implications for psychoanalytic theory and technique. *Journal of the American Psychoanalytic Association, 47*: 113–151.

Akhtar, S. (1999b). *Immigration and Identity: Turmoil, Treatment, and Transformation*. Northvale, NJ: Jason Aronson.

Akhtar, S. (1999c). Psychodynamic dimension of terrorism. *Psychiatric Annals, 29*: 350–355.

Akhtar, S. (2000). Mental pain and the cultural ointment of poetry. *International Journal of Psychoanalysis, 81*: 229–243.

Akhtar, S. (2003). Dehumanization: origins, manifestations, and remedies. In: S. Varvin & V. D. Volkan (Eds.), *Violence or Dialogue? Psychoanalytic Insights on Terror and Terrorism* (pp. 131–145). London: The International Psychological Association.

Akhtar, S. (Ed.) (2005a). *Freud Along the Ganges: Psychoanalytic Reflections on the People and Culture of India*. New York: Other Press.

Akhtar, S. (2005b). Hindu-Muslim relations in India: past, present, and future. In: S. Akhtar (Ed.), *Freud Along the Ganges* (pp. 91–137). New York: Other Press.

Akhtar, S. (2005c). *Objects of Our Desire*. New York: Harmony.

Akhtar, S. (2006). Technical challenges faced by the immigrant analyst. *Psychoanalytic Quarterly, 75*: 21–43.

Akhtar, S. (2007a). Four roadblocks in approaching Masud Khan. *Psychoanalytic Quarterly, 76*: 991–995.

Akhtar, S. (2007b). From unmentalized xenophobia to messianic sadism: some reflections on the phenomenology of prejudice. In: H. Parens, A. Mahfouz, S. W. Twemlow, & D. E. Scharff (Eds.), *The Future of Prejudice: Psychoanalysis and the Prevention of Prejudice* (pp. 7–19). Lanham, MD: Jason Aronson.

Akhtar, S. (2008a). Muslims in the psychoanalytic world. In: S. Akhtar (Ed.), *The Crescent and the Couch: Cross-currents Between Islam and Psychoanalysis* (pp. 315–333). Lanham, MD: Jason Aronson.

Akhtar, S. (Ed.) (2008b). *The Crescent and the Couch: Cross-currents Between Islam and Psychoanalysis*. Lanham, MD: Jason Aronson.

Akhtar, S. (2008c). A bit of prose about poetry. *International Journal of Applied Psychoanalytic Studies, 5*: 90–96.

Akhtar, S. (Ed.) (2009a). *Freud and the Far East: Psychoanalytic Perspectives on the People and Culture of China, Japan, and Korea*. Lanham, MD: Jason Aronson.

Akhtar, S. (2009b). *Comprehensive Dictionary of Psychoanalysis*. London: Karnac.

Akhtar, S. (2011a). *Immigration and Acculturation: Mourning, Adaptation, and the Next Generation*. Lanham, MD: Jason Aronson.

Akhtar, S. (2011b). *Matters of Life and Death: Psychoanalytic Reflections*. London: Karnac.

Akhtar, S. (2012). *The African American Experience: Psychoanalytic Perspectives*. Lanham, MD: Jason Aronson.

Akhtar, S. (2013). *Psychoanalytic Listening: Methods, Limits, and Innovations*. London: Karnac.

Akhtar, S. (2014). Mental pain of minorities. *British Journal of Psychotherapy, 30*: 136–153.

Akhtar, S. (2015). Editor's introduction: challenging the Western caricature of Muslim women. *International Journal of Applied Psychoanalytic Studies, 12*: 357–358.

Akhtar, S. (2016). Editorial: Charlie is no Chaplain! *International Journal of Applied Psychoanalytic Studies, 13*: 213.

Akhtar, S., & Brown, J. (2003). Animals in psychiatric symptomatology. In: *The Mental Zoo: Animals in the Human Mind and Its Pathology* (pp. 3–38). Madison, CT: International Universities Press.

Akhtar, S., & Choi, L. (2004). When evening falls: the immigrant's encounter with middle and old age. *American Journal of Psychoanalysis, 64*: 183–191.

Akhtar, S., & Tummala-Narra, P. (2005). Psychoanalysis in India. In: S. Akhtar (Ed.), *Freud Along the Ganges: Psychoanalytic Reflections on the People and Culture of India* (pp. 3–25). New York: Other Press.

Akhtar, S., & Twemlow, S. (2018). *Textbook of Applied Psychoanalysis*. London: Karnac.

Alderdice, J. L. (2018). Terror and terrorism. In: S. Akhtar & S. W. Twemlow, *Textbook of Applied Psychoanalysis* (pp. 183–198). London: Karnac Books.

All That Jazz (1979). Directed by Bob Fosse, produced by Columbia Pictures Corporation.

Alperovitz, G. (1995). *The Decision to Use the Atomic Bomb: the Architecture of an American Myth*. New York: Alfred A. Knopf.

Altman, N. (2004). *The Analyst in the Inner City: Race, Class, and Culture Through a Psychoanalytic Lens*. Hillsdale, NJ: Analytic Press.

Amati-Mehler, J., Argentieri, S., & Cansestri, J. (1993). *The Babel of the Unconscious: Mother Tongue and Foreign Languages in the Psychoanalytic Dimension*. J. Whitelaw-Cucco (Trans.). Madison, CT: International Universities Press.

Antokolitz, J. C. (1993). A psychoanalytic view of cross-cultural passages. *American Journal of Psychoanalysis, 53*: 35–54.

Atran, S. (2003). Genesis of suicide terrorism. *Science, 299*: 1534–1539.

Auerhahn, N. C., & Laub, D. (1987). Play and playfulness in Holocaust survivors. *Psychoanalytic Study of the Child, 42*: 45–58.

Auster, L. (1990). *The Path to National Suicide: An Essay on Immigration and Multiculturalism*. Monterey, VA: The American Immigration Control Foundation.

Aviram, R. (2009). *The Relational Origins of Prejudice: A Convergence of Psychoanalytic and Social Cognitive Perspectives*. Lanham, MD: Jason Aronson.

Awad, G. (2003). The minds and perceptions of "the others". In: S. Varvin & V. D. Volkan (Eds.), *Violence or Dialogue? Psychoanalytic Insights on Terror and Terrorism* (pp. 153–176). London: The International Psychological Association.

Bach, S. (1977). On narcissistic fantasies. *International Review of Psychoanalysis, 4*: 281–293.

Back to the Future (1985). Directed by R. Zemeckis, produced by Universal Pictures.

Bacon, D. (2008). *Illegal People: How Globalization Creates Migration and Criminalizes Immigration*. Boston, MA: Beacon.

Bailey, B. (2000). Communicative behavior and conflict between African-American customers and Korean immigrant retailers in Los Angeles. *Discourse and Society, 11*(1): 86–108.

Barthes, R. (2009). *Mourning Diary*. New York: Hill & Wang.

Bawer, B. (2007). *While Europe Slept: How Radical Islam Is Destroying the West from Within*. New York: Anchor.

Beginners (2010). Directed by M. Mills, an Olympics Pictures production.

Begley, L. (1993). *The Man Who Was Late*. New York: Alfred A. Knopf.

Bergler, E. (1949). *The Basic Neurosis: Oral Regression and Psychic Masochism*. New York: Grune & Stratton.

Berkeley-Hill, O. (1921). The anal-erotic factor in the religion, philosophy, and character of the Hindus. *International Journal of Psychoanalysis*, 2: 306–338.

Berry, J. W., & Kim, U. (1988). Acculturation and mental health. In: P. Dasen, J. Berry, & N. Sartorius (Eds.), *Health and Cross-Cultural Psychology: Towards Applications* (pp. 207–236). London: Sage.

Bion, W. R. (1957). Differentiation of the psychotic from the non-psychotic personalities. *International Journal of Psychoanalysis*, 38: 266–275.

Bion, W. R. (1962a). A theory of thinking. *International Journal of Psychoanalysis*, 43: 306–310.

Bion, W. R. (1962b). *Learning From Experience*. London: Karnac, 1984.

Bion, W. R. (1967). *Second Thoughts*. London: Heinemann.

Bird, B. (1957). A consideration of the etiology of prejudice. *Journal of the American Psychoanalytic Association*, 5: 490–513.

Blos, P. (1967). The second individuation process of adolescence. *Psychoanalytic Study of the Child*, 22: 162–186.

Blue (1993). Directed by K. Kie lowski, an International co-production.

Blumenfeld, L. (2002). *Revenge: A Story of Hope*. New York: Washington Square.

Bohleber, W. (2003). Collective phantasms, destructiveness, and terrorism. In: S. Varvin & V. D. Volkan (Eds.), *Violence or Dialogue? Psychoanalytic Insights on Terror and Terrorism* (pp. 111–130). London: The International Psychological Association.

Bollas, C. (1992). *Being a Character*. New York: Hill & Wang.

Bonovitz, J. (1998). Reflections of the self. In: S. Akhtar & S. Kramer (Eds.), *The Colors of Childhood: Separation-Individuation Across Cultural, Racial, and Ethnic Differences* (pp. 169–188). Northvale, NJ: Jason Aronson.

Booth, W. (2016). Israel angered over diplomat's comment. *Philadelphia Inquirer*, January 20, p. A-2.

Borum, R. C. (2004). *Psychology of Terrorism*. Tampa, FL: University of South Florida Press.

Brearley, M. (2018). Sports. In: S. Akhtar & S. W. Twemlow (Eds.), *Textbook of Applied Psychoanalysis* (pp. 129–138). London: Karnac.

Brenner, I. (1988). Multisensory bridges in response to object loss during the Holocaust. *Psychoanalytic Review*, 75: 573–587.

Brenner, I. (2001). *Dissociation of Trauma: Theory, Phenomenology, and Technique*. Madison, CT: International Universities Press.

Brenner, I. (2004). *Psychic Trauma: Dynamics, Symptoms, and Treatment*. Northvale, NJ: Jason Aronson.

Burston, D. (2002). Erich Fromm. In: E. Erwin (Ed.), *The Freud Encyclopedia* (pp. 231–232). New York: Routledge.

Cadge, W., & Ecklund, E. H. (2007). Immigration and religion. *Annual Review of Sociology, 33*: 359–379.

Card, D. (1990). Impact on the Mariel Boatlift on the Miami labor market. *Industrial and Labor Relations Review, 43*: 245–257.

Carter, J. (1987). *Palestine: Peace Not Apartheid.* New York: Simon & Schuster, 2006.

Chang, L. (2009). *Factory Girls: From Village to City in a Changing China.* New York: Spiegel & Grau.

Chasseguet-Smirgel, J. (1984). *Creativity and Perversion.* New York: W. W. Norton.

Cheng, F. (1985). Le cas du chinois. In: J. Bennani (Ed.), *Du Bilinguisme* (pp. 13–27). Paris: Denoel.

Choi-Kain, L. (2009). Second-generation Korean Americans. In: S. Akhtar (Ed.), *Freud and the Far East: Psychoanalytic Perspectives on the People and Culture of China, Japan, and Korea* (pp. 215–233). Lanham, MD: Jason Aronson.

Chomsky, A. (2007). *They Take Our Jobs and 20 Other Myths about Immigration.* Boston, MA: Beacon.

Chomsky, N. (1992). What Uncle Sam really wants. In: *How the World Works* (pp. 1–73). London: Penguin, 2011.

Chomsky, N. (1994). Secrets, lies, and democracy. In: *How the World Works* (pp. 136–205). London: Penguin, 2011.

Chomsky, N. (2003). *Hegemony or Survival: America's Quest for Global Dominance.* New York: Henry Holt.

Citizen Kane (1941). Directed by O. Welles, an RKO Radio Pictures production.

Clarke, R. A. (2004). *Against All Enemies: Inside America's War on Terrorism.* New York: Free Press.

Coltart, N. (2000). *Slouching Towards Bethlehem.* New York: Other Press.

Cooper, A. M. (1988). The narcissistic-masochistic character. In: R. A. Glick & D. Myers (Eds.), *Masochism: Current Psychoanalytic Perspectives* (pp. 117–138). Hillsdale, NJ: Analytic Press.

Cox, T. (2001). *Creating the Multicultural Organization.* San Francisco, CA: Jossey-Bass.

Curtis, M. (2003). *Web of Deceit: Britain's Real Foreign Policy.* New York: Vintage.

Dahl, C. (1989). Some problems of cross-cultural psychotherapy with refugees seeking treatment. *American Journal of Psychoanalysis, 49*: 19–32.

Dangar-Daly, C. (1930). The psychology of revolutionary tendencies. *International Journal of Psychoanalysis, 11*: 193–210.

Davids, F. (2006). Internal racism, anxiety, and the world outside: Islamophobia post 9/11. *Organizational and Social Dynamics, 6*: 63–85.

Davids, F. (2011). *Internal Racism: A Psychoanalytic Approach to Race and Difference*. New York: Palgrave Macmillan.

De Montagnac, F. J. L. (1885). *Lettres d'un Soldat: Neuf Annees de Campagnes en Afrique*. Paris: Destremeau, 1998.

Deo, M. E., Lee, J. J., Chin, C. B., Milman, N., & Yuen, N. W. (2008). Missing in action: "framing" race on prime-time television. *Social Justice, 35*: 145–162.

Deraniyagala, S. (2013). *Wave*. New York: Vintage.

Diagnostic and Statistical Manual for Mental Disorders-IV (1994). Washington, DC: American Psychiatric Publishing.

Didion, J. (2006). *The Year of Magical Thinking*. New York: Vintage.

Doi, T. (1962). Amae: a key concept for understanding Japanese personality structure. In: R. J. Smith & R. K. Beardsley (Eds.), *Japanese Culture: Its Development and Characteristics* (pp. 121–129). Chicago, IL: Aldine.

Doi, T. (1989). The concept of amae and its psychoanalytic implications. *International Review of Psychoanalysis, 16*: 349–354.

Ebaugh, H. R. F., & Chafetz, J. S. (2000). *Religion and the New Immigrants: Continuities and Adaptations in Immigrant Congregations*. Walnut Creek, CA: Alta Mira.

Ehrenfeld, R. (2003). *Funding Evil: How Terrorism Is Financed and How to Stop It*. New York: Taylor Trade Publishing.

Ellis, B. (1991). *The American Psycho*. New York: Vintage.

Ellison, R. (1947). *The Invisible Man*. New York: Random House, 1952.

Elovitz, P., & Kahn, C. (1997). *Immigrant Experiences: Personal Narrative and Psychological Analysis*. Cranbury, NJ: Associated University Presses.

Elshtain, J. B. (1992). Reflections on war and political discourse: realism, just war, and feminism in a nuclear age. In: J. B. Elshtain (Ed.), *Just War Theory* (pp. 260–279). New York: New York University Press.

Emily, J. (2002). Mom locked girl in closet to forget. *The Dallas Morning News*, November 7.

Erikson, E. H. (1950). *Childhood and Society*. New York: W. W. Norton, 1963.

Erikson, E. H. (1954). The dream specimen of psychoanalysis. *Journal of the American Psychoanalytic Association, 2*: 5–56.

Erikson, E. H. (1956). The problem of ego identity. *Journal of the American Psychoanalytic Association, 4*: 56–121.

Erikson, E. H. (1958). *Young Man Luther: A Study in Psychoanalysis and History*. New York: W. W. Norton.

Erikson, E. H. (1959). *Identity and the Life Cycle: Psychological Issues Monograph: I*. New York: International Universities Press.

Erikson, E. H. (1969). *Gandhi's Truth: On the Origins of Militant Nonviolence*. New York: W. W. Norton.

Erikson, E. H. (1975). *Life History and the Historical Moment.* New York: W. W. Norton.

Erikson, E. H. (1980). Elements of a psychoanalytic theory of psychosocial development. In: S. I. Greenspan & G. H. Pollock (Eds.), *The Course of Life: Psychoanalytic Contributions Toward Understanding Personality Development, Volume I: Infancy and Early Childhood* (pp. 11–61). Adelphi, MD: National Institute of Mental Health.

Erikson, E. H. (1982). *The Life Cycle Completed: A Review.* New York: W. W. Norton.

Esposito, J. L., & Mogahed, D. (2007). *Who Speaks for Islam?: What a Billion Muslims Really Think.* New York: Gallup.

Faimberg, H. (2005). *Telescoping of Generations: Listening to the Narcissistic Links Between Generations.* London: Routledge.

Fanon, F. (1952). *Black Skin, White Masks.* R. Philcox (Trans.). New York: Grove, 2008.

Fanon, F. (1959). *A Dying Colonialism.* H. Chevalier (Trans.). New York: Grove, 1994.

Fanon, F. (1963). *The Wretched of the Earth.* New York: Grove.

Father of the Bride (1991). Directed by C. Shyer, a Touchstone Pictures production.

Feder, S. (1981). Gustav Mahler: the music of fratricide. *International Review of Psychoanalysis, 8*: 257–284.

Fenichel, O. (1946). Elements of a psychoanalytic theory of anti-Semitism. In: *The Collected Papers of Otto Fenichel, Vol. II* (pp. 335–348). New York: W. W. Norton, 1954.

Fitzgerald, F. S. (1925). *The Great Gatsby.* New York: Scribner, 2010.

Fivush, R. (2001). Owning experience: the development of subjective perspective in autobiographical memory. In: P. Miller & E. Scholnick (Eds.), *The Self In Time: Developmental Perspectives* (pp. 85–106). New York: Cambridge University Press.

Fivush, R. (2010). Speaking silence: the social construction of silence in autobiographical and cultural narratives. *Memory, 18*: 88–98.

Fivush, R., & Nelson, K. (2004). Culture and language in the emergence of autobiographical memory. *Psychological Science, 15*: 586–590.

Fonagy, P., & Higgitt, A. C. (2007). The development of prejudice: an attachment theory hypothesis explaining its ubiquity. In: H. Parens, A. Mahfouz, S. Twemlow, & D. E. Scharff (Eds.), *The Future of Prejudice: Psychoanalysis and the Prevention of Prejudice* (pp. 63–79). Lanham, MD: Jason Aronson.

Fonagy, P., & Target, M. (1997). Attachment and reflective function: their role in self-organization. *Development and Psychopathology, 9*: 679–700.

Frances (1982). Directed by K. Reisz, a Brooksfilms production.

Frank, J. (2004). *Bush on the Couch: Inside the Mind of the President*. New York: Regan.

Franklin, S., & Little, D. (2006). Fear of retaliation trumps pain: deaths, injuries on the job soar for illegal immigrants. *Chicago Tribune*, September 3.

Freedman, D., & Thussu, D. (2012). *Media and Terrorism: Global Perspectives*. Thousand Oaks, CA: Sage.

Freeman, D. M. A. (1993). Looking, precocious individuation and appeal behavior portrayed in Ukiyo-e Art of the 17th-19th centuries. Presented at The American Psychoanalytic Association Interdisciplinary Colloquium on Child Development and Amae, December.

Freeman, D. M. A. (1996). Child development and shame experiences. In: O. Kitayama (Ed.), *Haji* (Shame) (pp. 65–102). Tokyo: Seiwa Shoten.

Freeman, D. M. A. (1998). Emotional refueling in development, mythology, and cosmology. In: S. Akhtar & S. Kramer (Eds.), *The Colors of Childhood: Separation-Individuation Across Cultural, Racial, and Ethnic Differences* (pp. 18–60). Northvale, NJ: Jason Aronson.

Freeman, D. M. A. (2009). Amae: East and West. In: S. Akhtar (Ed.), *Freud and the Far East: Psychoanalytic Perspectives on the People and Culture of China, Japan, and Korea* (pp. 71–88). Lanham, MD: Jason Aronson.

Freud, A. (1946). The psychoanalytic study of infantile feeding disturbances. *Psychoanalytic Study of the Child, 2*: 119–132.

Freud, S. (1900a). *The Interpretation of Dreams. S. E., 4–5*. London: Hogarth.

Freud, S. (1905d). *Three Essays on the Theory of Sexuality. S. E., 7*: 135–243. London: Hogarth.

Freud, S. (1907a). *Delusions and Dreams in Jensen's 'Gradiva'. S. E., 9*: 7–95. London: Hogarth.

Freud, S. (1908c). On the sexual theories of children. *S. E., 9*: 209–226. London: Hogarth.

Freud, S. (1910g). Contributions to a discussion on suicide. *S. E., 11*: 231–232. London: Hogarth.

Freud, S. (1910h). A special type of choice of object made by men. *S. E., 11*: 163–165. London: Hogarth.

Freud, S. (1911c). Psycho-analytic notes on an autobiographical account of a case of paranoia (dementia paranoides). *S. E., 12*: 3–82. London: Hogarth.

Freud, S. (1912d). On the universal tendency to debasement in the sphere of love (Contributions to the psychology of love, II). *S. E., 11*: 178–190. London: Hogarth.

Freud, S. (1914b). The Moses of Michaelangelo. *S. E., 13*: 209–238. London: Hogarth.

Freud, S. (1915c). Instincts and their vicissitudes. *S. E., 14*: 117–140. London: Hogarth.

Freud, S. (1916–1917). *Introductory Lectures on Psycho-Analysis. S. E.*, *15–16*. London: Hogarth.

Freud, S. (1917e). Mourning and melancholia. *S. E.*, *14*: 237–258. London: Hogarth.

Freud, S. (1918a). The taboo of virginity. *S. E.*, *11*: 193–208. London: Hogarth.

Freud, S. (1921c). *Group Psychology and the Analysis of the Ego. S. E.*, *18*: 65–144. London: Hogarth.

Freud, S. (1923b). *The Ego and the Id. S. E.*, *19*: 1–66. London: Hogarth.

Freud, S. (1924d). The dissolution of the Oedipus complex. *S. E.*, *19*: 171–188. London: Hogarth.

Freud, S. (1926d). *Inhibitions, Symptoms and Anxiety. S. E.*, *20*: 75–175. London: Hogarth.

Freud, S. (1930a). *Civilization and Its Discontents. S. E.*, *21*: 59–145. London: Hogarth.

Freud, S. (1931a). Libidinal types. *S. E.*, *21*: 215–220. London: Hogarth.

Freud, S. (1933a). *New Introductory Lectures on Psycho-Analysis. S. E.*, *22*: 7–182. London: Hogarth.

Freud, S. (1933b). Why War? (letter to Albert Einstein). *S. E.*, *22*: 203–215. London: Hogarth.

Freud, S. (1936a). A disturbance of memory on the Acropolis. *S. E.*, *22*: 239–248. London: Hogarth.

Freud, S. (1937d). Constructions in analysis. *S. E.*, *23*: 255–269. London: Hogarth.

Freud, S. (1950a). Project for a scientific psychology. *S. E.*, *1*: 295–343. London: Hogarth.

Fried, R. (1982). The psychology of the terrorist. In: B. M. Jenkins (Ed.), *Terrorism and Beyond: An International Conference on Terrorism and Low Level Conflict* (pp. 119–124). Santa Monica, CA: Rand.

Fromm, E. (1941). *Escape from Freedom*. New York: Henry Holt.

Fukuyama, F. (1994). Immigrants and family values. In: N. Mills (Ed.), *Arguing Immigration: The Debate Over the Changing Face of America* (pp. 151–158). New York: Touchstone.

Furman, E. (1974). *A Child's Parent Dies: Studies in Childhood Bereavement*. New Haven, CT: Yale University Press.

Ganley, E. (2016). Muslim professionals speak out in France. *Philadelphia Inquirer*, August 3, p. A-12.

Garcia, M. O., & Rodriguez, P. F. (1989). Psychological effects of political repression in Argentina and El Salvador. In: D. R. Koslow & E. P. Salett (Eds.), *Crossing Cultures in Mental Health* (pp. 64–83). Washington, DC: SIETAR International.

Garza-Guerrero, C. (1974). Culture shock: its mourning and the vicissitudes of identity. *Journal of the American Psychoanalytic Association*, *22*: 408–429.

Gates, E. (2015). In the name of God: UVA team develops new approach to battling religion-based violence. *Virginia: The UVA Magazine*, Winter 2015: 41–45.

Gay, P. (1988). *Freud: A Life for Our Time.* New York: W. W. Norton.

Gitelson, M. (1952). Re-evaluation of the role of the Oedipus complex. *International Journal of Psychoanalysis, 33*: 351–354.

Gorkin, M. (1996). Countertransference in cross-cultural psychotherapy. In: R. Perez-Foster, M. Moskovitz, & R. Javier (Eds.), *Reaching Across Boundaries of Culture and Class* (pp. 47–70). Northvale, NJ: Jason Aronson.

Grand, S. (2000). *The Reproduction of Evil: A Clinical and Cultural Perspective.* Mahwah, NJ: Analytic Press.

Great Santini, The (1979). Directed by L. J. Carlino, produced by Bing Crosby Productions.

Green, A. (1999). The death drive, negative narcissism and the disobjectalising function. In: *The Work of the Negative.* A. Weller (Trans.). London: Free Association.

Griffin, F. (2016). *Creative Listening and the Psychoanalytic Process: Sensibility, Engagement, and Envisioning.* London: Routledge.

Grinberg, L., & Grinberg, R. (1989). *Psychoanalytic Perspectives on Migration and Exile.* N. Festinger (Trans.). New Haven, CT: Yale University Press.

Griswold, D. (2010). US needs to let more workers in. *Philadelphia Inquirer,* April 27, p. A-15.

Grubrich-Simitis, I. (1984). From concretism to metaphor: thoughts on some theoretical and technical aspects of the psychoanalytic work with children of Holocaust survivors. *Psychoanalytic Study of the Child, 39*: 301–319.

Gu, M. D. (2006). The filial piety complex: variations on the Oedipus theme in Chinese literature and culture. *Psychoanalytic Quarterly, 75*: 163–195.

Guskin, J., & Wilson, D. L. (2007). *The Politics of Immigration: Questions and Answers.* New York: Monthly Review Press.

Guzder, J. (2011). Second skins: family therapy agendas of migration, identity, and cultural change. *Fokus Pa Familien, 39*: 160–179.

Halstead, M. (1988). *Education, Justice, and Cultural Diversity: An Examination of the Honeyfield Affair 1984–1985.* London: Flamer.

Hamid, H. (2008). Basic history and tenets of Islam: a brief introduction. In: S. Akhtar (Ed.), *The Crescent and the Couch: Cross-Currents between Islam and Psychoanalysis* (pp. 3–20). Lanham, MD: Jason Aronson.

Hamid, M. (2007). *The Reluctant Fundamentalist.* New York: Harcourt.

Hartmann, H. (1939). *Ego Psychology and the Problem of Adaptation.* New York: International Universities Press.

Hartung, J. (1995). Love thy neighbour: the evolution of in-group morality. *Skeptic, 3*: 86–99.

Henry, C. (Ed.) (1996). *Ralph J. Bunche: Selected Speeches and Writings*. Ann Arbor, MI: University of Michigan Press.

Hitler, A. (1925–1926). *Mein Kampf*. Boston, MA: Houghton Mifflin, 1943.

Hoffman, B. (1998). *Inside Terrorism*. London: Victor Gollancz.

Hollander, N. (2010). *Uprooted Minds: Surviving the Politics of Terror in the Americas*. New York: Routledge.

Holmes, D. E. (1992). Race and transference in psychoanalysis and psychotherapy. *International Journal of Psychoanalysis, 73*: 1–11.

Holmes, D. E. (1999). Race and countertransference: two "blind spots" in psychoanalytic perception. *Journal of Applied Psychoanalytic Studies, 1*: 319–332.

Holmes, D. E. (2006). Success neurosis: what race and social class have to do with it. In: R. Moodley (Ed.), *Race, Culture, and Psychotherapy* (pp. 189–199). London: Routledge.

Holmes, D. E. (2012). Racial transference reactions in psychoanalytic treatment: an update. In: S. Akhtar (Ed.), *The African American Experience: Psychoanalytic Perspectives* (pp. 363–376). Lanham, MD: Jason Aronson.

Holmes, D. E. (2016). Come hither, American psychoanalysis: our complex multicultural America needs what we have to offer. *Journal of the American Psychoanalytic Association, 64*: 569–586.

Homayounpour, G. (2013). *Doing Psychoanalysis in Tehran*. Cambridge, MA: MIT Press.

Horney, K. (1937). *The Neurotic Personality of Our Times*. New York: W. W. Norton.

Horney, K. (1939). *New Ways in Psychoanalysis*. New York: W. W. Norton.

Houchins, L., & Houchins, C. S. (1974). The Korean experience in America, 1903–1924. *Pacific Historical Review, 43*: 548–573.

Huddle, D. (1993). *The Cost of Immigration*. Houston, TX: Carrying Capacity Network.

Huntington, S. P. (1996). *Clash of Civilizations and the Remaking of the World Order*. New York: Simon & Schuster.

Hurvich, M. (2003). The place of annihilation anxieties in psychoanalytic theory. *Journal of the American Psychoanalytic Association, 51*: 579–616.

Idliby, R., Oliver, S., & Warner, P. (2016). *The Faith Club: A Muslim, a Christian, and a Jew—Three Women Search for Understanding*. New York: Atria.

Imaginary Crimes (1994). Directed by A. Drazan, a Morgan Creek production.

Israelam.com. //www.timesofisrael.com/netanyahus-full-remarks-at-un-general-assembly. Accessed on April 15, 2017.

Jackson, J. J. (1988). Competition between blacks and immigrants. In: D. Simcox (Ed.), *U.S. Immigration in the 1980s: Reappraisal and Reform* (pp. 247–253). Washington, DC: Center for Immigration Studies.

Jacobson, E. (1954). The self and the object world: vicissitudes of their infantile cathexes and their influence on ideation and affective development. *Psychoanalytic Study of the Child, 9:* 75–127.

Jeong, D.-U. (2011). The Korean psychoanalytic movement and the IPA (1980–2010). In: P. Loewenberg & N. L. Thompson (Eds.), *100 Years of IPA: The Centenary History of the International Psychoanalytical Association 1910–2010: Evolution and Change* (pp. 404–411). London: Karnac.

Jeong, D.-U, & Sachs, D. (2009). Psychoanalysis in Korea. In: S. Akhtar (Ed.), *Freud and the Far East: Psychoanalytic Perspectives on the People and Culture of China, Japan, and Korea* (pp. 27–42). Lanham, MD: Jason Aronson.

Jones, E. (1929). Fear, guilt, and hate. *International Journal of Psychoanalysis, 10:* 383–397.

Jones, E. (1931). The problem of Paul Morphy—a contribution to the psychoanalysis of chess. *International Journal of Psychoanalysis, 12:* 1–23.

Jones, E. (1936). *The Elements of Figure Skating.* London: Methuen.

Jones, E. (1948). The death of Hamlet's father. *International Journal of Psychoanalysis, 29:* 174–176.

Judge, The (2014). Directed by D. Dobkin, a Warner Brothers production.

Kakar, S. (1990a). *Intimate Relations: Exploring Indian Sexuality.* Chicago, IL: University of Chicago Press.

Kakar, S. (1990b). *The Inner World: a Psychoanalytic Study of Child and Society in India.* London: Oxford University Press.

Kakar, S. (1991a). *The Analyst and the Mystic.* New Delhi: Viking.

Kakar, S. (1991b). *Shamans, Mystics, and Doctors: A Psychological Inquiry into India and Its Healing Traditions.* Chicago, IL: University of Chicago Press.

Kakar, S. (1993). *Identity and Adulthood.* London: Oxford University Press.

Kakar, S. (1996). *The Colors of Violence: Cultural Identities, Religion and Conflict.* Chicago, IL: University of Chicago Press.

Kaplan, S. (2008). *Children in Genocide: Extreme Traumatization and Affect Regulation.* London: Karnac.

Kareem, J., & Littlewood, R. (1992). *Intercultural Therapy: Themes, Interpretations, and Practice.* Oxford: Blackwell Scientific Publications.

Kayatekin, S. (2008). Christian Muslim relations: the axis of Balkans and the West. In: S. Akhtar (Ed.), *The Crescent and the Couch: Cross-currents Between Islam and Psychoanalysis* (pp. 199–216). Lanham, MD: Jason Aronson.

Kernberg, O. F. (1975). *Borderline Conditions and Pathological Narcissism.* Lanham, MD: Jason Aronson.

Kernberg, O. F. (1984). *Severe Personality Disorders: Psychotherapeutic Strategies.* New Haven, CT: Yale University Press.

Kernberg, O. F. (2012). Suicide prevention for psychoanalytic institutes and societies. *Journal of the American Psychoanalytic Association, 60:* 707–719.

Kestenberg, J., & Brenner, I. (1996). *The Last Witness: the Child Survivor of the Holocaust*. Washington, DC: American Psychiatric Press.

Khan, M. M. R. (1963). The concept of cumulative trauma. *Psychoanalytic Study of the Child*, 18: 286–306.

Khanna, R. (2004). *Dark Continents: Psychoanalysis and Colonialism*. Chapel Hill, NC: Duke University Press.

Kirmayer, L., Narasiah, L., Munoz, M., Rashid, M., Ryder, A., & Guzder, J. (2011). Common mental health problems in immigrants and refugees: general approach to the patient in primary care. *Canadian Medical Association Journal*, 183: 959–967.

Kirsner, D. (2000). *Unfree Associations: Inside Psychoanalytic Institutes*. London: Process Press.

Kirsner, D., & Snyder, E. (2009). Psychoanalysis in China. In: S. Akhtar (Ed.), *Freud and the Far East: Psychoanalytic Perspectives on the People and Culture of China, Japan, and Korea* (pp. 43–60). Lanham, MD: Jason Aronson.

Kitayama, O. (1991). The wounded caretaker and guilt. *International Review of Psycho-Analysis*, 18: 229–240.

Kitayama, O. (1997). Psychoanalysis in shame culture. *Bulletin of the American Society of Psychoanalytic Physicians*, 85(2): 47–50.

Kitayama, O. (1998). Transience: its beauty and danger. *International Journal of Psychoanalysis*, 70: 937–953.

Kitayama, O. (2004). Cross-cultural varieties in experiencing affect. In: S. Akhtar & H. Blum (Eds.), *The Language of Emotions* (pp. 33–48). Northvale, NJ: Jason Aronson.

Kitayama, O. (2009). Psychoanalysis in the "shame culture" of Japan: a "dramatic" point of view. In: S. Akhtar (Ed.), *Freud and the Far East: Psychoanalytic Perspectives on the People and Culture of China, Japan, and Korea* (pp. 89–103). Lanham, MD: Jason Aronson.

Kitayama, O. (2011). The "Japanese ways" in psychoanalysis. In: P. Loewenberg & N. L. Thompson (Eds.), *100 Years of IPA: The Centenary History of the International Psychoanalytical Association 1910–2010: Evolution and Change* (pp. 402–403). London: Karnac.

Klein, M. (1929). Personification in the play of children. *International Journal of Psychoanalysis*, 19: 193–214.

Klein, M. (1932). *The Psychoanalysis of Children*. New York: Free Press, 1975.

Klein, M. (1940). Mourning and its relation to manic depressive states. In: *Love, Guilt and Reparation and Other Works—1921–1945* (pp. 344–369). New York: Free Press, 1975.

Klein, M. (1946). Notes on some schizoid mechanisms. In: J. Riviere (Ed.), *Developments in Psychoanalysis* (pp. 292–320). London: Hogarth, 1952.

Klein, M. (1948). On the theory of anxiety and guilt. In: *Envy and Gratitude and Other Works—1946–1963* (pp. 25–42). London: Hogarth, 1975.

Klein, M. (1975). Love, guilt, and reparation. In: *Love, Guilt, and Reparation and Other Works—1921–1945* (pp. 306–343). New York: Free Press.

Kluft, R. P. (1985). Childhood multiple personality disorder: predictors, clinical findings, and treatment results. In: R. P. Kluft (Ed.), *Childhood Antecedents of Multiple Personality* (pp. 167–196). Washington, DC: American Psychiatric Press.

Kluft, R. P. (1993). Clinical approaches to the integration of personalities. In: R. P. Kluft & C. G. Fine (Eds.), *Clinical Perspectives on Multiple Personality Disorder* (pp. 101–134). Washington, DC: American Psychiatric Press.

Kogan, I. (1995). *The Cry of Mute Children—A Psychoanalytic Perspective of the Second Generation of the Holocaust*. New York: Free Association.

Kohut, H. (1972). Thoughts on narcissism and narcissistic rage. *Psychoanalytic Study of the Child, 27*: 360–400.

Kosawa, H. (1931). Two kinds of guilt feelings: the Ajase complex. In: S. Akhtar (Ed.), *Freud and the Far East: Psychoanalytic Perspectives on the People and Culture of China, Japan, and Korea* (pp. 61–70). Lanham, MD: Jason Aronson, 2009.

Kramer, S., & Akhtar, S. (1988). The developmental content of pre-oedipal internalized object relations. *Psychoanalytic Quarterly, 42*: 547–576.

Kris, E. (1952). *Psychoanalytic Explorations in Art*. New York: International Universities Press.

Kristeva, J. (1988). *Etrangers à nous mêmes*. Paris: Fayard.

Kristol, I. (1995). *Neoconservatism: The Autobiography of an Idea*. New York: Free Press.

Krogstad, J. M., & Radford, J. (2017). *Key Facts about Refugees to the US*. Philadelphia, PA: Pew Research Center.

Krystal, H. (1968). *Massive Psychic Trauma*. New York: International Universities Press.

Kurien, P. (1998). Becoming American by becoming Hindu: Indian-Americans take their place at the multicultural table. In: R. S. Warner & J. G. Wittner (Eds.), *Gatherings in Diaspora: Religious Communities and the New Immigration* (pp. 37–70). Philadelphia, PA: Temple University Press.

Kurien, P. (2001). Religion, ethnicity, and politics: Hindu and Muslim Indian immigrants in the United States. *Ethnic and Racial Studies, 24*: 263–293.

Lambert-Hurley, S., & Sharma, S. (2010). *Atiya's Journey: a Muslim Woman from Colonial Bombay to Edwardian Britain*. New Delhi: Oxford University Press.

Laub, D. (1998). The empty circle: children of survivors and the limits of reconstruction. *Journal of the American Psychoanalytic Association, 46*: 507–529.

Layton, L., Hollander, N. C., & Gutwill, S. (Eds.) (2006). *Psychoanalysis, Class and Politics: Encounters in the Clinical Setting*. London: Routledge.

Leary, K. (1995). Interpreting in the dark: race and ethnicity in psychoanalytic psychotherapy. *Psychoanalytic Psychology, 12*: 127–140.

Leary, K. (1997). Race, self-disclosure, and "forbidden talk": race, ethnicity in contemporary practice. *Psychoanalytic Quarterly, 66*: 163–189.

Leuzinger-Bohleber, M., Rickmeyer, C., Tahiri, M., Hettich, N., & Fischmann, T. (2016). What can psychoanalysis contribute to the current refugee crisis? *International Journal of Psychoanalysis, 97*: 1077–1093.

Lewis, C. S. (1961). *A Grief Observed*. New York: HarperCollins, 2015.

Lichtenstein, H. (1961). Identity and sexuality: a study of their interrelationship in man. *Journal of the American Psychoanalytic Association, 9*: 179–260.

Lichtenstein, H. (1963). The dilemma of human identity: notes on self-transformation, self-objectivation, and metamorphosis. *Journal of the American Psychoanalytic Association, 11*: 173–223.

Lien, P. (2004). Religion and political adaptation among Asian Americans: an empirical assessment from the Pilot National Asian American Political Survey. In: T. Carnes & F. Yang (Eds.), *Asian American Religions: The Making and Remaking of Borders and Boundaries* (pp. 263–284). New York: New York University Press.

Lipka, M. (2017). Muslims and Islam: key findings in the United States and around the world. *Pew Research Center FactTank*. Accessed March 9, 2017.

Listen Up, Philip (2014). Directed by A. R. Perry, a Sailor Bear production.

Liu, C. (2011). The Formosa model: an emerging tradition of developing psychoanalysis in Taiwan. In: P. Loewenberg & N. L. Thompson (Eds.), *100 Years of IPA: The Centenary History of the International Psychoanalytical Association 1910–2010: Evolution and Change* (pp. 412–418). London: Karnac.

Loewenberg, P. (1995). *Fantasy and Reality in History*. New York: Oxford University Press.

Lyman, R. (2017). Already hostile to migrants, Hungary starts detaining them. *The New York Times*, April 19, A-1, A-8.

Mack, J. (1976). *A Prince of Our Disorder: The Life of T. E. Lawrence*. Boston, MA: Little, Brown.

Mahdawi, A. (2017). The 712 page Google document that proves Muslims do condemn terrorism. *The Guardian*, March 26. www.theguardian.com, accessed April 4, 2017.

Mahler, M. S., Pine, F., & Bergman, A. (1975). *The Psychological Birth of the Human Infant: Symbiosis and Individuation*. New York: Basic Books.

Marcus, P. (2015). *Sports as Soul-Craft: How Playing and Watching Sports Enhances Life*. Milwaukee, WI: Marquette University Press.

Marcuse, H. (1955). *Eros and Civilization*. New York: Athenaeum Library of Philosophy.

McCarthy, K. F., & Burciaga Valdez, R. (1985). *Current and Future Effects of Mexican Immigration in California*. Santa Monica, CA: Rand Corporation.

McCauley, C., Stitt, C. L., & Segal, M. (1980). Stereotyping: from prejudice to prediction. *Psychological Bulletin, 87*: 195–208.

Me, Myself, and Irene (2000). Directed by B. Farrelly and P. Farrelly, a Twentieth Century Fox production.

Meyer, B. C. (1970). *Joseph Conrad: A Psychoanalytical Biography*. Princeton, NJ: Princeton University Press.

Meyer, B. C. (1976). *Houdini: A Mind in Chains: a Psychoanalytic Portrait*. New York: Dutton.

Mikhail, A. (2017). Old world order: how a quartet of powerful 16th century rulers shaped a continent. *The New York Times Book Review*, May 7, p. 19.

Miles, J. (1994). Blacks vs browns. In: N. Mills (Ed.), *Arguing Immigration: The Debate over the Changing Face of America* (pp. 101–142). New York: Touchstone.

Mines, R. (1985). Undocumented immigrants and California industries: reflections on research. *Hearings of the Intergovernmental Relations Committee*, November 1.

Mish, F. C. (Ed.) (1998). *Merriam-Webster's Collegiate Dictionary (10th Edition)*. Springfield, MA: Merriam-Webster.

Mitra, D. (2008). Punjabi-American taxi drivers: the new white working class? *Journal of Asian American Studies, 11*: 303–336.

Mohammad-Arif, A. (2002). *Salaam America: South Asian Muslims in New York*. London: Anthem.

Mommy (2014). Directed by X. Dolan, produced by Les Films Séville.

Money, J., & Ehrhardt, A. (1972). *Man, Woman, Boy, and Girl*. Baltimore, MD: Johns Hopkins University Press.

Montville, J. (1987). The arrow and the olive branch: a case for track II diplomacy. In: J. W. McDonald, Jr. & D. B. Bendahmane (Eds.), *Conflict Resolution: Track II Diplomacy* (pp. 5–20). Washington, DC: US Government Printing Office.

Montville, J. (1991). Psychoanalytic enlightenment and the greening of diplomacy. In: V. D. Volkan, J. V. Montville, and D. A. Julius (Eds.), *The Psychodynamics of International Relationships, Vol II* (pp. 177–192). Lexington, MA: Lexington.

Montville, J. (2008). Jewish-Muslim relations: Middle East. In: S. Akhtar (Ed.), *The Crescent and the Couch: Cross-currents Between Islam and Psychoanalysis* (pp. 217–230). Lanham, MD: Jason Aronson.

Moore, M. (2009). Wa: harmony and sustenance of the self in Japanese life. In: S. Akhtar (Ed.), *Freud and the Far East: Psychoanalytic Perspectives on the People and Culture of China, Japan, and Korea* (pp. 79–88). Lanham, MD: Jason Aronson.

Moore, S., Gallaway, L., & Vedder, R. (1994). Immigration and unemployment: new evidence. *Melting Pot, 7*: 103.

Mori, S. (2011). Globalization and the importation of psychoanalysis into Japan. In: P. Loewenberg & N. L. Thompson (Eds.), *100 Years of IPA: The Centenary History of the International Psychoanalytical Association 1910–2010: Evolution and Change* (pp. 390–401). London: Karnac.

Movahedi, S. (1996). Metalinguistic analysis of therapeutic discourse: flight into a second language when the analyst and the analysand are multilingual. *Journal of the American Psychoanalytic Association, 44*: 837–862.

Muller, T., & Espenshade, T. J. (1985). *The Fourth Wave: California's Newest Immigrants*. Washington, DC: Urban Institute Press.

My Girl (1991). Directed by H. Zieff, produced by Columbia Pictures Corporation.

Nacos, B. (2016). *Mass Media Terrorism: Mainstream and Digital Media in Terrorism and Counterterrorism*. Lanham, MD: Rowman Littlefield.

Nagel, J. J. (2007). Melodies of the mind: Mozart in 1778. *American Imago, 64*: 23–36.

Nagel, J. J. (2010). Melodies in my mind. *Journal of the American Psychoanalytic Association, 58*: 649–662.

Nagel, J. J., & Nagel, L. (2005). Animals, music, and psychoanalysis. In: S. Akhtar & V. D. Volkan (Eds.), *Cultural Zoo: Animals in the Human Mind and Its Sublimations* (pp. 145–176). Madison, CT: International Universities Press.

Nandi, A. (1983). *The Intimate Enemy: The Loss and Recovery of Self under Colonialism*. Oxford: Oxford University Press.

Nash, J. R. (1998). *Terrorism in the 20th Century*. New York: M. Evans.

Nemeth, C. J. (1985). Dissent, group process, and creativity. *Advances in Group Processes, 2*: 57–75.

Neubauer, P. B. (1960). The one-parent child and his Oedipal development. *Psychoanalytic Study of the Child, 15*: 286–309.

Newton, M. (2002). *Savage Girls and Wild Boys*. Philadelphia, PA: Faber and Faber.

Ng, M. (2002). Seeking the Christian tutelage: agency and culture in Chinese immigrants' conversion to Christianity. *Sociology of Religions, 63*: 195–214.

Niederland, W. (1968). Clinical observations on the "survivor syndrome". *International Journal of Psychoanalysis, 49*: 313–315.

Niemann, Y. F. (2003). The psychology of tokenism: psychosocial realities of faculty of color. In: G. Bernal, J. Trimble, A. K. Burlew, & F. T. Leong

(Eds.), *Handbook of Racial and Ethnic Minority Psychology* (pp. 100–118). Thousand Oaks, CA: Sage.

Nin, A. (1976). *In Favor of the Sensitive Man, and Other Essays*. New York: Harcourt, Brace, 1976.

Noonan, P. (1994). Why the world comes here. In: N. Mills (Ed.), *Arguing Immigration: The Debate over the Changing Face of America* (pp. 176–180). New York: Touchstone.

Ogden, T. H. (1997). Listening: Three Frost poems. *Psychoanalytic Dialogues*, 7: 619–639.

Ogden, T. H. (1998). A question of voice in poetry and psychoanalysis. *Psychoanalytic Quarterly*, 67: 426–448.

Ogden, T. H. (1999). "The music of what happens" in poetry and psychoanalysis. *International Journal of Psychoanalysis*, 80: 979–994.

Okinogi, K. (2009). Psychoanalysis in Japan. In: S. Akhtar (Ed.), *Freud and the Far East: Psychoanalytic Perspectives on the People and Culture of China, Japan, and Korea* (pp. 9–26). Lanham, MD: Jason Aronson.

Olsson, P. (2007). *The Cult of Osama: Pyschoanalyzing Bin Laden and His Magnetism for Muslim Youth*. New York: Praeger.

Ordinary People (1980). Directed by R. Redford, produced by Paramount Pictures.

Pacella, B. (1980). The primal matrix configuration. In: R. F. Lax, S. Bach, & J. A. Burland (Eds.), *Rapprochement: The Critical Subphase of Separation-Individuation* (pp. 117–131). New York: Jason Aronson.

Papadopoulos, R. K. (2002). *Therapeutic Care for Refugees: No Place Like Home*. London: Karnac.

Pape, R. A. (2005). *Dying to Win: the Strategic Logic of Suicide Terrorism*. New York: Random House.

Paper Moon (1973). Directed by P. Bogdanovich, produced by The Directors Company.

Parens, H. (1998). Prejudice: benign and malignant. Paper presented at Grand Rounds at the Department of Psychiatry and Human Behavior at Jefferson Medical College, Philadelphia, PA.

Parens, H. (1999). Toward the prevention of prejudice. In: *At the Threshold of the Millennium: A Selection of the Proceedings of the Conference, Vol. II* (pp. 131–141). Lima: Prom Peru.

Parens, H. (2007). Toward understanding prejudice: benign and malignant. In: H. Parens, A. Mahfouz, S. W. Twemlow, & D. E. Scharff (Eds.), *The Future of Prejudice: Psychoanalysis and the Prevention of Prejudice* (pp. 21–36). Lanham, MD: Jason Aronson.

Parens, H., Mahfouz, A., Twemlow, S. W., & Scharff, D. E. (2007). *The Future of Prejudice*. Lanham, MD: Jason Aronson.

Passel, J. S. (1994). *Immigrants and Taxes: A Reappraisal of Huddle's "The Cost of Immigrants"*. Washington, DC: Urban Institute.

Passel, J. S. (2006). The size and characteristics of the unauthorized migration population in the United States. *Pew Hispanic Center Bulletin*, March 7.

Perez-Foster, R., Moskowitz, M., & Javier, R. A. (1996). *Reaching Across Boundaries of Culture and Class*. Northvale, NJ: Jason Aronson.

Picture of Dorian Gray, The (1945). Directed by A. Lewin, produced by Metro-Goldwyn-Mayer.

Pine, F. (1988). The four psychologies of psychoanalysis and their place in clinical work. *Journal of the American Psychoanalytic Association, 36*: 671–696.

Pollock, G. H. (1970). Anniversary reactions, trauma, and mourning. *Psychoanalytic Quarterly, 39*: 347–371.

Pollock, G. H. (1972). On mourning and anniversaries: the relationship of culturally constituted defensive systems to intrapsychic adaptive process. *Israel Annals of Psychiatry, 10*: 9–40.

Pollock, G. H. (1976). Manifestations of abnormal mourning: homicide and suicide following the death of another. *Annals of Psychoanalysis, 4*: 225–249.

Ponette (1996). Directed by J. Doillon, produced by Les Films Alain Sarde.

Portes, A., & Jensen, L. (1989). The enclave and entrants: patterns of ethnic enterprise in Miami before and after Mariel. *American Sociological Review, 54*: 929–949.

Portes, A., & Rumbaut, R. G. (1996). *Immigrant America: A Portrait*. Berkeley, CA: University of California Press.

Powell, D. (2012). Psychoanalysis and African Americans: past, present, and future. In: S. Akhtar (Ed.), *The African American Experience: Psychoanalytic Perspectives* (pp. 59–84). Lanham, MD: Jason Aronson.

Prakash, K. M., & Lo, Y. L. (2004). The role of clinical neurophysiology in bioterrorism. *Acta Neurologica Scandinavica*, December 9.

Prathikanti, S. (1997). East Indian American families. In: E. Lee (Ed.), *Working with Asian Americans: A Guide to Clinicians* (pp.79–100). New York: Guilford.

Proust, M. (1913). *A Remembrance of Things Past*. London: Wordsworth, 2006.

Raising Cain (1992). Directed by B. de Palma, produced by Pacific Western.

Rajagopal, A. (2000). Hindu nationalism in the United States: changing configurations of political practice. *Ethnic and Racial Studies, 23*: 467–496.

Ramana, C. V. (1964). On the early history and development of psychoanalysis in India. *Journal of the American Psychoanalytic Association, 12*: 110–134.

Random House Dictionary of the English Language, The (1996). New York: Random House.

Rickman, J. (1924). Photography as a pseudo-perversion. *International Journal of Psychoanalysis, 6*: 238.

Roheim, G. (1934). *Origins and Functions of Culture*. New York: Anchor, 1971.

Roheim, G. (1943). *Fire in the Dragon and Other Psychoanalytic Essays on Folklore*. Princeton, NJ: Princeton University Press, 1992.

Roheim, G. (1947). *Psychoanalytic and Social Sciences*. New York: Holley, 2011.

Roland, A. (1996). *Cultural Pluralism and Psychoanalysis: The Asian and North American Experience*. New York: Routledge.

Roland, A. (2011). *Journeys to Foreign Selves: Asians and Asian Americans in a Global Era*. New Delhi: Oxford University Press.

Romano, C. (2006). Author sees growing Muslim enclaves hoping to rule Europe: review of "While Europe Slept: How Radical Islam is Destroying the West from Within" by B. Bawer. *Philadelphia Inquirer*, February 19, p. H-12.

Rubin, T. (2016). Fight jihad with hope in Molenbeek. *Philadelphia Inquirer*, March 23, p. A-15.

Rudnytsky, P. L. (2011). *Rescuing Psychoanalysis from Freud and Other Essays in Re-Vision*. London: Karnac.

Rushdie, S. (1980). *Midnight's Children*. London: Penguin, 1988.

Ryan, M. (2017). US owns up to Iraq strike. *Philadelphia Inquirer*, March 26, p. A-15.

Sachs, S. (2002). Interview of Laura Blumenfeld. *New York Times*, April 6, p. B-9.

Sagerman, M. (2004). *Understanding Terrorist Networks*. Philadelphia, PA: University of Pennsylvania Press.

Said, A. A., & Jensen, B. (2006). Islam and the West trapped in lies told about each other. *Philadelphia Inquirer*, February 9, p. A-19.

Said, E. (1978). *Orientalism*. New York: Pantheon.

Sanchez-Mazas, M., & Casini, A. (2005). Egalité formelle et obstacles informels à l'ascension professionnelle: les femmes et l'effet "plafond de verre". *Social Science Information, 44*: 141–173.

Sanchez-Mazas, M., & Casini, A. (2009). "To climb or not to climb?: when minorities stick to the floor. In: F. Butera & J. M. Levine (Ed.), *Coping with Minority Status: Responses to Exclusion and Inclusion* (pp. 38–54). New York: Cambridge University Press.

Sandler, J. (1960). The background of safety. *International Journal of Psychoanalysis, 41*: 352–363.

Sartre, J.-P. (1946). *No Exit and Three Others Plays*. New York: Vintage.

Schreiber, F. R. (1973). *Sybil*. New York: Warner, 2009.

Settlage, C. F. (1992). Psychoanalytic observations on adult development in life and in the therapeutic relationship. *Psychoanalytic Contemporary Thought*, *15*: 349–374.

Settlage, C. F. (1998). A cross-cultural perspective on separation-individuation theory. In: S. Akhtar & S. Kramer (Eds.), *The Colors of Childhood: Separation-Individuation Across Cultural, Racial, and Ethnic Differences* (pp. 61–78). Northvale, NJ: Jason Aronson.

Shaheed, F., & Shaheed, A. L. (2011). *Great Ancestors*. Karachi, Pakistan: Oxford University Press.

Shapiro, E., & Pinsker, H. (1973). Shared ethnic scotoma. *American Journal of Psychiatry*, *130*: 1338–1341.

Sharma, A. (2000). *Kya Chahti Hai Shivani?* Radio play relayed on BBC Worldwide Hindi Service, April.

Sheikh, R. (2015). Review of "Atiya's Journey: a Muslim Woman from Colonial Bombay to Edwardian Britain" by S. Lambert-Hurley and S. Sharma. *International Journal of Applied Psychoanalytic Studies*, *12*: 363–366.

Shengold, L. (1989). *Soul Murder: The Effects of Childhood Abuse and Deprivation*. New Haven, CT: Yale University Press.

Shengold, L. (1995). *Delusions of Everyday Life*. New Haven, CT: Yale University Press.

Shine (1996). Directed by S. Hicks, produced by Australian Film Finance Corporation.

Shriver, L. (2003). *We Need to Talk about Kevin*. New York: HarperCollins.

Shukla, P. (2015). Review of "Great Ancestors" by F. Shaheed and A. Shaheed. *International Journal of Applied Psychoanalytic Studies*, *12*: 359–362.

Simpson, V. L., & Hadjicostis, M. (2010). Vatican: Mideast Christians at risk. *Philadelphia Inquirer*, June 7, p. A-2.

Singh, J. A. L., & Zingg, R. M. (1939). *Wolf Children and Feral Man*. New York: Harper & Row.

Sklarew, B., Twemlow, S. W., & Wilkinson, S. (2004). *Analysts in the Trenches: Streets, Schools, War Zones*. New York: Routledge.

Sletvold, J. (2014). *The Embodied Analyst: from Freud and Reich to Relationality*. London: Routledge.

Smith, J. P., & Edmonston, B. (1997). *The New Americans: Economic, Demographic, and Fiscal Effects of Immigration*. Washington, DC: National Academy Press.

Sophocles (429 BC). *Oedipus Rex*. New York: Dover Thrift Editions, 1991.

South Pacific (1949). Musical composed by R. Rodgers, lyrics by O. Hammerstein. Directed by J. Logan.

Spanking the Monkey (1994). Directed by D. O. Russell, produced by Buckeye Films.

Spitz, R. (1946). The smiling response: a contribution to the ontogenesis of social relations. *Genetic Psychology Monographs, 34*: 57–125.

Spitz, R. (1965). *The First Year of Life*. New York: International Universities Press.

Spivak, G. C. (1988). Can the subaltern speak? In: C. Nelson & L. Grossberg (Eds.), *Marxism and the Interpretation of Culture* (pp. 283–298). Champagne-Urbana, IL: University of Illinois Press.

Sripada, B. (1999). A comparison of failed supervision and a successful supervision of the same psychoanalytic case. *Annual of Psychoanalysis, 26*: 219–241.

Steele, J. (2010). Chilcot inquiry accused of fixating on west and ignoring real victims. *The Guardian*, August 27.

Sterba, R. (1947). Some psychological factors in Negro race hatred and in anti-Negro riots. *Psychoanalysis and Social Sciences, 1*: 411–427.

Stevenson, R. L. (1886). *The Strange Case of Dr Jekyll and Mr Hyde*. New York: Dover, 1991.

Still Walking (2008). Directed by H. Koreeda, produced by Bandai Visual Company.

Sullivan, D. (2016). Obama should be honest about combat role in Mid East. *Philadelphia Inquirer*, May 12, p. A-14.

Szekely, L. (1954). Biological remarks on fears originating in early childhood. *International Journal of Psychoanalysis, 35*: 57–69.

Taketomo, Y. (1996). An American-Japanese transcultural psychoanalysis and the issue of teacher transference. *Journal of the American Academy of Psychoanalysis, 17*: 427–450.

Taylor, C. (1989). *Sources of the Self: The Making of the Modern Identity*. Cambridge, MA: Harvard University Press.

Taxi Driver (1976). Directed by M. Scorsese, produced by Columbia Pictures Corporation.

Telhami, S. (2016). *American Attitudes on Refugees from the Middle East*. Washington, DC: Brookings Institution Press.

Thirteen (2003). Directed by C. Hardwicke, produced by Fox Searchlight Pictures.

Thompson, C. (1996). The African-American patient in psychodynamic treatment. In: R. P. Foster, M. Moskowitz, & F. A. Javier (Eds.), *Reaching Across Boundaries of Culture and Class: Widening the Scope of Psychotherapy* (pp. 115–142). Northvale, NJ: Jason Aronson.

Thomson, J. A. (2003). Killer apes on American Airlines, or how religion was the main hijacker on September 11. In: S. Varvin & V. D. Volkan (Eds.), *Violence or Dialogue? Psychoanalytic Insights on Terror and Terrorism* (pp. 73–84). London: International Psychoanalytical Association.

Thomson, J. A., Harris, M., Volkan, V. D., & Edwards, B. (1993). The psychology of Western European neo-racism. *International Journal of Group Rights*, 3: 1–30.

Three Faces of Eve, The (1957). Directed by N. Johnson, produced by Twentieth Century Fox.

Tirman, J. (2011). *The Deaths of Others: The Fate of Civilians in America's Wars.* New York: Oxford University Press.

Top Gun (1986). Directed by T. Scott, produced by Paramount Pictures.

Traub, J. (2016). Europe wishes to inform you that the refugee crisis is over but the humanitarian and political crises of the great Syrian exodus are just beginning. *foreignpolicy.com*, October 18. Accessed April 27, 2017.

Trouble with the Curve (2012). Directed by R. Lorenz, produced by Warner Brothers.

Tschalaer, M. H. (2017). *Muslim Women's Quest for Justice: Gender, Law, and Activism in India.* Cambridge: Cambridge University Press.

Tucker, C. (2010). GOP should join Democrats in immigration-reform push. *Philadelphia Inquirer*, April 4, p. C-5.

Twemlow, S. W. (2009). Zen, martial arts, and psychoanalysis in training the mind of the psychotherapist. In: S. Akhtar (Ed.), *Freud and the Far East: Psychoanalytic Perspectives on the People and Culture of China, Japan, and Korea* (pp. 175–195). Lanham, MD: Jason Aronson.

Twemlow, S. W., & Sacco, F. (2008). *Why School Anti-Bullying Programs Do Not Work.* Lanham, MD: Jason Aronson.

Twemlow, S. W., & Sacco, F. (2012). *Preventing Bullying and School Violence.* Washington, DC: American Psychiatric Press.

US Department of State Bureau of Population, Refugees, and Migration (2017). *Refugee Arrivals by Region.* Washington DC: US Department of State.

Van Waning, A. (2007). Naikan—a Buddhist self-reflective approach: psychoanalytic and cultural reflections. *Japanese Contributions to Psychoanalysis*, 2: 158–178.

Varma, V. K., Akhtar, S., Kulhara, P. N., & Kaushal, P. (1973). Measurement of authoritarian traits in India. *Indian Journal of Psychiatry*, 15: 156–175.

Varvin, S. (1995). Genocide and ethnic cleansing: psychoanalytic and social-psychological viewpoints. *Scandinavian Psychoanalytic Review, 18*: 192–210.

Varvin, S. (2003). Extreme traumatization: strategies for mental survival. *International Forum of Psychoanalysis, 12*: 5–16.

Varvin, S., & Gerlach, A. (2011). Development of psychodynamic psychotherapy and psychoanalysis in China. In: P. Loewenberg & N. L. Thompson (Eds.), *100 Years of IPA: The Centenary History of the International Psychoanalytical Association 1910–2010: Evolution and Change* (pp. 356–365). London: Karnac.

Varvin, S., & Volkan, V. D. (Eds.) (2005). *Violence or Dialogue? Psychoanalytic Insights on Terror and Terrorism.* London: International Psychoanalytical Association.

Vedantam, S. (2003). When violence masquerades as virtue: a brief history of terrorism. In: S. Varvin & V. D. Volkan (Eds.), *Violence or Dialogue? Psychoanalytic Insights on Terror and Terrorism* (pp. 7–30). London: International Psychoanalytical Association.

Volkan, V. D. (1981). *Linking Objects and Linking Phenomena: A Study of the Forms, Symptoms, Metapsychology, and Therapy of Complicated Grief.* New York: International Universities Press.

Volkan, V. D. (1988). *The Need to Have Enemies and Allies: From Clinical Practice to International Relationships.* Northvale, NJ: Jason Aronson.

Volkan, V. D. (1997). *Bloodlines: From Ethnic Pride to Ethnic Terrorism.* New York: Farrar, Straus and Giroux.

Volkan, V. D. (2004). *Blind Trust: Large Groups and Their Leaders in Times of Crises and Terror.* Charlottesville, VA: Pitchstone.

Volkan, V. D. (2006). *Killing in the Name of Identity: A Study of Bloody Conflicts.* Charlottesville, VA: Pitchstone.

Volkan, V. D. (2014). *Psychoanalysis, International Relations, and Diplomacy.* London: Karnac.

Volkan, V. D., & Itzkowitz, N. (1984). *The Immortal Ataturk.* Chicago, IL: University of Chicago Press.

Volkan, V. D., Itzkowitz, N., & Dodd, A. (2001). *Richard Nixon: A Psychobiography.* New York: Columbia University Press.

Volkan, V. D., Montville, J. V., & Julius, D. A. (Eds.) (1991). *The Psychodynamics of International Relationships, Vol. 2: Unofficial Diplomacy at Work.* Lexington, MA: Lexington.

Von Feuerbach, P. J. A. (1832). *Kaspar Hauser: Beispiel eines Verbrechens am Seelenleben des Menschen.* Berlin: Anspach.

Waelder, R. (1936). The principle of multiple function: observations on multiple determination. *Psychoanalytic Quarterly, 5:* 45–62.

Waters, M. C. (1999). *Black Identities: West Indian Immigrant Dreams and Immigrant Realities.* New York: Russell Sage Foundation.

Webster's Ninth New Collegiate Dictionary (1987). Springfield, MA: Merriam-Webster.

Weiner, J., Anderson, J. A., & Danze, E. A. (2006). *Psychoanalysis and Architecture.* New York: Mental Health Resources.

Wharton, E. (1913). *The Custom of the Country.* New York: Vintage, 2012.

Wheelis, A. (1975). *On Not Knowing How to Live.* New York: Harper & Row.

Wheelis, A. (1994). *The Way Things Are.* New York: Baskerville.

Winnicott, D. W. (1953). Transitional objects and transitional phenomena: a study of the first not-me possession. *International Journal of Psychoanalysis, 34:* 89–97.

Winnicott, D. W. (1956). Primary maternal preoccupation. In: *Collected Papers: Through Paediatrics to Psychoanalysis* (pp. 300–305). New York: Basic Books, 1958.

Winnicott, D. W. (1960a). Ego distortion in terms of true and false self. In: *The Maturational Processes and the Facilitating Environment* (pp. 140–152). New York: International Universities Press, 1965.

Winnicott, D. W. (1960b). The theory of parent-infant relationship. *International Journal of Psychoanalysis, 41*: 585–595.

Winnicott, D. W. (1962). Ego integration in child development. In: *Maturational Processes and the Facilitating Environment* (pp. 45–53). New York: International Universities Press.

Winnicott, D. W. (1963). The development of the capacity for concern. In: *The Maturational Processes and the Facilitating Environment* (pp. 73–82). New York: International Universities Press, 1965.

Wirth, L. (1945). The problem of minority groups. In: R. Linton (Ed.), *The Science of Man in the World Crisis* (pp. 345–361). New York: Columbia University Press.

Wissing, D. A. (2012). *Funding the Enemy: How US Taxpayers Bankroll the Taliban.* New York: Prometheus.

Wolman, T. (2005). Human space, psychic space, analytic space, geopolitical space. In: M. T. Savio Hooke & S. Akhtar (Eds.), *The Geography of Meanings: Psychoanalytic Perspectives on Place, Space, Land, and Dislocation* (pp. 23–45). London: International Psychoanalytical Association.

Wolman, T., & Thompson, T. (1998). Adult and later-life development. In: A. Stoudemire (Ed.), *Human Behavior: An Introduction for Medical Students, Third Edition* (pp. 350–363). Philadelphia, PA: Lippincott-Raven.

Woodward, R. (2004). *Plan of Attack.* New York: Simon & Schuster.

Wright, L. (2006). *The Looming Tower: al-Qaeda and the Road to 9/11.* New York: Vintage.

Wyche, S. (2012). An African American's becoming a psychoanalyst: some personal reflections. In: S. Akhtar (Ed.), *The African American Experience: Psychoanalytic Perspectives* (pp. 321–336). Lanham, MD: Jason Aronson.

Yang, F., & Ebaugh, H. R. (2001). Religion and ethnicity among new immigrants: the impact of majority/minority status in home and host countries. *Journal for the Scientific Study of Religion, 40*: 367–378.

Young Adult (2011). Directed by J. Reitman, produced by Paramount Pictures.

Young-Bruehl, E. (1996). *The Anatomy of Prejudices.* Cambridge, MA: Harvard University Press.

Zoepf, K. (2017). *Excellent Daughters: The Secret Lives of Young Women Who Are Transforming the Arab World.* London: Penguin.

INDEX

Abbasi, A., 17–18, 68, 118
Abend, Sander, 13
Abraham, K., 5, 19
Abuelaish, I., 144
academic candidates, 191–192
    track, 192
Ad-Dab'bagh, Y., 96–97, 110, 190
Ad-Dab'bagh's Proposal, 96–97
Adorno, T., 7–8, 94, 101
adulthood, consolidation of, 174
Afghani Muslims, 59
African Americans, 23
    tension with new immigrants,
        38–42
Ahmad, Nina, 44
Ahmed, L., 119, 150
Ajase complex, 13
Akhtar, S., 12, 16–18, 23–25, 43, 52,
        59, 61–62, 66, 68, 75, 77, 80,
        93, 98–99, 101, 106, 111, 114,
        122, 139–140, 144, 150–151,

160, 167, 173–179, 183, 185,
    188, 190, 192
Alderdice, J. L., 148
Alexis de Tocqueville Institution, 33
Alf Layla wa-Layla, 118
Ali Jinnah, Mohammad, 119
All That Jazz, 181
Alperovitz, G., 90
Altman, N., 15, 18, 61, 178
amae, 13–14
Amati-Mehler, J., 17, 72, 177
American culture, 34
American military interventions, 129
American Psycho, The, 181
American Psychoanalytic
    Association, 174
analytic ego, 62
Anderson, J. A., 20, 133
anthropological psychoanalysis, 9–16
    vs. psychoanalytic anthropology,
        16

223

Parens, Henri, 67, 69
Passel, J. S., 48, 50
Path to National Suicide: An Essay on Immigration and Multiculturalism, The, 37, 74
Perez-Foster, R., 61
Picture of Dorian Gray, The, 181
Pine, F., 17, 52, 97, 100, 153
Pinsker, H., 62, 176
Pollock, G. H., 182
Ponette, 182
Portes, A., 30, 64
positive prejudice, 90
Powell, D., 178, 187
Prakash, K. M., 114
Prathikanti, S., 62
preconceived judgment, 88
pre-genital drives, disownment of, 100
prejudice, 88, 91, 109
    classification, 94
    culturally syntonic and culturally dystonic prejudices, 92
    manifestations of, 103–104
    monolithic phenomenon, 92–93
    obsessive, hysterical, and narcissistic types, 94
    origins of, 95
Proust, M., 182
pseudo-perversion, 5
psychoanalysis
    and culture, 3–19
    anthropological, 9–16
    applied, 5
    community-directed applications of, 18–19
    contemporary culturalization, 12
    transformation of, 17
    wild, 5
psychoanalytic anthropology, 4–9, 171
    era of, 8–9
    vs. anthropological psychoanalysis, 16

Psychoanalytic Center of Philadelphia, The, 193
psychoanalytic developmental theory, 7
psychoanalytic self, 8, 12
psychobiography, 16
Psychological Birth of the Human Infant, The, 153
psychosocial ostracism, 10
purified pleasure ego, 81
"purity" of white European identities, 127

Quran, 115–116

racism, 92, 109
Radford, J., 54
radical Islamic terrorism, 124
Rahman, Sheikh Mujibur, 46
Raising Cain, 182
Rajagopal, A., 27
Ramadan, 116
Ramana, C. V., 19
Random House Dictionary of the English Language, The, 88
Rashid, M., 18
refugee(s), 52–59
    definition of, 53
    global agreements for, 53–54
    situation in Europe, 55–58
    situation in other parts of the world, 58–59
    situation in the United States, 54–55
regression-based dehumanization, 155–156
rehumanization, 164–165
religion
    and immigration, 24–29
    place of, 24–25
    role in post-immigration identity change, 25–26